THE LAST JUDGMENT

To my parents, Tad and Wanda: the first and best teachers

The Last Judgment
Christian Ethics in a Legal Culture

ANDREW SKOTNICKI
Manhattan College, USA

Routledge
Taylor & Francis Group
LONDON AND NEW YORK

First published 2012 by Ashgate Publishing

Published 2016 by Routledge
2 Park Square, Milton Park, Abingdon, Oxon OX14 4RN
711 Third Avenue, New York, NY 10017, USA

First issued in paperback 2017

Routledge is an imprint of the Taylor & Francis Group, an informa business

British Library Cataloguing in Publication Data
Skotnicki, Andrew.
The last judgment : Christian ethics in a legal culture.
1. Christianity and law. 2. Bible and law. 3. Law
(Theology)--Biblical teaching. 4. Christian ethics.
I. Title
241.2-dc23

Library of Congress Cataloging-in-Publication Data
Skotnicki, Andrew.
The last judgment : Christian ethics in a legal culture / by Andrew
Skotnicki.
p. cm.
Includes bibliographical references (p.) and index.
ISBN 978-1-4094-3574-7 (hardcover)
1. Christianity and law. I. Title.
BR115.L28S66 2012
241'.2--dc23

2011037829

ISBN 13: 978-1-138-11070-0 (pbk)
ISBN 13: 978-1-4094-3574-7 (hbk)

Contents

Acknowledgments

I am most grateful to my wise and generous colleagues who read and commented on portions of the manuscript: Richard Emerson, Eoin O'Connell, William O'Neill, S.J., Jeff Pettis, Stephen Pope, and Claudia Setzer. Also, versions of the manuscript were presented at the annual meeting of the Catholic Theological Society of America, to the staff of Prison Fellowship International, and at the world conference of Prison Fellowship International in Toronto. Insights of the various scholars and practitioners at these assemblies were gratefully received and incorporated into the final text. It was also a privilege to spend part of 2009 as a Visiting Scholar at New York University. During that time, I benefited from the expertise of the renowned faculty at the Law and Society Program, particularly Sally Engle Merry and David Garland. Their ideas and bibliographic suggestions were extremely valuable. Finally, my wife Vivian has been a sounding board for the project since its inception. Both her legal expertise as an attorney and her practical wisdom have added grace and refinement to the ideas presented.

Prologue

This is a book about judgment, specifically legal judgment and the resultant penalties imposed upon those who break the law. It is also a book about Christian ethics and the decided impact the church has had upon the evolution of legal thought and the practice of punishment. It is finally a critique of Christian support of law and its judicial apparatus, particularly when human conduct is evaluated and reproved in terms different than those presented in the gospel.

The immediate motivation for this study is the unprecedented growth in many countries, most particularly the United States, in both the number of incarcerated persons and the length and severity of their sentences. Inasmuch as law reflects to a significant degree the values and norms of a given culture, and given the fact that a significant majority of Americans identify themselves as Christian, it can be said that many rank and file Christians ally themselves with these punitive trends.[1]

While, from a purely pragmatic point of view, the emphasis on order and law enforcement among Christians is of small surprise, it provokes serious inquiry when read against the backdrop not only of the New Testament, but also against the thrust of much of church history where, despite legalistic strains, fears of heresy, and frequent demonstrations of harsh judgment, a wariness, if not outright fear of judging others, coupled with a frequently pronounced antinomianism, are very much in evidence. All meta-analysis, especially one observing patterns in a subject as vast as the history of Christianity, must proceed with a large dose of intellectual humility and the awareness that generalizations always require careful qualification. This is categorically true of the present topic, but the conclusion that Christians of an earlier age often felt morally and spiritually incompetent to judge malevolence and support its punishment has much evidence in its support. This is particularly of interest in those periods in the first and early second millennia when ecclesiastical officials wielded much power in the social realm and, of perhaps greater interest, when the church began in the twelfth century to transform legal geography with the world's first universal code of law, the development of the first school of law, and other rudiments of jurisprudence that have had such a significant impact on subsequent secular legal development.[2]

---

[1] According to a 2004 Gallup Poll in the United States, 71 percent of Protestants and 66 percent of Catholics support the use of capital punishment. See http://deathpenaltyinfo.org/religion-and-death-penalty. See also Anne-Marie Cusac, *Cruel and Unusual: The Culture of Punishment in America* (New Haven: Yale University Press, 2009), ch. 1.

[2] Harold Berman argues that the "legal revolution" instituted by Pope Gregory VII is the defining moment in Western legal history, and very possibly in the history of the West.

Part of the present task is descriptive: first, to enunciate the origins and resonance of a Christian ethical stance of a non-judgmental, compassionate presence to those who are threatening or even harmful and, second, to describe the widespread abandonment of that stance in favor of one that in many instances fervently supports repressive legal sanctions and punishments.

The other task is prescriptive. The intent here is not only to inform but also to challenge Christians to revisit the ethical norms concerning law and judgment—based on what I will suggest is Christ's own contemplative and empathic attentiveness—that many of their ancestors in the faith held as sacred obligations. This objective is propelled by a desire not simply to abjure the idea of inflicting punishment, but to re-envision the entire narrative wherein sin and crime are understood to one patterned, not on law, still less on a polarized distance between the reputedly good and the malevolent, but on essential theological truths for Christians, the most central of which is the cross. Christ provides the model for what Christians and, dare it be said, humans are to do with suffering and pain, even pain incurred without moral provocation. Suffering borne with love and a sense of ontological communion overcomes anger, transforms the offense into a ritual of pardon, and invites imitation. Christian faith encourages that imitation since, in many respects, one sides either with the persecuted or those who persecute them; one either forbears and forgives or stands in judgment; or, in the words of Richard Rohr, one either transforms pain or transmits it.[3]

Each person is mired in divisive and destructive patterns of anger and reprisal which can neither be avoided nor willed into submission, but each person, nevertheless, has been enveloped by the mercy and love of God, has been loved without measure, and forgiven despite culpability. Meekness, humility, and patient endurance are essential Christian virtues because they are apropos of a people who know essential truths about themselves and about God.

Such an ethic will undoubtedly be of small consequence to those empowered by the state to judge and execute sentence on those found guilty in courts of law. Nor will it be of great consequence to the ones whose personal narrative is shaped largely by the values of some other community, such as the nation, where, in most instances, the commitment to an alternative set of prima facie goods, for example life, liberty, and the pursuit of happiness, and to the punitive social structures aligned with them, take precedence over the insistence in the gospel that Christians dare not judge the speck in the eye of another knowing full well that a log is lodged in their own (Mt 7: 3), that the measure with which they measure will be measured back to them (Lk 6: 38), and wherein Christ himself stated, "friend, who set me up as your judge or arbiter?" (Lk 12: 14).

Thankfully, the task of the Christian is in no way diminished by popular opinion or the interests of those wielding political and economic power. Christians are born out of a desire to be faithful to the story of Christ, to mirror the peace and

---

See *Law and Revolution* (Cambridge, MA: Harvard University Press, 1983), Introduction.

[3] Richard Rohr, *Adams's Return* (New York: Crossroad, 2004), pp. 36–37.

pardon he emitted with each breath, and to witness to the power of the cross as the transformative agent in history and, in the present case, as the model for how one ought to view law, judgment, and punishment.

The introductory chapter will begin with a discussion of the cultural patterns, in which the Christian churches have played a critical role, that have produced a pronounced desire to judge and to define justice in terms of bringing harm upon those who break the law. The central argument of the book that a univocal focus on the Christian narrative cannot countenance a judgment willing harm upon those found guilty of legal infractions will then be spelled out in greater detail.

The exploration of Christian attitudes to law and judgment will commence in Chapters 1 and 2 with an investigation of these issues in the Old and New Testaments. I will maintain that the Hebrew Scriptures summon varied responses to the centrality of law, but fundamentally the devout believer either sees obedience to divine law as the primary truth against which all other things are measured, or measures all things, including fidelity to law itself, in terms of love. In brief, Christ chose the latter approach and commanded his followers to do the same.

Chapter 3 comprises a summary of theological opinion in the early Christian community. The accommodation versus paradox model surfaces with force in the first Christian communities; it will be argued that despite the widespread presence of the former, the paradoxical claims of the gospel to renounce both judgment and law as antecedents to punishment are held in place, largely due to the development of the sacrament of penance and the penal ethos established in the first monastic communities.

The period commencing in the early second millennium and culminating with the Enlightenment at the end of the seventeenth century, surveyed in Chapter 4, presents several important variations on this subject. The first is the classic theory of natural law most authoritatively proposed by Thomas Aquinas. Another is found in nominalism as developed among Franciscan theologians, most notably William of Ockham. Still another can be traced to the Jesuit theologian Francisco Suarez, who, in an attempt to reconcile natural law and nominalism, set much of the tone for later positivist legal thinking with his concept of "purely penal law." Most importantly, legal developments in this era initiated the movements that have proved most decisive in fracturing the primitive Christian ethical template, and making law a supervening, objective force blurring the immediate call to love one's neighbor, especially the enemy, as one's self. Here, for the first time, law emerged as an independent and self-validating force for inflicting punishment.

The chapter continues with a discussion of the influence of the Reformation. Protestant thought, especially as derived from the theologies of Luther and Calvin, was extremely influential in the development of jurisprudence in the West. Whereas the Catholic Church elevated ecclesiastical law as a discrete tool of judgment and punishment, separate from the teaching of the gospel, Protestant theology tended to provide the same legitimacy for laws enacted by the state.

The chapter will conclude with summary observations from the evidence provided. The primary conclusion will be that dualism, a conscious commitment to separate the sacred from the profane, God from the world, and the good from the evil, led to a shattering of the comprehensive, "enchanted" Christian narrative that refrained from judgment to the exact degree that Christians were aware of both their sinfulness and God's unabashed benevolence and mercy.

The fifth chapter addresses the relation between Christian and secular understandings of law and judgment during the Enlightenment. The main focus will be upon those philosophical and theological movements that withdrew God from intimate revelatory contact with the cosmos and all within it. Disenchantment and desacralization coincided with the birth of the nation and the various intellectual movements that, as Marcel Gauchet and Charles Taylor have proposed, elevated political authority to a near deified status, whether in the guise of the absolute ruler in Hobbes, Bodin, and Rousseau, or the democratic republic as envisioned by Marsilius of Padua and exemplified most influentially in Locke.[4] That deification found its analogue and bridges the thought of disparate thinkers such as Rousseau and Hegel in the concept of civil religion. A God who is distant, stern, and judgmental replaced the God of love and agape incarnated in Jesus and, of equal importance, law and judgment became at the same time both tools of social order and instruments of divine punishment.

Chapter 6 provides an overview of contemporary theories of law and judgment. It centers on British and American law as these nations, particularly the latter, exemplify the harsh and punitive approach to breaches of the law that are the motivation for this volume. Emphasis will be placed upon legal positivism or, as it is sometimes termed, legal agnosticism. The ascension of law as an instrument of justice and judgment aimed at providing security for the material flourishing of the citizenry, and independent of theories of ethics or theology, mirrors the disenchantment of the political process and the transference of the power of the divine to the state.

Other theories of law will also be discussed in this chapter, notably, the various strains of legal realism which provide a critique of the way interest and ideology shape legal statutes, and narrative understandings of law that offer important and potentially fruitful connections with the approach to Christian ethics being espoused in these pages.

The chapter will conclude with an overview of law and judgment in contemporary criminology. A noted writer in the field once stated that criminology creates crime.[5] Theories in this discipline have the capacity to become self-fulfilling prophecies as an exasperated public and opportunistic political officials respond to what is at least perceived to be the problem of unfettered delinquency. In an atmosphere of cautiousness and trepidation, legislators, jurists, and penal officials often embrace

---

4 Marcel Gauchet, *The Disenchantment of the World*, trans. Oscar Burge (Princeton, NJ: Princeton University Press, 1997); Charles Taylor, *A Secular Age* (Cambridge, MA: Belknap Press, 2007).

5 John Braithwaite, *Crime, Shame, and Reintegration* (Cambridge: Cambridge University Press, 1989), pp. 5–8.

the theory of the moment in shaping criminal justice policy, regardless of its truth-value or efficacy. The background to the imprisonment boom, especially in the United States, will be reiterated as well as the influential changes in sentencing policy that have been the most striking efficient cause of this carceral expansion.

The seventh and final chapter will summarize the position concerning law, judgment, and Christian ethics proposed throughout the book. It is a perspective that at once finds resonance with proponents of narrative ethics and Christian pacifism, and also with a common thread running through both Christian and Eastern approaches to contemplative prayer that rejects all forms of dualism, proclaims the unity and sacredness of all life, and embraces a spirituality of unqualified presence to the other. In this stance, typified in Jesus breathing peace and the Holy Spirit upon the disciples who abandoned him (Jn 20: 22–23), it is impossible to objectify the wrongdoer, condemn him or her, and use the law as a tool to separate the good and the bad, justifying the punishment of the latter.

Albert Camus once stated that it is the task of the humanist to do something Christianity has never done: show mercy and care for the damned.[6] His words are an indictment of those of us who consider ourselves Christians, and who have fallen prey to a story of the world that divides the legally innocent from the legally guilty in much the same way as it divides good and evil. But the words of Camus are also a challenge, an important challenge, to retell the story of the universal human penchant to choose division over unity and harm over care. It is the story of God's own response in Jesus: a relentless self-emptying on our behalf, a love, to paraphrase Thomas Merton, that blesses everyone and judges no one.[7] This is the vision of Christian ethics and of law and judgment that will be presented in this book.

6 Taylor, *Secular Age*, pp. 585–86.

7 Thomas Merton, "Rain and the Rhinoceros," in *Raids on the Unspeakable* (New York: New Directions, 1964), pp. 9–10.

Introduction: Crime, Harm, and the Cultural Landscape

Many Christians, like their social counterparts, have concerns over personal safety and the protection of their rights and possessions. The valence of those concerns and their relation to spiritual commitments, specifically gospel commitments such as detachment and simplicity, nonviolence, and the abnegation of rights in deference to the needs of others are topics that will be addressed in the pages to come. What also prompts discussion and, frankly, alarm is the deep antipathy many Christians reveal toward those whose conduct is judged to threaten their safety, rights, and possessions.

Approximately 70 percent of American Christians favor the use of the death penalty; and even in a time of stable and often reduced crime rates, the majority of these same Christians support many of the programs that have made Americans the most imprisoned people on earth.[1]

Nor can one simply attribute the desire to punish those found guilty of illegal behavior to social conservatives who traditionally take a more punitive attitude in criminal justice matters, especially toward those found guilty of what are termed "street crimes" such as stealing, assaults, and selling narcotics. Liberals have perhaps outdone their conservative colleagues in spearheading an unprecedented expansion of the criminal code. One study recently noted that the new legal regime that has arisen from this impulse to punish "has given birth to criminal penalties in … every area of government interaction with society and the economy." All of these new laws are in addition to the 300,000 federal regulations whose violation can lead to prosecution and imprisonment.[2]

In what has been termed a "prosecutor's paradise," judges are required by strict sentencing guidelines to disallow human emotions such as sympathy and compassion to enter into determinations of punishment. Furthermore, these same guidelines are driven by the concept of "strict liability" that rules out traditional elements of justice such as *mens rea* and equity that have accompanied judicial

1 See Prologue, note 1. See also, Pew Center on the States, *One in 100: Behind Bars in America 2008*; United States Department of Justice, Bureau of Justice Statistics, "Prison Statistics," http://www.ojp.usdoj.gov/bjs.

2 James V. DeLong, "The New 'Criminal' Classes: Legal Sanctions and Business Managers," in Gene Healy (ed.), *Go Directly to Jail* (Washington, DC: The Cato Institute, 2004), p. 9.

sentences over the centuries, the former dating back to the time of Augustine and the latter at least to the thought of Aristotle.[3]

The absence of these legal "goods" and a concomitant desire to punish and imprison the malevolent and the threatening has created a social dynamic where, as one scholar has noted, the law on the books in the United States makes every adult citizen a felon.[4] The ramifications of this unprecedented expansion of punishable offenses have not, however, been applied equally. To rephrase a line from Abraham Heschel, all are guilty but few are responsible.[5] In other words, the demographic profile of the imprisoned reveals that the nets of the carceral regime have been calibrated in most cases only to catch a certain kind of prey, namely, poor members of racial minorities who make up the large percentage of the prison population (nearly 70 percent) in the United States, even though they comprise only thirty percent of the citizenry.[6] One study in legal anthropology surmises that in the exercise of discretion as to what cases will be prosecuted and what types of punishment will be offered in the plea-bargaining process, district attorneys often "rely on models of normal crimes; what makes crime normal is often less statutory definition and more time/location or the social characteristics of the victim or defendant."[7]

---

3 *Mens rea* refers to the belief that intent has as much to do with the gravity of an action as does the action itself (*actus reus*). It was a principle tenet of the ethics of Peter Abelard but can be traced to a quote of St Augustine: "the tongue is not made guilty unless the mind is guilty." See W. Cole Durham, "Religion and Criminal Law: Types and Contexts of Interaction" in John Witte, Jr. and Frank S. Alexander (eds), *The Weightier Matters of the Law* (Atlanta: Scholars Press, 1988), pp. 221–22. Abelard wrote: "For God thinks not of what was done but in what mind it may be done." See Peter Abelard, *Peter Abelard's Ethics*, trans. D.E. Luscombe (Oxford: Clarendon Press, 1971), pp. 28–29. Erik Luna states: "the common law required a convergence of harmful conduct (*actus reus*) and a culpable mental state (*mens rea*) … Today, however, criminal responsibility can be doled out without a culpable mental state through the concept of 'strict liability.'" See "Overextending the Criminal Law" in Healy, *Go Directly to Jail*, p. 4. Equity was a fundamental requirement of what Aristotle (and later Aquinas) termed special justice. See Aristotle, *Ethics*, trans. J.A.K. Thompson (Harmondsworth, UK: Penguin, 1955), V, x; St Thomas Aquinas, *Summa Theologica*, trans. Fathers of the English Dominican Province (New York: Benziger, 1947), II-II, Q. 58, a. 7.

4 William J. Stuntz, "The Pathological Politics of Criminal Law," *Michigan Law Review* 100 (2001), p. 511.

5 "Above all, the prophets remind us of the moral state of people. Few are guilty, but all are responsible." Abraham Heschel, *The Prophets* (New York: Harper & Row, 1962), p. 16.

6 Census data is available through the U.S. Census Bureau, "Census 2010," http://www.census.gov. Prison population statistics are available at the U.S. Department of Justice, Bureau of Justice Statistics, "Prison Statistics," http://www.ojp.usdoj.gov/bjs.

7 Patricia Ewick and Susan S. Sibley, *The Common Place of Law* (Chicago: University of Chicago Press, 1998), p. 16.

A recent volume on white-collar crime observes that while the latter has risen dramatically in recent decades, especially in former industrialized nations that have seen a significant rise in professional and managerial workers, the public, by and large, identifies with criminals of their own race and social status and is far more fascinated and appalled by crime in the streets as opposed to "crime in the suites."[8]

Nor does it matter in this new penal economy whether the offense is poised to do immediate harm. What are termed "nuisance crimes" more and more form the substance of offenses that merit arrest and confinement: e.g., the United States Supreme Court upheld a jail sentence for a person who refused to wear a seat belt;[9] police in Washington, DC arrested a young adult for eating a hamburger in a Metro Station; the state of Illinois has outlawed sleeping near a highway;[10] and the State of California imprisoned a man for life for stealing a pair of socks.[11] Legal interventions such as the ones just mentioned are not isolated incidents meant to mar an otherwise tolerant justice system. They are more and more the everyday practice of law enforcement throughout the United States and symptomatic of an accusatory stance toward others that infects societies throughout the globe.[12] Authors across the criminal justice discipline have been marking these trends for the last two decades.[13]

---

8 Terry L. Leap, *Dishonest Dollars* (Ithaca and London: Cornell University Press, 2007), pp. 18–19.

9 James Whitman, *Harsh Justice* (New York: Oxford University Press, 2003), p. 3.

10 Luna, "Overextending," pp. 1–2.

11 Nicholas D. Kristof, "Priority Test: Health Care or Prisons?" *New York Times*, August 18, 2009.

12 Writing of the social climate in France that reflects a more general moral trend, Jean Delumeau states: "Our era constantly speaks about liberating itself from guilt feelings without noticing that, in the entire history of guilt, the accusation of others has never been as strong as it is today." See *Sin and Fear*, trans. Eric Nicholson (New York: St. Martin's, 1983), p. 5.

13 Malcolm Feeley and Jonathan Simon detected this paradigm shift some years ago, remarking in a memorable phrase that the new penology has evolved in the minds of many of its proponents into a form of "waste management." See "The New Penology: Notes on the Emerging Strategy of Corrections and its Implications," *Criminology* 30 (1992), p. 470. John Irwin writes of the desire to rid the streets of the "rabble." See *The Jail: Managing the Underclass in American Society* (Berkeley: University of California Press, 1985), ch. 1; *The Warehouse Prison* (Los Angeles: Roxbury, 2005). Steve Bogira describes an evening at the booking dock at the Cook County Jail in Chicago where the arrested featured people selling watches on the subway. See *Courtroom 302* (New York: Alfred A. Knopf, 2005), p. 15. Erik Luna writes: "Over criminalization leads to enormous police discretion to stop pedestrians or motorists by using legal pretexts that serve as cover for discriminatory enforcement based on class, race, or ethnicity." See "Overextending," p. 6. See also David Garland, *The Culture of Control* (Chicago: University of Chicago Press, 2001); Mark Mauer, *Race to Incarcerate* (New York: New Press, 1999).

A culture zealous to judge and prosecute is also a culture with less and less regard for fundamental guidelines meant to insure a just hearing for the defendant. Aside from the abrogation in many jurisdictions of concepts essential to a Christian understanding of justice such as intention and equity, observers have noted a lessening of legal attention to due process both at the time of arrest and after conviction. It is as if those arrested are presumed to be guilty by the very fact that they have been arrested, while those incarcerated for criminal activity forfeit their right to a fair hearing for their grievances regardless of the substance of their claim.[14] As a report on inmates recently processed at the Cook County Jail in Chicago states: "Those marched into the basement are cloaked in the presumption of innocence—in theory. The prevailing wisdom down here, however, is: if they're so innocent, why'd they arrive in handcuffs?" A sergeant then comments: "We get the dregs of humanity here … If these people moved in next to you, your lawn would die."[15]

Nor does the punishment end once a person is released from custody. Unlike the prevailing practice in some European countries, Americans who commit felonies are deprived of virtually all civil rights upon their release. As James Whitman has observed, American justice attacks not simply the action in question but "the very personhood of offenders."[16] And to put an exclamation point on all of this, the large majority of those polled believe that the guilty deserve everything they get.[17]

This deeply troubling state of affairs is the background for the discussion of law and judgment and their relation to Christian ethics, not only historically but also theologically. The history of law moves through many phases in Western history, much of it a reflection of a shifting continuum within the church between antinomian tendencies rooted in New Testament teaching and pragmatic

---

14 The Prison Reform Litigation Act of 1996 was designed to retard the filing of frivolous lawsuits by prisoners. Its effect, however, has been to hinder severely the claims of prisoners for fundamental human rights. For example, the suit of 18 inmates in a Louisiana jail whose cells had neither a toilet nor running water, only a hole in the floor covered by an iron grate and a gallon of water for drinking and toilet maintenance, was dismissed by both state and federal courts because the prisoners "had not identified a single human need of which they were deprived." When a Texas inmate sued because he was refused therapy for his hepatitis B and C on the grounds that he was mentally ill, the U.S. Court of Appeals for the Fifth Circuit dismissed his case as "frivolous." See Jens Soering, *The Church of the Second Chance* (New York: Lantern Books, 2008), pp. 66–67. James Whitman notes: "[W]e have forgotten the old Christian precepts according to which a morally justifiable system must protect *both* the innocent *and* the guilty." See *The Origins of Reasonable Doubt* (New Haven: Yale University Press, 2008), p. 209.

15 Bogira, *Courtroom 302*, p. 7.

16 Whitman, *Harsh Justice*, p. 9.

17 "In practice, in the face of ever-increasing criminal sentences, many decision-makers and spectators of the criminal justice system have found … that offenders deserve as much punishment as they get." See Alice Ristroph, "Desert, Democracy, and Sentencing Reform," *Journal of Criminal Law and Criminology* 96 (2006), p. 1295.

compromises with ruling authorities. The influence of the church on law became pronounced with legislation enacted by Christian emperors after the fourth century, often in explicitly Christian language, and often at the behest of and in service to ecclesiastical needs. The insertion of law, both formally and materially, into Christian theology and organizational practice began in earnest during the twelfth and thirteenth centuries. It was in the same period that the use of legal regulations as a means of social control came into prominence in the church and within the emerging state. In the new juridical economy promoted by these developments that reached its culmination in the Enlightenment, law, and the material well-being of those under its authority, began to assume the ultimate focus once directed, ideally, to God alone. The self-validating warrant to judge and punish, without a hint of humility or remorse, that has just been documented is the product of this change of theological and political course.

Christian ethical practice in may respects splits along the fault-line of law. Specific Christians and their denominational spokespersons are informed and shaped by cultural assumptions regarding law and punishment just as they, in turn, impact the cultures in which they live. The hyper-retributive penal philosophy in many countries in the world today has influenced and been influenced by Christian theology and ethics, in the same way that the more transcendent approach to law with its concomitant wariness to convert perception into harm and its conscious remembrance of the sacrifice of the cross recalls the sobriety concerning judgment common in an earlier era.

History, if not common sense, reveals that conflict with the state and the surrounding culture are inevitable if a non-violent and non-judgmental vision of justice rooted in the teaching of Christ is to be embraced. St Ambrose captured the essence of that necessary tension in a reference to his ever uneasy relationship with Emperor Theodosius: "I am ready to bear the usual fate of a bishop if he follows the usual practice of kings."[18] This may have some explanatory significance in the quest to determine how law and its surrogate values of security and retribution have so often challenged the gospel in defining the parameters and even the content of Christian ethics. As Robert Cover maintains, each system of law is narrative-based and contains both a world-envisioning and a world-maintaining dimension.[19] The need for order within the state, its monopoly on the use of violent force, and its self-justifying narrative have persuaded many Christians to reshape the dimensions of faith to accommodate the legal structure and maintain their "freedoms," including the freedom to practice their religion, or risk finding themselves living outside the law.[20]

---

18 St Ambrose, "Sermon against Auxentius," in Oliver O'Donovan and Joan Lockwood O'Donovan (eds), *From Irenaeus to Grotius: A Sourcebook in Christian Political Thought* (Grand Rapids, MI: Wm. B. Eerdmans, 1999), Ep. 75A, 1.

19 Robert Cover, "Nomos and Narrative," *Harvard Law Review* 97 (1983), pp. 12–13.

20 Stanley Hauerwas, "The Politics of Freedom: Why Freedom of Religion is a Subtle Temptation," in *After Christendom* (Nashville: Abingdon, 1991), pp. 69–92.

Many who have sought to fit their lives into its narrow contours have come to know, often painfully, that the Christian narrative is not a given, nor is it socially beneficial, in much the same way that they know that Christ's willingness to embrace the pain and failure of the cross was not a given; it must be a choice over other far more popular conceptions of the good life.

Christian ethics, understood properly, is not a set of laws but a way of shaping one's vision to see the other as a part of oneself, and both as a part of the divine. Karl Rahner expresses this way of seeing specifically with regard to convicted criminals: "But suppose that our sober everyday eyes should look at this neighbor of ours and see through all his physical degeneracy, through the screen of his instinctual life ... Suppose that our eyes seeing through all of this, should seek and find that which is most real and ultimate in this other person: God, with his love and his mercy, who has conferred an eternal dignity upon this person and offers himself to him, without repentance, in the incomprehensible prodigality of the divine foolishness of love."[21]

Accompanying, with equal emphasis, this stance of limitless care is the contention that seeing is itself predicated upon the ascetic practice of presence to the divine in each moment and in each breath. To be present to another is to lose one's self in much the same way as Christ stated that if you love your life you will lose it (Mk 8: 35). It is what Martin Buber calls the "I-Thou," or what the phenomenologist Alfred Schutz characterizes as "growing old together."[22] Mostly, however, it is what mystical theologians call contemplation. It is an embracing of the unity of all creation in love and in the fervent belief that the other cannot in any truthful way be encountered without a practiced abandonment of objective analysis, self-interest, and self-seeking.

The method of Christian judgment that necessarily follows from this can only be expressed after the other has been met in an atmosphere of complete openness. It cannot be dualistic, based on an imaginary divide between reason and the other components of the psyche or the soul. The response to the other is wholistic, intuitive, and guided by the Spirit. When one breathes peace and non-violence, when an offense brings forth patience, tolerance, and tenderness, one breathes the Spirit of God, participates in the unity and love of the Trinity, and judges rightly.

Christ was not a lawgiver because, as St Paul repeatedly insists, people are not made better by the law; they are made better by picking up their cross and following in the footsteps of the Savior, by imitating his charity, humility, forbearance, and

---

Thomas Merton, referencing the Syrian hermit Philoxenos, states that for the Christian contemplative "there is no justification for the solitary life, since it is without a law. To be a contemplative therefore is to be an outlaw. As was Christ. As was Paul." See "Rain and the Rhinoceros," p. 14.

21 Karl Rahner, "The Prison Pastorate," in *Justice Reflections* 6 (2004), pp. 6–7.

22 Martin Buber, *I and Thou*, trans. Walter Kaufman (New York: Charles Scriber's Sons, 1970); Alfred Schutz, *On Phenomenology and Social Relations* (Chicago: University of Chicago Press, 1970), p. 187.

forgiveness. Christ was a rabbi, a storyteller. He did not issue legal directives as much as he met the challenges of his friends, listeners, and persecutors with stories meant to reach their imagination and enable them to see new possibilities in their manner of thought and action.[23]

Certainly, law has played a central role in the development of Christianity both in a theological sense and within Christian social experiments. Even antinomians such as William of Ockham and some of his Franciscan theological colleagues showed a deep respect for law, particularly where given popular support, and especially when echoing the moral guidelines presented in the Bible.[24] One need only think of the profound effect natural law thinking has had on the shape of Christian thought, particularly the moral theology and social thought of the Catholic Church, and the similar impact Lutheran and Calvinist legal concepts have had on the development of Western jurisprudence, to realize that Christians cannot invoke a political theology or, more to the point, a theological understanding of criminal justice without attentiveness to and some degree of appreciation for the role law plays in society.[25]

Having said that, this book argues that law can be no more than a heuristic device, a reminder, as Sts Paul and Augustine insisted, later to be invoked by Luther, of our profound weakness in the face of our moral and spiritual responsibilities, and an intervening agent in defense of those being harmed or abused.[26] This will be discussed in detail later, but briefly put, while law is needed in an immediate sense to separate those who do harm from their actual or intended victims, it can serve no other moral purpose than to echo the moral imperatives Christians know to be incumbent upon them from divine revelation in the Scriptures. The elevation of law (and the nation it serves and the interests it protects) to a transcendent status in contemporary society has led not only to the punitive and racist practices mentioned earlier, it has provided citizens in general, and many Christians in particular, a false sense of moral superiority and a warrant to inflict harm on those the law finds culpable. Sin has, in other words, once again become linked with crime; and the lawful have deluded themselves into thinking that because their sins and crimes have not been punished, they are somehow superior to the imprisoned,

---

23 See, e.g., Harvey Cox, *When Jesus Came to Harvard* (Boston: Mariner Books, 2004), pp. 23–31; William Spohn, *Go and Do Likewise* (New York: Continuum, 1999), pp. 9–15.

24 See A.S. McGrade, *The Political Thought of William of Ockham* (Cambridge: Cambridge University Press, 1974), pp. 213–15.

25 John Witte writes: "Every major religious tradition strives to come to terms with law by striking a balance between the rational and the mystical, the prophetic and the priestly, and the structural and the spiritual." See "Introduction," in John Witte, Jr. and Frank S. Alexander (eds), *Christianity and Law: An Introduction* (Cambridge: Cambridge University Press, 2008), p. 1.

26 On the uses of the law in Luther and Calvin, see Harold Berman, *Law and Revolution II* (Cambridge, MA: Harvard University Press, 2003), pp. 75ff.

as if the parable of the Pharisee and the Publican (Lk 18: 9–14) was not intended for modern ears.[27]

The same set of coordinates should be invoked with regard to legal judgment and Christian attitudes in respect to it. To isolate those who do harm should never be understood as a desire to punish them. Such judgments cannot be justified from a Christian perspective in this author's opinion. The offender stands in the same radical relation to God and to divine grace as every other human being: no one can pay the ransom of his or her own life (Ps 49: 7–9); the gap between the actions of each and the perfect goodness of God can invite nothing other than humility and repentance. Grace, however, overcomes human shortcomings. God's love and desire to heal and reconcile sinners and all criminal offenders to the community, to themselves, and to God's own self is as unconditional as it is unwarranted.[28]

While such an interpretation of the gospel message may not prove compelling to many, the concerns of numerous scholars, activists, and concerned men and women, both in and outside of the church, coincide in the desire to create a consensual and empathic relation between those standing in judgment and those to be judged.[29]

It is the hope of this volume that the two strands of conversation, the one dealing with Christian attitudes to law and judgment, the other dealing with secular understandings of these same functions, can recognize some common ground and elicit motivation. Not in order to create a Christian commonwealth, not to dilute the example of justice and love that Jesus has provided, but to create a more sober, if not compassionate, response to those bearing the weight of their own misdeeds and, as is so often the case, the weight imposed by those who have willed them to suffer.[30]

---

[27] On the development of the concepts of sin and crime see Berman, *Law and Revolution*, pp. 183–87; Andrew Skotnicki, *Criminal Justice and the Catholic Church* (Lanham, MD: Rowman & Littlefield, 2008), pp. 41–42. On the re-conflation of sin and crime in American society, see Whitman, *Harsh Justice*, p. 201. On the theological commitments that create a notion of "essential difference" between the law-abiding and those who break the law, see T. Richard Snyder, *The Protestant Ethic and the Spirit of Punishment* (Grand Rapids: Eerdmans, 2001), pp. 55–73.

[28] Paul M. Zahl, *Grace in Practice* (Grand Rapids: Eerdmans, 2007), pp. 208–09.

[29] One area of legal scholarship particularly sensitive to these matters is what has been termed "legal realism." See Karl Llewellyn, *Jurisprudence: Realism in Theory and Practice* (Chicago: University of Chicago Press, 1962), pp. 112–14. See also Lon Fuller, *The Morality of Law* (New Haven: Yale University Press, 1964); Cover, "Nomos and Narrative."

[30] Harold Berman is among those who argue that a synthesis of the different strands of Western law, especially those influenced by Christian theology, is a necessary goal. See Berman, *Law and Revolution II*, p. 11; and "An Ecumenical Jurisprudence" in John Witte, Jr. and Frank S. Alexander (eds), *The Teachings of Modern Christianity on Law, Politics, and Human Nature* (2 vols, New York: Columbia University Press, 2006), vol. 1, pp. 752–64.

We now proceed to the task of describing how Christians have thought about law and judgment, especially in the area of criminal justice. The evidence presented will in some ways be reminiscent of some elements of our present legal system, and will in other ways reveal how far contemporary judicial and penal practice have departed from what our ancestors often believed about law and judgment, and how much needs to be done if that ancient vision is again to inform the theory and practice of Christian ethics.

Chapter 1
Law and Judgment in the Hebrew Scriptures

A thesis that argues that law and judgment, in all but the most restricted circumstances, are improper ideas for Christians must find its principal warrant in the biblical text and, since it provides so much of the basis for the Christian experience, the Hebrew Bible. Gunther Bornkamm has remarked that the Bible is not only the most popular book ever written, it is also the most misunderstood.[1]

Cognizant of that proviso, I will contend that there is a continuum of interpretation regarding the divine law in these paradigmatic texts. At one end, there exists a particular, austere and legal approach to creation and God's role within it; on the other, a unified, relational, and contemplative one.[2] The latter worldview lays the groundwork for the argument that will be sustained throughout the book concerning law and judgment. Here, one's love of God and God's creation, and one's silent contemplation of the divine mystery, provide the horizon wherein law is interpreted and judgments are rendered. The law is sacred but must be viewed in light of a deity who speaks to the attentive heart in a language that supersedes the literal language of the Torah, especially the promise that its obedient servants will prosper (Job 29: 12–17; 31: 5–40; Mal 3: 14–15). It is in this framework, reminiscent of the theology in the Book of Job, that Jesus approached the law.[3] In

---

1 Gunther Bornkamm, *The New Testament: A Guide to its Writings*, trans. Reginald H. Fuller and Ilse Fuller (Philadelphia: Fortress, 1973), p. 1.

2 Edward Peters notes that the influence of the Jewish Bible "reached a far wider audience than Plato or the Greek orators, and that audience paid particular attention to its vivid expressions of human helplessness and terror, particularly in its language of confinement and release, of captives ransomed by God, of refuge and sanctuary, and of exile and return." See "Prison Before The Prison" in Norval Morris and David J. Rothman (eds), *The Oxford History of the Prison* (New York: Oxford University Press, 1995), p. 14. Conversely, Moshe Chayim Luzzatto argues that the spiritual soul is "radiant," representing the shining of God's countenance, but the body is defective, and proceeds from "the absence of divine goodness" and the concealment of God's countenance. God is guiding the universe to perfection but only by creating these two orders of good and evil, rewarding the first and punishing the second. See *The Knowing Heart*, trans. Shraga Silverstein (Jerusalem and New York: Feldheim, 1982), pp. 105ff.

3 A number of authors criticize the reading of Job as an exercise in theodicy wherein God's justice and law are vindicated in the course of the narrative. See Alan Bernstein, *The Formation of Hell* (Ithaca: Cornell University Press, 1993), pp. 156–162; Roland Murphy, *The Book of Job* (New York: Paulist, 1999), p. 130; Paul Ricoeur, "Religion, Atheism, and Faith," in *The Conflict of Interpretations*, trans. Charles Freilich (Chicago: Northwestern University Press, 1974), pp. 460–61.

contrast, there exists a far more literal Deuteronomic view that the laws revealed in the Torah are a manifestation of God's inscrutable and unsearchable ways and are unconditionally binding regardless of circumstance or human disposition, unless amended by God Himself.[4]

Whatever variations of interpretation may be summoned by the range of opinion presented above, the people of ancient Israel understood law within the context of a covenant, implying a relationship between God and the people whom God chose to bear witness to a gracious and loving plan for the redemption of humankind (Isa 2: 2–4). The rules emanating from this covenant are thus deeply bound to the historical events that form the story of the Jewish people. Yet, in this long and hallowed history, God shows a willingness to reshape both the form and content of laws since they comprise a charter for the preservation and flourishing of life as it is conditioned by unfolding events, not simply a set of rigid, ahistorical mandates (Dt 30: 15–16). In parallel fashion, punishment, while often severe, cannot be separated either from the covenantal promise of restoration or from an unfailing love that makes good out of the human propensity to do evil and seeks to foster a humble serenity rather than rebellion in the face of life's painful limitations.

It is thus not my intention to comb the Hebrew Scriptures in order to find proof texts for a sharply drawn antinomian argument. Such a task would, first of all, be impossible in describing a faith whose character is defined so poignantly by its relation to law. Besides, as we will see and as many readers already know, the early Christian community was hardly of a single mind with regard to locating the place of law and judgment in an ethic faithful to Christ. And even among the most fervent antinomians, the Torah could not be rejected as both a religious and moral guide. Christians were incapable of ignoring the divine origin of the Pentateuch without at the same time setting themselves on heretical turf, as both Manichaeans and followers of Marcion were to reveal.[5] In whatever way early Christians approached the subject, law was in some form still an expression of God's justice and sovereignty. This was the common belief of their Jewish ancestors, not to mention all the peoples of the Ancient Near East whose influence on Hebrew legal formulations was significant.[6]

---

4 "[T]he rule of His will is absolute, allowing of no deterrent whatsoever at any time whatsoever." Luzzatto, *Knowing Heart*, p. 65.

5 See W.H.C. Frend, *The Rise of Christianity* (Philadelphia: Fortress, 1984), pp. 212–18; 314–18.

6 Parallels between the legal system of Ancient Israel and those of its neighbors were not accidental. Scholars have noted the influence of codes as early as that of Hammurabi in the Hebrew texts. Bernard Levinson precludes a "lex ex nihilo" approach to a study of ancient Israel, noting that the very idea of a legal collection shows the influence of neighboring peoples. See *Legal Revision and Religious Renewal in Ancient Israel* (New York and Cambridge: Cambridge University Press, 2008), p. 23. See also Ze'ev Falk, *Hebrew Law in Biblical Times* (Jerusalem: Wahrmann Books, 1964), p. 73; Terence E.

This chapter will first depict the traditional position that law, as imparted in the context of the Covenant, provides the only path God provides for the attainment of human and spiritual flourishing. As such, its provisions, as discerned within the tradition, are unconditionally binding. It will then develop the idea that law, despite its honorable place in the narrative of Judaism, is authoritative only within a deeper context of a contemplative and loving stance before God and creation. Finally, the implications of these two views for the punishment of lawbreakers will be discussed.

The Divine Origin of Law

For the Greeks, law was sacred. It expressed the structures of a permanent natural order, and in Plato that sense of divinity applied to the laws enacted by the community.[7] The same can be said for the people of Israel. The creation accounts reveal a belief that God has instilled laws into the very fabric of life. The Psalms announce that this soundless moral message of God extends from one end of the universe to the other (Ps 19: 4–6). Implied law can be found throughout Genesis: after Adam and Eve disobey God's command they hide and feel shame (Gen 3: 7–11); Cain, after killing Abel, laments that his sin is too great to be pardoned and that he can no longer endure the presence of God (Gen 4: 13–14); and Abraham is commended for his righteousness and obedience to the divine will even though the law had as yet not been proclaimed (Gen 26: 5).[8]

The word for judgment found throughout the Hebrew Scriptures, *mishpat*, coincides with what might be considered not an extraneous pattern of normative human behavior but a natural one.[9] Among its various meanings, including the case to be heard before a court and the judgment rendered, *mishpat* implies a "measured, balanced relatedness … to the whole of life."[10] This understanding also reveals a theological affirmation of the harmony between divine and human

---

Fretheim, *God and World in the Old Testament* (Nashville: Abingdon, 2005), p. 137; Paul Johnson, *A History of the Jews* (New York: Harper & Row, 1987), p. 32; Robert W. Shaffern, *Law and Justice from Antiquity to the Enlightenment* (Lanham, MD: Roman & Littlefield, 2009), pp. 3–5; Roland de Vaux, O.P., *Ancient Israel: Its Life and Institutions*, trans. John McHugh (New York: McGraw Hill, 1961), p. 152.

7 Remi Brague, *The Law of God*, trans. Lydia G. Cochrane (Chicago: University of Chicago Press, 2008), pp. 18, 26.

8 The obedience praised by the biblical author cannot simply be reduced to a literary device to employ Abraham in a *post hoc propter hoc* relationship with the Mosaic law. See Fretheim, *God and World*, pp. 98–100.

9 Brague, *Law*, p. 20.

10 Eliezer Berkovits, *Essential Essays on Judaism*, ed. David Hazony (Jerusalem: Shalem Press, 2002), p. 146.

life as well as between divine and human judgment when the fundamental laws of the Creator's universe are honored.[11]

Furthermore, the law is revealed to the ancient Hebrews in the context of their own liberation from slavery. A free as opposed to an enslaved people are the subjects of law; it is the gift given to a community capable of voluntary assent to its provisions to enable them to maintain their freedom against the impulses and political decisions that led to their enslavement in the first place.[12]

Law, therefore, must always be understood not simply in a social but also in a literary framework. Each of the commandments given to Moses on Sinai, for example, is related to a story emanating from the experience of the people of Israel.[13] This is not simply a charming stylistic device. The formative story of a people, not coercive force, is what provides law with the sacred character it so often possesses. A legal code always has a world-creating dimension. It carries the aspirations of a particular people and measures those aspirations against a mythical horizon, one that explains the meaning of the people themselves, the world they inhabit, and the god they serve.[14] "For every constitution there is an epic."[15] This summons the idea of ongoing interpretation in the face of epistemological crisis, when the meaning of the world created by the myth and sustained by the law is called into question by new and unsettling events.[16]

In Jewish culture, this interpretive role is associated with the rise of the synagogue, and eventually the rabbinate. After the exile, the authority of the local congregation grew and through it new sources of binding law began to develop.[17] This was evident in the movement of Pharisaism and the belief that God gave to Moses not only a written covenant but an oral one; it was the task of the teacher in the synagogue to place the law "in the mouths" of Jewish youth: "The practice of the Oral Law made it possible for the Mosaic code to be adapted to changing conditions and administered in a realistic manner."[18] One sees the first post-exilic

---

[11] Brague, *Law*, p. 58.

[12] Ibid. Michael Walzer maintains that the Exodus story provides the paradigmatic pattern for all revolutions in history wherein oppression leads to liberation, and liberation leads to law. See *Exodus and Revolution* (New York: Basic, 1994).

[13] Shaffern, *Law and Justice*, pp. 9–12.

[14] Jacob Neusner states that by late antiquity "the Torah" lost its capital letter and definite article and became "torah," a term signifying not only a scroll of laws but also the distinctive life and worldview of the Jewish people. See *Torah* (Philadelphia: Fortress, 1985), pp. xi, 5.

[15] Cover, "Nomos," pp. 4–5.

[16] On epistemological crisis, see Stanley Hauerwas, "The Nonviolent Terrorist," in Michael L. Budde and Robert W. Brimlow (eds), *The Church as Counterculture* (Albany: State University of New York Press, 2000), pp. 89–104.

[17] Abraham Heschel, *Between God and Man* (New York: Harper & Brothers, 1959), p. 160.

[18] Johnson, *History*, p. 106.

example of this when Ezra, who is not a prophet, re-reads and applies the text of the law in light of a people still under the jurisdiction of the King of Persia.[19] It is still the task of every human community. The narrative must be revered but also summoned and applied if a society, as well as an organization, is to continue to flourish.[20]

This dynamic of reinterpretation helps us understand the attitude assumed by legally conservative adherents in regard to the seeming contradictions in Scripture where God appears to take back earlier decrees or exhibit less than consistent guidelines on discrete occasions. Such examples of legal emendation do not yield a vacillating or "creative" approach to the divine law. In traditional Judaism, every command in the Pentateuch complements every other; contradictions may be apparent but are never real.[21] Levinson states that despite God changing His mind, making mistakes, and expressing regret in events such as the flood, the multiple betrayals during the sojourn in the desert, the events concerning Sodom and Gomorrah, and the fate of the city of Nineveh, many interpreters of sacred legal texts show God's authority as absolute and the supernatural commands as timeless.[22]

The divine care for human beings reinforces the claim that law, for the Jewish people, is not a service to a deity whose self-esteem is bruised by human negligence, as much as a mandatory code for the preservation of the sacred life that God created.[23] In similar fashion, the ethos of ancient Hebrew culture reveals no distinction between religion and legal compliance; the word *dat* expresses the meaning of both law and religion.[24] In other words, the religious person, in this framework, is he or she who has perceived and conformed their behavior to

---

19 David Novak, "Law and Religion in Judaism," in John Witte, Jr. and Frank S. Alexander (eds), *Christianity and the Law* (Cambridge: Cambridge University Press, 2008), pp. 38–39; James C. VanderKam, *An Introduction to Early Judaism* (Grand Rapids, MI: William B. Eerdmans, 2001), pp. 3–4.

20 Organizational psychology reveals the truth of this claim. The mission statement craze is not simply a fad. It is a sometimes formulaic but always necessary process if any institution is to avoid collapse in moments of crisis. Patricia Wittberg has studied this phenomenon from the viewpoint of Catholic religious orders. See *The Rise and Decline of Catholic Religious Orders* (Albany: State University of New York Press, 1994). Bowen McCoy has viewed the issue from the point of view of corporate culture: see "The Parable of the Sadhu," *Harvard Business Review* 103 (1983), pp. 103–08.

21 Novak, "Law and Religion," pp. 36–37.

22 Levinson, *Legal Revision*, pp. 48–49.

23 Fretheim, *God and World*, p. 133.

24 Falk, *Hebrew Law*, p. 19; Novak, "Law and Religion," p. 33; Yochanan Muffs, *The Personhood of God* (Woodstock, VT: Jewish Lights, 2005), p. 106.

the pattern established by the Creator. To do otherwise leads to malicious action against creation.[25]

The Covenant continues and ratifies this awareness that obedience to law is for the sake of people.[26] As Moses is quoted as saying, "do this and you will live!" (Dt 30: 19). Similarly, the covenant is conveyed in interpersonal language. The commands are not formal and abstract but a personal communication from God, each beginning with "you."[27] In this manner, God provides "the eternal example for meeting the other."[28] Thus, how each one reacts to this heavenly communication is a response to God bidding God's creatures to live a certain way.[29] The relational character of life is maintained at all times, whether or not one is aware of it or whether or not one obeys the commandments.

Unlike more immanent theologies, among them Christianity in many respects, commentators often maintain that in Judaism God is not encountered within the material and interpersonal. Rather, the Holy One is revealed as fully transcendent "and only accidentally immanent."[30] Even the Torah scroll itself is not holy, only the revelation that it contains.[31] Adherence to revealed law establishes a bridge whereby God becomes present to the daily events of life. Since the divine essence is hidden, God's involvement in human life as well as God's love for creation are manifested precisely in the act of giving the law.[32] It is in this way that God is "situated within a history."[33] As Abraham Heschel describes it: "The way to God is a way of God and the mitzvah [Jewish law] is a way of God, a way where the self-evidence of the Holy is disclosed."[34]

An important corollary of this approach, wherein the very sanctity of God enters the human sphere by way of the law, is the belief that it was actually God

---

25 Louis Ginzberg notes that the Ten Commandments are so closely interwoven that offenses against the first table of the Decalogue, concerning duties to God, are linked necessarily to offenses in the second table that are concerned with obligations to others. See *Legends of the Bible* (New York: Simon and Schuster, 1956), p. 389. Brague states that the idea that the people of Israel are priests (Ex 19: 6) means that "Israel is obliged to observe, at all times, the code of conduct that pertains to priests and behave as if in a sanctuary." See *Law*, pp. 55–56.

26 "[T]he law is the guarantee of God's continued interest in man. As long as God's law stands, he too remains involved in the destiny of man." Berkovits, *Essential Essays*, p. 5.

27 Muffs, *Personhood*, p. 25.

28 Berkovits, *Essential Essays*, p. 3.

29 Heschel, *Between God and Man*, p. 155.

30 Ibid., p. 94.

31 Neusner, *Torah*, p. 20.

32 Berkovits, *Essential Essays*, pp. 4–5.

33 Brague, *Law*, p. 65.

34 Heschel, *Between God and Man*, pp. 79–80.

who was ruling. Judges or kings simply put the divine decrees into effect.[35] The Torah was the "finger of God" (Ex 32: 16; Dt 9: 10).[36] It was this attitude of relating the divine to the normative foundations of life and the specific historical narrative of a people that formed the basis of the Greek word *nomos* and the English word "law."[37]

The devout Jew in this formulation is one who trusts that the law is good, has been revealed, and must be obeyed regardless of circumstance or consequence. To do less is to rupture the only line of communication between a loving and purposeful God and God's noble but tragically limited and dependant creation.

A Contemplative Understanding of Law

The centrality of the belief in a faithful adherence to law in the Hebrew Bible emphasizes the preeminence of obedience over rational deliberation, and action over intention; actions reveal one's thoughts and moral commitments.[38] It can thus be stated that as great an emphasis is placed upon character and virtue as on any lesser motivation for legal adherence such as fear or opportunistic calculation. In the biblical view, the ritual prescriptions, for example, are not simply a legal restraint upon human spontaneity but an attempt to create an overall mindfulness of the divine presence, inculcating "the awareness of God as a secondary instinct."[39] One is ultimately defined, therefore, not by citizenship, political affiliation, or by one's power to reason, but by response to the norms that summon a continued attentiveness even as they penetrate every area of life.[40]

Despite this sense of divine resonance in the mundane affairs of each day and the conscientious habits they often evoke in the individual believer, the primacy of obedience to an objective set of behavioral requirements, however piously they are perceived, often creates a pervasive sense of dualism. The God who cannot be named, "who has risen on high to His throne yet stoops from the heights to look down … upon heaven and earth" (Ps 113: 5–6), is finally a God whose transcendence precedes and defines His immanence. As Paul Johnson notes:

---

35 On God reigning in Israel, see Brague, *Law*, pp. 41, 47, 49; Falk, *Hebrew Law*, p. 20; Herbert Fingarette, "The Meaning of Law in the Book of Job," in Stanley Hauerwas and Alasdair McIntyre (eds), *Revisions* (South Bend, IN: Notre Dame University Press, 1983), p. 250; Johnson, *History*, pp. 32–33; Levinson, *Legal Revision*, pp. 26–27.

36 Brague, *Law*, p. 49.

37 Cover, "Nomos," p. 11.

38 Heschel, *Between God and Man*, p. 156.

39 Berkovits, *Essential Essays*, p. 30.

40 Berkovits writes: "Every important event in the life of the Jew is brought under the dominance of law. There seems to be no niche or nook into which the law has not penetrated. The law is present all the time and everywhere. The Jew is indeed surrounded by *mitzvot* on all sides." See *Essential Essays*, p. 7. See also Brague, *Law*, p. 68.

"The Israelites thus attributed a far greater power and distance to God than any other religion of antiquity."[41] This differentiation between God and the world, a difference so vast that the very idea of representing God was unthinkable, was bridged by a discrete system of legal statutes. Thus were created the conditions for an ethical stance that came to elevate to divine status the requirements associated with law and, as a consequence, the tendency to view external compliance as determinative of internal consent.[42] It is not within my capacity to measure the degree to which that identification shaped the Jewish worldview, but the brunt of the discussion in the chapters to come will discuss how the apotheosis of law, often regardless of its statutory requirements, came to dominate in a negative and regrettable way the context in which Christians came to understand the teachings of Christ.

In contrast, the stance of mindfulness to the presence of God in life's daily routine can widen the consciousness and change the moral and spiritual horizon of the individual believer. It can lead to an approach to life and to faith that transcends unimpeachable cosmic barriers; one based on an immediate loving response to reality that obviates the view of law as an objective force that must be obeyed and of judgment as an analytical determination of human guilt and of one's rightful measure of pain. It is a stance that can affirm from one's very core the divine pronouncements banning idolatry (Ex 20: 2–3) and yet recognize that idolatry itself can only proceed from a dualistic consciousness, never from one fully absorbed in love of the Creator and creation.

This latter view is particularly pertinent to the discussion concerning love and obedience to law. This very topic provides the substance of much of the discord that the subject of the Jewish law provokes in the New Testament. If obedience is understood as essential to religion and to human liberation, is the attitude of the obedient subject to God's law of much importance? Many writers argue that it is, centering on a particular appreciation of the relational nature of the covenant. They argue that compliance is the result of a love for God and for humankind; a loving gift invites a loving response.[43] God is holy and calls for holiness from the chosen people (Lev 11: 44). This is why Heschel argues that Judaism is "a

---

[41] Johnson, *History*, p. 39. Gerhard von Rad writes: "If one may say so, Israel paid a high price for her refusal to accept any form of metaphysical dualism, for by excluding from the world any traces of theomachic dualism, she was compelled to face the problem in her religious thought of accepting and explaining the dualism as a fact within the godhead itself." See, "Some Aspects of the Old Testament World-View," in *The Problem of the Hexateuch*, trans. E.W. Trueman Dicken (New York: McGraw Hill, 1966), p. 151.

[42] This is the argument made by Gauchet, *Disenchantment*; Taylor, *Secular*. It also advanced by Henri Bergson in *The Two Sources of Morality and Religion*, trans. R. Ashley Audra and Cloudesley Brereton (New York: Doubleday, 1935).

[43] Berkovits, *Essential Essays*, p. 5.

complex of obligations" yet, at the same time, to follow the law without love vitiates its meaning.[44]

By its nature, however, love always threatens to overwhelm the limits established by strict material codes of conduct. In the heart of the one who follows the psalmist in stilling and quieting the soul (Ps 131: 2), the one attentive to the divine utterance: "Be still and know that I am God" (Ps 46: 11), or the one who ponders the words of the prophet: "The Lord is in His holy temple. Let all the earth keep silence before Him" (Hab 2: 20), a path lies open for an experience of a God far different from the custodian of reward and retribution. Ricoeur portrays a deity who loves and initiates a love in the one created that bursts through the confines established by law: "The love of creation is a form of consolation which depends on no external compensation and which is equally remote from any form of vengeance. Love finds within itself its own compensation; it is itself consolation."[45]

A similar challenge to the particularity associated with a univocal focus upon dutiful submission to legal ordinance arises in the Book of Job. Herbert Fingarette suggests that the intent of the author of this profound ethical parable is to reveal "that law is an essentially human, not divine enterprise." The story teaches, through an analysis of the troubling contradictions often found within statutory observance, that "a passionate personal integrity" is the ground essential to achieving ultimate wisdom and salvation.[46] The author of the text seeks to underscore the inability of any legal system, in this case the Torah, to encompass the infinite shadings of human experience.[47] The intent of Job's repeated queries concerning the fractured relation of obedience and justice are an affirmation of the preeminence of life itself over law.[48] They remind the devout believer of a central truth in contemplative spirituality, one very much at the heart of Christian ethics and at the heart of its paradigmatic symbol, the cross: religion is fundamentally a path for understanding pain, and, specifically, of transforming pain into an act of humility, love, and forgiveness: "God's message comes in suffering; an appreciation of the meaning of the message comes only when we despair of our own powers, thus accepting the inevitability of the humbled human will."[49]

In like manner, Roland Murphy contends that the book is a protracted investigation of Satan's cynical interpretation of Job's faultless attendance to the

---

[44] Heschel, *Between God and Man*, pp. 159, 162. Muffs makes a similar claim: see *Personhood*, p. 37.

[45] Ricoeur, "Religion," p. 467. Johnson suggests that Elijah, too, mirrored this contemplative pattern not only in his perception of "the still small voice" on Mt. Horeb (I Kings 19: 12), but also in standing "for the individual conscience, perhaps the first man in Jewish history to do so." See *History*, p. 67.

[46] Fingarette, "Meaning of Law," p. 249.

[47] Bernstein, *Formation of Hell*, pp. 156–58.

[48] Fingarette, "Meaning of Law," p. 272.

[49] Ibid., p. 266.

law's decrees: "Is it for nothing that Job is God-fearing?" (Job 1: 9). The intent of the author is to have the reader ponder whether one can be motivated solely by love without any hope of recompense; whether, in effect, love is its own reward. Murphy thinks this is the challenge of the tale for us all: "Even if doubt is cast on the credibility of Job's replies in 1:21 and 2:10, they are recorded there and present a possible stage of selfless love of God, and this question remains as a challenge for every human being."[50]

Of course, these authors do not represent all, nor perhaps even the majority of views on the meaning of the book. Berkovits, for example, concurs with the valence of the "suffering as test" thesis. He states that God is just but also must consider other issues in the "management of the universe," among them "the terrifying testing of the faith of the righteous, as was the case with Job."[51] The point of our investigation is, however, to reveal that the ability for each person to perceive God in all of creation and to express a love of God beyond compliance or non-compliance with law, beyond reward and punishment, has its roots in Jewish poetry, spirituality, and theology. These are the beliefs that shaped a love of the law and, ultimately, a love beyond the law in the life of Jesus.

Law and Punitive Judgment

We now must look specifically at the process of rendering punitive judgment for legal violations and its relation to what we have thus far discussed. The God of Israel is quite unlike the gods of other nations, not only "slow to anger and abounding in kindness," but also deeply upset at human injustice. Whereas the gods of Mesopotamia are only driven to rage by the foibles of the king, the slightest human misdeed can stir the divine ire. This is not a sign of pettiness or the whims of power, but a reaction to betrayal and infidelity in an intimate relationship (Hos 11: 1–2).[52] What some have termed the "wrath of God" must then be seen, according to Muffs, in light of the fact that we only grow angry with the ones for whom we care deeply. The poor and powerless are of no concern to other deities, but the God of Israel sees any affront to human dignity, especially by the heirs of the covenant, as an abomination.[53] The Hebrew term *psh* relates to the idea of violating these sacred ties; it connotes a rebellion, a breach, or a breaking away.[54] Crime and sin were thus indistinguishable: all sins were crimes and all crimes

---

50 Murphy, *Job*, p. 109.

51 Berkovits, *Essential Essays*, p. 151. For a Jewish perspective on suffering that takes exception to the suffering as test thesis, see Harold S. Kushner, *When Bad Things Happen to Good People* (New York: Avon, 1981), pp. 24–26.

52 Heschel, *Prophets*, pp. 5–26.

53 Muffs, *Personhood*, p. 42.

54 Mark E. Biddle, *Missing the Mark: Sin and Its Consequences in Biblical Theology* (Nashville: Abingdon, 2005), p. 20. See also Fretheim, *God and World*, p. 149.

were sins.[55] Acts of disregard for covenantal responsibilities not only consciously elevated a false set of behavioral norms that could do no other than harm the doer and others; they also threatened to annul, at least temporarily, the divine promises that were the basis for Israel's existence.[56]

Nowhere is this intolerance for sin, especially sins against the well-being of others, more evident than in the prophets. Heschel writes that most parallel theologies either avoid the subject of human misery or seek to provide divine justification for it, but the biblical prophet manifests God's scrupulous concern with human conduct and magnifies the smallest act of cruelty or injustice to such a degree that as a result of the transgression, "the whole world appears as a slum."[57]

If small affronts to the sanctity of life provoked God to righteous anger, there is little reason to doubt the divine reaction to egregious acts of mischief and cruelty. Capital punishment is prescribed for a large number offenses, none more serious than willful murder (Nm 35: 31–34; Josh 7: 25–26). Here no compensation was sufficient to undo the harm caused; and divine justice is exacted not only against the enemies of God's people but also against this very people.[58] Johnson takes the view that precisely because human life was of the utmost value to God, the wealthy could not use social privilege as a means of buying their way out of their just desserts, even if their victim was a servant or a slave.[59]

Although scholars remind us that most acts of violent punishment, especially the death penalty, are rarely in evidence in post-exilic Jewish society, a strong punitive current still exists for unlawful conduct in the Hebrew Bible.[60] Yet there is also much evidence to support an interpretation of law and judgment that addresses human misdeeds in a way that conforms to the ethic being proposed in this book.

If one takes a creational view of law, that patterns of truthful living are embedded in the fabric of reality, that there is a divine presence in the human heart that challenges the human ego and seeks to direct each to purposes harmonious with divine love, one can ascertain not an active judgment from God to a set of externally imposed rules but a set of consequences already inherent in the primal order of things (Lam 1: 2–13; Hos 9: 7–9). Violations of this pattern are destructive of the doer, of the natural environment, and of the entire community: "The sinner

---

55 Johnson, *History*, p. 33.

56 Falk, *Hebrew Law*, p. 23.

57 Heschel, *Prophets*, p. 5.

58 Israel Drapkin, *Crime and Punishment in the Ancient World* (Lexington, MA: Lexington Books, 1989), pp. 54–83.

59 Johnson, *History*, p. 33.

60 On the infrequent practice of violence in post-exilic Israel see E. Christian Brugger, *Capital Punishment and Roman Catholic Tradition* (Notre Dame: University of Notre Dame Press, 2003); Lee Griffith, *The Fall of the Prison* (Grand Rapids: Eerdman's, 1993), pp. 91–92; James J. Megivern, *The Death Penalty: An Historical and Theological Survey* (New York: Paulist, 1987), pp. 10–12; De Vaux, *Ancient Israel*, pp. 149–50.

need not await a day of judgment; sin begins to exact its price immediately."[61] This interpretation places law as an instrumental device to safeguard human well-being, not as a vehicle of deliberate social control or reprisal. It also honors human nature, both in its beauty and pathos.

Overreliance on a punitive juridical metaphor, even in a religion as legally complex as Judaism, also does not give proper attention to other issues that arise in the human response to legislative decrees. It simply cannot do "justice" to human frailty, as sin is often not willfully committed at all, nor does it honor the relentless openness of the human person to transcendence.[62]

The administration of justice in ancient Israel also reveals the tension between a legalist and a more nuanced and tolerant approach to human failing. There existed the clear possibility to judge harshly within the orbit of the law but so too was there a constant call to allow love for the other to guide the response to delinquent behavior.

Justice was based on the adversarial model, one that would remain in effect in virtually all parts of the Western world until the thirteenth century.[63] A complaint would be brought by a private person. There was no public prosecutor. Plaintiff and defendant argued their cases and were able to direct questions to one another (Dt 25: 7–8; Prov 25: 8). In a capital case, a conviction could not be substantiated without at least two reliable witnesses (Nm 35: 30; Dt 17: 6).[64] It was the Mosaic teaching that the witness upon whose testimony the conviction of death was substantiated would be the first one required to hurl the fatal stone (Dt 17: 7).

There were several different jurisdictions: a communal assembly of elders was appointed in each town, usually the heads of the various families in the clan. They would assist a judge, or at times judges, who would hear cases and render their decisions. The king also had a judicial function (Isa 16: 5), as did the Levites (I Chron 24).[65] Juridical procedure was carried out in public, either at the city gate

---

[61] Biddle, *Missing the Mark*, p. 20. Reinhold Niebuhr argues in similar fashion that the "original sin" is the human anger over the natural limitations God has placed on humans who then react with a destructive embrace of either power or self-indulgence. See *The Nature and Destiny of Man* (2 vols, New York: Charles Scribner's Sons, 1949), vol. 1, pp. 16–18. See also Heschel, *Between God and Man*, p. 193.

[62] Biddle, *Missing the Mark*, p. 95. See also Kevin Jung, "Fallibility and Fragility," in Jonathan Rothchild, Matthew Myer Boulton and Kevin Jung (eds), *Doing Justice to Mercy* (Charlottesville: University of Virginia Press, 2007), pp. 206–21. This is clearly not the only way to interpret the punitive justice that is evident until the end of the monarchy. The public prosecution of serious offenses is also seen as necessary to preserve the purity of the community and the land as well as the sanctity of human life as revealed in the Mosaic Codes. See Falk, *Hebrew Law*, pp. 20–23; Johnson, *History*, pp. 33–34.

[63] Shaffern, *Law and Justice*, p. 36. The inquisitorial system emerged with the development and implementation of canon law in the Middle Ages. See Berman, *Law and Revolution*, pp. 50, 64; Whitman, *Origins*, p. 54.

[64] De Vaux, *Ancient Israel*, pp. 155–56.

[65] Ibid., p. 152; Falk, *Hebrew Law*, p. 58.

(Ex 21: 6; Job 29: 7; Ps 127: 5; Ruth 4: 1–12; Prov 24: 7) or in a holy place or a sanctuary (I Sam 7: 16).

The goal repeatedly invoked was *mishpat*, not a strict retributive justice but righteousness, to which Isaiah gives such memorable words: "He will not judge by appearance, nor pass sentence based on hearsay. He will judge the lowly with justice and defend the rights of the poor of the land" (Isa 11: 3–4). Throughout the Hebrew Bible God executes *mishpat* for the fatherless, the widow, the orphan, and the alien (Dt 10: 18; Ex 23: 6–7; Jer 5: 28–29). One author claims that the purpose of judgment itself "is to save the innocent from injustice. The idea is so deeply anchored in scriptural thought that 'to judge' becomes the equivalent of 'to save'."[66]

Even in the most commonly referenced passages of a crude vengeance, such as the *lex talionis*, the "eye for an eye" (Ex 21: 23–25), the verses are located between two decrees, the latter mandating compensation for a slave who has lost an eye or a tooth (Ex 21: 6–7) and the former stating that wounds sustained in a quarrel were to be recompensed by means of a fine (Ex 21: 18–19). Furthermore, the law was enacted in order to constrain the common practice of blood vengeance that exacted guilt not only to the perpetrator but also to their kin.[67]

God's requirement of justice, therefore, mirrors not only God's perfect holiness and the desire to impart a moral reminder to the disobedient, but also a deep concern for those so easily exploited by the powerful and, often, by the implementation of the law itself. For whatever other divisions may have existed between tribes and classes, between priests, prophets, and the poor, the law of God given to Israel was scrupulous in its declaration of the equality of all in legal matters.[68] There are many angry biblical laments directed to judges whose decisions lack fairness and equity; these indictments are normally accompanied by a passionate summons for the judicial office to do nothing to further the burdens already borne by the poor of the land (Ps 72: 2; 82: 2–5; 94: 20–21; Isa 10: 1–4).

Imprisonment was rarely practiced. Of the 17 instances of forcible confinement in the Hebrew Bible, 12 occur in descriptions of life during periods of exile.[69] The use of a punitive detention, aside from several personal acts of aggression as seen in the confinement of Jeremiah (Jer 20: 12; 32: 2–5; 37: 13–16) and that of the prophet Micah (I Kings 22: 26–28), is only witnessed in Jewish society as a result of foreign rule. The Book of Ezra, for instance, contains a judicial decree from Artaxerxes II mandating exile, death, confiscation of goods, or imprisonment as fitting punishments for legal violations (Ez 7: 26). The few remaining instances were normally forms of detention while the will of God was sought as a response to a legal infraction, as when Moses temporarily confined a reputed blasphemer (Lev 24: 10–12) and detained one who had gathered sticks on

66 Berkovits, *Essential Essays*, p. 135; see also Falk, *Hebrew Law*, p. 25.

67 Falk, *Hebrew Law*, pp. 80–81.

68 Johnson, *History*, p. 40.

69 Peters, "Prison," p. 11.

the Sabbath as "there was no clear decision as to what should be done with him" (Nm 15: 32–36). Overall, forcible detention, in whatever form, is overshadowed by a divine justice wherein the pain of separation is overcome by God's repeated desire for the return of the exile and the liberation of the captive (Isa 42: 6–7; Ps 107: 16).

We thus see that in the concrete practices of judicial procedure, just as in the determination of the meaning and binding force of the law, two distinct and often interrelated interpretations were at play: one proceeding from the unquestionable duty to obey divine statutes and punish those who fail to honor them, the other from a loving awareness of God's immanent presence in all of creation that precedes and, at times, requires that the provisions of law be amended, or even disregarded.

Summary

Von Rad sees the different worldviews of Israel that we have been discussing in terms of the dialectic between unity and universality on one hand and, on the other, the growing emphasis, particularly with the enactment of the Torah, upon particularity and "dogmatic considerations" that foster a more enclosed stance toward the rest of the world.[70] The former view is often expressed in passages with a noticeable contemplative tone: "The heavens are telling the glory of God … Day to day pours forth speech, And night to night declares knowledge" (Ps 19: 1–2). Von Rad notes that a "whole world separates this ancient hymn from a later addition to the same psalm" in praise of the Mosaic law: "The law of the Lord is perfect, refreshing the soul; The decree of the Lord is trustworthy, giving wisdom to the simple" (Ps 19: 8–9). He adds that the "change of style is unmistakable" and "is a profoundly conceived theological addition."[71]

Admitting these disparate views of divine intention and of the way to honor God among our Jewish ancestors, it is evident that the approach to law and judgment proposed in this volume finds a firm footing in the revelation made to the people of Israel. There will be significant departures in theology and ethics in the New Testament and in later Christian history, but the thesis that a mindful and compassionate presence to the other that transcends both law and judgment in the immediate encounter finds more in the Hebrew Bible in which to root itself than much of later Christian history will suggest. For the proscriptions enacted there against the culpable cannot function faithfully, in fact lose much of their divine authority, outside a commitment to the sacredness of each life that has been confirmed by God's own decree. Berkovits notes that *mishpat* keeps "comfortable company" in the Bible with *hesed* (love), *rahamin* (mercy and compassion), and *tzedaka* (charity and supererogatory acts).[72]

---

70 Von Rad, "Old Testament World-View," pp. 154, 156.

71 Ibid., p. 157.

72 Berkovits, *Essential Essays*, p. 138.

Certainly, in the Book of Job one finds an extended meditation on the belief that personal integrity and a fervent unwillingness to judge, given the profound inadequacy of human reason before the divine mind, take precedence over law. In fact, the author clearly implies that Job is innocent and God is unjust if the Mosaic law is given priority of honor in forging a theological ethic in general, and an ethic of justice in particular.[73]

Job comes to meet God not by obedience, and certainly not by judging, but through a spirituality of suffering: a humble acceptance of life's capriciousness (an acceptance of the cross, if you will), a cultivation of silence, patience, and hope (cf. Isa 30: 15), and a radical curtailment of his own ego.[74]

From origins such as these, a Christian ethic can emerge wherein justice seeks first to honor what can never be broken, human and creational solidarity, and wherein one cannot envision a punitive judgment in any other terms than accompanying the offender on the inner journey to find liberation and reconciliation through personal repentance. From these origins, too, can emerge a contemplative Christian spirituality: one that shuns division and dualism—each fostered as much by legalism as by the memory of unfortunate events—and one that stands in awe of the infinite God, and the beauty of all that God has created, with nothing more than a quiet mind and a loving heart.

Yochanan Muffs comments that Judaism in its approach to law and judgment successfully brings together a triad of normative commitments that had not been harmonized before, nor have they since. He speaks of the union of power, justice, and love. He then states that Christianity reconfigured the three values, making only one central to its belief system, eclipsing the value of the other two. That one supreme ethical commitment is love.[75] Its ascendence as a rule of life in the person of Jesus and its preeminence over law and judgment will now be discussed, after which we will speak of its decline.

73 Fingarette, "Meaning of Law," pp. 249, 255.

74 Ibid., pp. 264, 266.

75 Muffs, *Personhood*, pp. 85, 87.

Chapter 2
Law and Judgment in the New Testament

Christ suffered a horrible and ignominious death. He was condemned by a Roman prefect—abetted by the Temple aristocracy—and was abandoned by virtually all of his friends and associates. He was a lawbreaker and his death was neither accidental nor a theological construct.[1] It is noteworthy that virtually all of the early Roman documents referring to Jesus and his disciples are records of disturbances and "police actions."[2] Jesus was also a Jew. The actions that led to his condemnation were, in part, violations of Roman law but also of the law of God his father and of the people he loved (Mk 15: 60–64; Jn 19: 7). The Pharisees regarded Jesus as a sinner due to his lack of legal observance (Jn 9: 24).[3]

Christians, in particular, must consider these things in seeking to construct a proper approach to law and judgment. Paul states, "absolute fullness resides in him" (Col 1: 19). Christians worthy of the name, as Martin Luther King insisted, must measure their attitudes, their decisions, and their very lives against the life of Christ; and the conclusions reached are of great significance not only for those who profess the Christian faith but, increasingly, for the countless millions who are judged, punished, and sometimes executed for violations of law.[4]

Scripture scholars are in near unanimous agreement that the main theme of the preaching of Jesus was the "reign of God."[5] God's final revelation not only dominates the sayings of Jesus and forms the substance of some of his most

---

1 Gerd Theissen writes that Christ "was responsible for this own execution." He states: "No religious group depicts its redeemer as a criminal who died a dishonorable death on the cross unless it has to." See *Fortress Introduction to the New Testament* (Minneapolis: Fortress, 2003), p. 22. Jon Sobrino calls theological attempts to minimize the political nature of Christ's execution an "abstraction;" see *Christology at the Crossroads* (Maryknoll, NY: Orbis, 1976), p. 72. See also Curt Cadorette, "Legion and the Believing Community: Discipleship in an Imperial Age," in Michael Budde and Robert Brimlow (eds), *The Church as Counterculture* (Albany: State University of New York Press, 2000), pp. 153–70; Ched Myers, *Binding the Strong Man: A Political Reading of Mark's Story of Jesus* (Maryknoll, NY: Orbis, 1988), pp. 152–56, 176–77; Mark Lewis Taylor, *The Executed God* (Minneapolis: Fortress, 2001), pp. 70–98.

2 Donald Senior, *Jesus: A Gospel Portrait* (New York: Paulist, 1992), p. 12.

3 Craig R. Koester, *The Word of Life: A Theology of John's Gospel* (Grand Rapids, MI: William B. Eerdmans, 2008), p. 69.

4 Martin Luther King, "Letter from the Birmingham Jail" in *Why We Can't Wait* (New York: Harper & Row, 1964), pp. 77, 88–89.

5 Donald Senior writes: "Every New Testament scholar would agree that the central theme of Jesus' ministry was the Kingdom of God." See *Jesus*, p. 48. See also Gunther

compelling parables, it is also considered an impending event and the decision to accept or reject it of immediate importance.[6] The idea of the "kingdom" is not foreign to Jewish texts, but there it is forecast as a future event and carries the hope of deliverance from Gentile rule.[7] Jesus, on the other hand, proclaims that the Messianic reign has arrived in his coming (Lk 17: 21): the ancient prophecies of Isaiah concerning the fulfillment of God's promises are now taking place (Lk 4: 16–21).[8] Rather than a defeat of the alien and the foreign oppressor, the message of Jesus places the alien and the Gentile on an equal footing with the people of Israel and, even more, often portrays the former as possessing the life of the new age before the ones originally chosen by God (Lk 13: 29).[9]

This is a central message of the "good news" or "gospel." The term is not original with the early Christians; it was a common linguistic device, utilized by the Romans in reference to the emperor. Significant occurrences in imperial life, such as the day of his birth or his military conquests, were proclaimed as gospel. The New Testament writers appropriated the term in describing the life of Christ not only as literal good news, but also, some feel, as a deliberate attempt to upstage the emperor while affirming a seminal theological truth concerning the true "king of kings."[10]

The Christian gospel is a message of liberation for the captive and the oppressed, a pronounced "option for the poor," one in which the violent practices of worldly politics give way to a dominion of peace upon God's holy mountain (Isa 2: 2–4; 11: 2–10).[11] It is a declaration that the human tendency to engage in polarized judgment is not only untruthful but also that the new age in which all creation is one in Christ has appeared and supplanted it. This good news proclaims an end to political and psychological systems that divide the world into the good and the bad, the powerful and the weak, the worthy and the unworthy. It also

---

Bornkamm, *The New Testament*, p. 12; Rudolf Bultmann, *Theology of the New Testament*, trans. Kendrick Grobel (2 vols, New York: Charles Scribner's Sons, 1951), vol. 1, p. 4.

6 Theissen, *Fortress*, p. 12; Senior, *Jesus*, p. 48.

7 W.D. Davies, *Invitation to the New Testament* (Garden City, NY: Doubleday, 1966), p. 153; Theissen, *Fortress*, p. 18.

8 Davies, *Invitation*, p. 163.

9 Theissen, *Fortress*, p. 18.

10 This is how Bornkamm distinguishes the gospel (the good news of fulfillment and salvation in Christ) from the gospels (the specific narratives about his life). See *New Testament*, pp. 19–22. Davies acknowledges this view in certain texts in the New Testament, particularly in Luke (2: 1; Acts 17: 7), but prefers the interpretation that the "good news" referred to in the gospels is more an attempt to echo sentiments in the Hebrew Bible (Jer 20: 15; I Sam 31: 8–10). See *Invitation*, pp. 148–49.

11 God's preference for the poor is visible in stories such as the rich man and Lazarus (Lk 16: 19–31), and the Pharisee and the Publican (Lk 18: 9–14), as well as in teachings such as the widow's mite (Mk 12: 41–44) and the beatitudes (Lk 6: 20–26). Senior, *Jesus*, pp. 62–63.

announces an end to the tendency of religions to project the fulfillment of the divine plan solely as a future event and then employ it as an extension of the reward/punishment system.[12]

All things must now be reconsidered; all things are now made new (Rev 21: 5).

The gospel is a proclamation narrative unlike anything in ancient literature.[13] Law and judgment are not invalid concepts but henceforth must be reinterpreted in conformity to "the way, the truth, and the life" who has appeared to guide, console, and unite humankind (Jn 14: 6; Eph 1: 10; Col 1: 20). In this new age, the last are now first (Mt 20: 16).

Jesus, St Paul, and the Law

As was noted at the beginning of the chapter, Jesus often ignored legal obligations or legitimated non-compliance. The question that has frequently occupied scholars is not whether Jesus was a lawbreaker, but why he deliberately broke the law. Most conclude that Jesus did not flaunt the Torah out of some anarchic commitment to antinomianism but rather, as was appropriate for a rabbi, continually viewed the law in light of the scriptural narrative. In his case, however, it was the fulfillment of that narrative in his human incarnation.[14]

Jesus was a teacher of the law. It has been suggested that Matthew crafts his entire gospel with an eye to portraying Jesus as a second Moses. The Sermon on the Mount, for instance, is consciously set on a mountain, a deliberate reference to Sinai, and contains the new and final rendition of the law. This is seen in Jesus' repeated use of the phrases "you have heard it said," followed by "but I say unto you."[15]

Matthew is as much arguing against the Christian Hellenists and antinomians of his day as he is arguing for a continuation of the law in Jesus, nowhere more so than when Christ insists that he has not come to abolish the law and the prophets (Mt 5: 17).[16] For Matthew, as for any devout Jew, the law is eternal, but what makes it eternal is the context of love in which each of its provisions must now be placed. Perhaps the most compelling evidence of this principle is found in the

---

[12] Richard Rohr, *The Naked Now* (New York: Crossroad, 2009), pp. 100–01.

[13] Bornkamm, *New Testament*, p. 41.

[14] Harvey Cox, *When Jesus Came to Harvard*, pp. 23–31; Fretheim, *God and World*, p. 154.

[15] Gunther Bornkamm, "End Expectation and Church in Matthew," in Gunther Bornkamm, Gerhard Barth, and Heinz Joachim Held (eds), *Tradition and Interpretation in Matthew*, trans. Percy Scott (London: SCM, 1982), p. 35. The theme of Matthew's gospel presented here is not shared by all scholars. See, e.g., Robert Charles Branden, *Satanic Conflict and the Plot of Matthew* (New York: Peter Lang, 2006).

[16] Gerhard Barth, "Matthew's Understanding of the Law," in *Tradition and Interpretation in Matthew*, pp. 67, 70.

extended meditation on forbearance and forgiveness in the Sermon on the Mount (Mt 5: 21–48). Here, those who would imitate Christ are counseled not only to avoid anger at anyone and seek reconciliation with everyone, no matter how grievous the offense, but also to view the enemy and the persecutor, no less than any other person, with purity of heart and, above all, with love.[17]

The frequent conflicts with the Pharisees are not over love of the Torah but over whether love is its fulfillment. What Jesus asks for in regard to the law is radical obedience, but the obedience is to an all-embracing and uncompromising ethic of care contained in the only law Jesus ever gave, that his disciples love one another as they were loved by him (Jn 13: 34).[18] This is a counsel that "surpasses every legal demand; it knows no boundary or limit" (James 2: 8–13).[19] It is a loving response to the outpouring of love that the grateful heart receives from God, a childlike sense of wonder and total dependence that defines those who belong to the reign of God (Mk 10: 15), and a challenge to those who believe that they are saved by their own merits (Lk 16: 15).[20] In similar fashion, Paul also stressed that love fulfills all of the requirements of the Torah (Gal 5: 4–6), and that those who live in the Spirit of Jesus have already fulfilled whatever legitimate function law may possess (Rom 8: 4).

Jesus, devout in his Jewish faith, rarely acted contrary to the letter of the Mosaic precepts without consciously invoking a passage in the Hebrew Bible in which a more inclusive interpretation is then offered (Mt 5: 21ff, 27ff, 33ff, 38ff). This is the format of the contemplative approach to law that was spoken of in the last chapter, wherein the directives governing daily activities summon a loving attentiveness to all that one does and all with whom one interacts. Legal constraints become reminders that there are no actions lacking significance and, more importantly, that one must adopt a reverence for the sacredness of God's creation.[21]

Rather than an unconditional devotion to particular material commands, Jesus tended to view the entire legal edifice as a whole, a communication from God depicting a world filled with the divine glory as opposed to one wherein simple obedience could easily lead to a division between the devout and the reprobate, or the sacred and the profane.[22] From this perspective, as Bultmann suggests, Jesus

---

17 Ibid., p. 98.

18 Bultmann, *Theology*, p. 12. C.H. Dodd states that all of the precepts that Jesus taught must be regarded as indicating "the quality and direction of action which shall conform to the standard set by the divine *agape*." See *Gospel and Law* (New York: Columbia University Press, 1951), p. 73.

19 Bultmann, *Theology*, p. 18.

20 Ibid., p. 14.

21 Berkovits maintains that the purpose of the ritual laws, in particular, was not the inherent validity of the practices themselves as much as the inculcation of a mindfulness of the presence of God. See *Essential Essays*, p. 30.

22 Senior, *Jesus*, p. 96.

emphasized that the Pharisees and their companions at times failed to make a proper distinction between what is lawfully required and what is morally true. In so doing, they hallowed ordinances that had lost the meaning they once had and regarded "a plethora of cultic and ritual demands" as "God's command, or an ethical demand," thus overshadowing the *real* ethical demands required in a given situation.[23]

Therefore, Jesus speaking to women, to prostitutes, and to tax collectors; his touching of lepers and the unclean; and his frequent healings on the Sabbath are not entries in a catalogue of legal indifference but instances of the victory of the "suffering servant" who shall "decide aright for the land's afflicted" (Isa 11: 4), and signs of the love, inclusiveness, and forgiveness that are destined to permeate all of creation. The new age has arrived in Christ and its nascent quality is a summons, a challenge to all, especially to Christians, to bring the reign of God to life in repetition of his example.[24] For the disciple, as with the master, the example to be emulated is not one of lawless behavior but a reminder to place law in service to the truth that God is present everywhere and is to be loved and embraced wherever one's eyes are turned. This is what some believe Jesus is referring to when he states: "until heaven and earth pass away, not the smallest letter of the law … shall be done away with" (Mt 5: 18). What will endure forever is the interpretation of the law that Christ announces.[25]

In like manner, the continual subverting by Jesus of the established order of things that triggered so much consternation among his foes (Mk 2:16; Lk 7: 39; 15: 1–2; 19: 7) was not intended as a rejection of some in preference to others. Rather, in hallowing poverty over riches, weakness over strength, humility over pride, and mercy over judgment he makes an affirmation of treasures that endure (Mt 6: 20) and provides an invitation to "taste and see" (Ps 34: 9) that by imitating the way of God one finally overcomes the fear, isolation, and narcissistic indulgence that entrap so many.

It is often remarked that even this "command" to love is not a command at all but an instance of the way Jesus inspired his listeners to refashion the way they see God, themselves, and the world. More than any other term used to describe him, whether the "son of God," or the "son of man," or the "divine logos," Harvey Cox contends that the most licit and accurate description of Jesus is that he was a rabbi.[26] The way that Jesus taught reveals not only his moral message but also his moral methodology. Rabbis, in Cox's view, are first of all storytellers; and this is by and large what Jesus did.[27] In the face of honest human questions concerning

[23] Bultmann, *Theology*, p. 11.

[24] Thomas Schreiner states that law in the gospel of Mark should always be interpreted against this paradigm. See *New Testament Theology* (Grand Rapids, MI: Baker Academic, 2008), p. 618.

[25] Bornkamm, "End Expectation," pp. 37–38.

[26] Cox, *When Jesus Came*, pp. 23–24.

[27] Ibid., pp. 25–26.

the division of an estate, the extent of care owed to one's neighbor, or the limits of forgiveness, he told stories that invited his hearers to ponder a way of life that begins in the imagination, revealing a psychology of human motivation in which each person first embraces an image of the kind of person he or she wants to be, and then adopts the appropriate dispositions and motivations to allow that image to claim one's very identity.[28]

Accompanying this narrative approach, Jesus continually offered hypothetical imperatives rather than direct commands: "if you wish to enter eternal life," "if you want to be perfect" (Mk 10: 21).[29] Some ethicists maintain that the parable of the Good Samaritan (Lk 10: 25–37) best exemplifies this emphasis on openness to others, dialogue, and the attempt to provide a new context wherein the seeker can come to a deeper appreciation of the grace offered in the moment on his or her own. Jesus entertains the question of the lawyer regarding who is one's neighbor, but never answers the query because it is at root an inappropriate question. He simply challenges his hearer to strive to become a neighbor in service to whomever is encountered along the way, regardless of personal cost.[30]

It is important to restate, in light of this conversation, that love was by no means foreign to Jewish interpretations of the law. A century before Jesus, Hillel had summed up the Torah in the command to love.[31] Similarly, in rabbinic Judaism, love is often used to convey the meaning of fidelity to covenantal guidelines. Those who adhered to such an interpretation, however, would probably not have been the ones offended by Jesus' teaching. As noted in the previous chapter, there were strict factions in the Jewish community for whom scrupulous adherence to the law was the precondition for one claiming to love God. They therefore felt justified in concluding that Jesus could not have come from God (Jn 9: 16).[32]

This tension between understanding law in the light of love as opposed to viewing love in light of legal observance is very much in evidence in the writings of St Paul. E.P. Sanders concludes that Paul's thought on the relevance of the law can be summarized in one dominant formula: "getting in and staying in."[33] Humans are saved in Christ; in him, they enter the people of God. If they sin

---

[28] Numerous Christian ethicists maintain the centrality of this storytelling function of Jesus and the importance of the imagination in regard to it. See ibid., pp. 32–45; Stanley Hauerwas, *A Community of Character* (Notre Dame: University of Notre Dame Press, 1981), pp. 9–52; Philip Keane, *Christian Ethics and the Imagination* (Ramsey, NJ: Paulist, 1984); Spohn, *Go And Do Likewise*, pp. 9–32.

[29] Brague, *Law*, p. 70; Cox, *When Jesus Came*, pp. 26–28.

[30] Ivan Illich and David Cayley, *The Rivers North of the Future* (Toronto: Anansi, 2005), pp. 50–51, 206–07; Paul Ramsey, *Basic Christian Ethics* (New York: Scribner's, 1954), pp. 92–108.

[31] Brague, *Law*, p. 69. See also Heschel, *Between God and Man*, p. 162.

[32] Senior, *Jesus*, p. 95.

[33] E.P. Sanders, *Paul, the Law, and the Jewish People* (Philadelphia, Fortress, 1983), p. 6. Not all Pauline scholars agree with Sanders in this matter; see Steve Moyise, *Evoking*

they can be chastised and "stay in;" they can repent of their sins and "stay in," or they can refuse to reform and be excluded from the community of salvation.[34] Paul consistently focuses not on the merits of specific works but on what one must do to be incorporated into the people of God.[35] The final answer is always faith (Gal 3: 11).

Paul is not engaged in an argument with, and certainly not a diatribe against, the Jews, for "despite all the difficult passages, Paul was absolutely convinced that God sent Christ to save all humanity on the same basis."[36] Besides, Paul pays too much attention to his own conflict with fellow Christians, for example the controversy over circumcision, or the very unholy behavior of many in the church in Corinth, to warrant such an anti-Semitic claim. The focus is on those who claim that to be a child of Abraham one must adhere to the Law of Moses.[37] Paul insists that the promises made to Abraham have nothing to do with the law, which does not appear until 400 hundred years after Abraham's death (Gal 3: 15–18). Strict legal interpreters within the people of Israel made an error common to all in stumbling over the stone that is Christ in their insistence that behavioral compliance rather than faith was the central moral requirement (Rom 9: 30–33). The fault was not in the law as such, only in the inability to recognize that in Christ "the very righteousness of God" was now before them (Rom 10: 3–4).[38]

Although Paul works diligently to correct the errors of his contemporaries about the final end of law, he is just as influential on subsequent Christian thought in his proximate understanding of its value. The well-known directive to obey governing authorities since all authority is legitimated by divine decree (Rom 13: 1–5) was given decisive importance in the political theology of Martin Luther and his followers; and it is still utilized today as a Christian legitimation of law, judgment, and willful punishment of criminals.[39] Scholars have debated the centrality of this passage, some concluding that its principal intent was the employment of an analogy to then current "household ethics" that was then magnified to suit

---

Scripture (London and New York: T&T Clark, 2008), p. 76; F. Watson, *Paul and the Hermeneutics of Faith* (London and New York: T&T Clark, 2004), p. 324.

34 Sanders, *Paul*, p. 7.

35 Ibid., p. 18.

36 Ibid., p. 81.

37 Ibid., p. 19.

38 Luke Timothy Johnson, *Reading Romans* (New York: Crossroad, 1997), p. 158; Ernst Kasemann, *Commentary on Romans*, trans. Geoffrey W. Bromily (Grand Rapids, MI: William B. Eerdmans, 1980), p. 281.

39 Martin Luther, "Secular Authority," in *Martin Luther: Selections from His Writings*, ed. John Dillenberger (New York: Anchor, 1961), pp. 63–402. Oliver O'Donovan writes: "For the proposition that the authority of government resides *essentially* in the act of judgment, we must turn to the New Testament where St Paul described the function of civil authority as to reward the just and punish the evil (Rom 13: 4)." See *The Ways of Judgment* (Grand Rapids, MI: William B. Eerdmans, 2005), p. 4.

"reactionary" and "totalitarian" political interests.[40] It will be my argument that the strict approach to legal obedience that this passage depicts need not devalue the primacy of love and forgiveness for the Christian, nor need it endow a primary significance either to law or to judgment. The Pauline affirmation that those who bring evil upon others are reminded by law (and by God through its promulgation) of the incoherence of such behavior with the primacy of relationships in human life, and restrained by its statutes that such harm may not continue, coincides with what I propose is law's only legitimate function, as an instrumental or exhortative device. This approach is consistent not only with the teaching of Christ, who recommends the cutting of the infected tree (Lk 13: 6–7) and warns that unpaid debts will land one in prison (Lk 12: 58–59), but also with the humble attitude of Jesus toward those who punished him for breaking the law.

The question for Jesus and for Paul is never whether the law has any legitimacy, only whether the legalistic Pharisee or Hellenist is correct in affirming that it justifies and leads to life.[41] A literal interpretation of Paul's directive in Romans 13 would force one to conclude that both the Roman and Temple authorities who conspired in the execution of Jesus were justified in doing so by divine ordinance. Law and judgment do not take precedence over the life and example of Christ, nor should Christians place them on an equal plane with the very essence of who God is and who we aspire to be.

Law often serves to unite a particular people, but this parochial and unitive function is almost invariably at the expense and exclusion of those within its domain who fail to observe it, and just as often those outside of its jurisdiction who do not conform to its expectations. In contrast to this, as Paul states in Ephesians, the wall of enmity erected by the law between Jew and Gentile, citizen and foreigner, free person and slave, and woman and man, must now fall so that "now, united to Christ Jesus by the blood that he shed, you who were once aliens have now come together in peace" (Eph 2: 11–13).

---

40 Johnson writes that the passage has been used "to justify totalitarian and wicked regimes." He adds that it is "too much weight for a few words of contingent remarks to bear." See *Reading Romans*, pp. 185, 189–90. Kasemann states that the words are largely "an alien body" in the corpus of Paul's writing which were subsequently used by Christians to open doors "not only to conservative but also to reactionary views even to the point of political fanaticism." Kasemann contends that Paul is "not so much thinking of institutions as of organs and functions ranging from the tax collector, to the police, magistrates, and Roman officials." See *Commentary*, pp. 351, 354. For a contrasting view arguing that Paul "never purchases his high doctrine of the church at the expense of a low doctrine of the state," see John A.T. Robinson, *Wrestling with Romans* (Philadelphia: Westminster Press, 1979), p. 137.

41 Koester, *Word*, p. 69.

Terminal Illness and the Divine Doctor

The critique of strict legal observance by Jesus and St Paul cannot be teamed with a moral assumption concerning the demerits of those who find meaning and solace in such unqualified obedience.[42] That is to say, those mired in sin should not judge others in the same condition; and *all* are mired in that condition. Each, from the least to the greatest, is guilty of preferring darkness to the light (Jn 3: 19–20). "[This] is an evil and adulterous generation" (Mt 16: 4), and Jesus has come "to save his people from their sins" (Mt 1:21). He is the "doctor" who has come to heal the sick (Mk 2: 17), give sight to the blind, and hearing to the deaf (Mt 11: 4–5). Jesus even includes himself among the sinful when he tells the rich young man, "Why do you call me good? No one is good but God alone" (Mk 10: 18). Paul's exhortation that faith rather than law brings justification not only strikes a note of comfort to the habitually sinful, but also, as Kasemann suggests, it is a humbling indictment "because it fundamentally sets even a religious person in the place of the godless" (Rom 3: 27–28).[43]

Sin in the Bible has a number of meanings and various words are used to portray it. Scholars note, however, that the basic term utilized is the Greek word *hamartia* or the Hebrew word *hata* that are usually translated as "missing the mark." The Pharisees, for instance, use these terms in the gospels in their denunciation of the actions of Jesus.[44] What is vital to theology and the ethics of judgment and punishment is that this definition of sin does not coincide with lawbreaking. Although these terms, as we will see, become synonymous in some strands of Christian medieval thought, and this synthesis is certainly present in legal absolutism, sin in the Bible should not be viewed as a crime. Mark Biddle reveals that in Genesis, God does not impose a set of "artificial penalties;" rather sin, as in the command concerning the tree of the knowledge of good and evil in the garden of Eden, brings its own suffering to bear on its perpetrators (Gen 2: 16–17): "To violate the moral order is to injure, first of all, oneself and simultaneously one's environment and relationships."[45] What Adam and Eve feel before God says or does anything in accord with some divine juridical equation is shame, not

---

[42] Sin is not an ontological category in the Bible. It is a function of will, not of nature. See R.R. Reno, "Doctrine of Sin," in *Dictionary for Theological Interpretation of the Bible*, ed. Kevin J. Vanhoozer (Grand Rapids, MI: Baker Academic, 2005), p. 749.

[43] Kasemann, *Commentary*, p. 102.

[44] The following words appear in the biblical text to denote the idea of sin: *hamartia* (missing the mark), *parabasis* (transgression), *adikia* (unrighteousness), *asebeia* (impiety), *anomia* (lawlessness), *poneria* (depravity), *and epithymia* (evil desire). See Reno, "Doctrine," p. 749. The word that most often appears in Scripture to convey the idea of sin is *hamartia*. See John M. Court, *Dictionary of the Bible* (London: Penguin, 2007), s.v. "sin"; Biddle, *Missing the Mark*, p. 51.

[45] Ibid., p. 14.

only before their maker, but before one another. Their guilt is "internal, personal, immanent, and imminent."[46]

Rather than a legal infraction, sin carries more the sense of a failure to honor the sacred bond with God and creation, an interpretation with deep roots in the Hebraic theology of the covenant. In St Paul, sin is the failure to offer praise and thanks to God (Rom 1: 21).[47] In St John's gospel, it is a failure to respond faithfully in a loving relationship.[48] To the degree one is lost in the cares and petty desires of the world, one causes harm to one's inherent connection with others and with God (Jn 7: 7; 15: 22–24). Such self-preoccupation consists in a failure to see properly, specifically, to see God in one's neighbor and in one's surroundings. Ivan Illich maintains that the most fitting portrayal of sin is in those who failed to come to the aid of their fallen brother in the parable of the Good Samaritan (Lk 10: 25–37). Neither the priest nor the Levite broke the law but they sinned in failing to respond to the need of their neighbor, and, more cogently, in failing "to see" that the bloody man in the ditch *was* their neighbor.[49]

This portrayal of sin is, however, incomplete until forgiveness is added as its rightful companion. Just as all commit sin, forgiveness is offered to all. Jesus is Emmanuel; he has come to free his people from their sins (Mt 1: 21). No one who turns to him will be rejected, nor should those who follow him reject anyone, regardless of what they have done or how often they have done it (Mt 18: 21–22). This is not to say that there are no disciplinary regulations in the sayings of Jesus, or especially in the teaching of St Paul, but just as love defines the meaning and extent of law, so does forgiveness define the meaning and extent of sin. Thus the influential passage in Matthew's gospel in which Christ provides the proper method to admonish and chastise the errant Christian (Mt 18: 15–17) is preceded and followed by two passages on forgiveness—the seeking of the lost sheep and the endless mercy to be shown to a brother or sister who causes harm (Mt 18: 12–14; 18: 19–35). Forgiveness is a practice, a virtue that, as suggested in the introduction, relates to a way of living and especially breathing. One must learn to breathe peace and forgiveness as surely as Christ breathed peace and forgiveness on his cowardly disciples (Jn 20: 19–22). This topic will be taken up repeatedly by Christian mystics throughout the history of the church. Focusing on God and on God's intimate presence in all of creation with each breath is not an exotic vocation for the spiritual elite; it is the practical way to learn to be a disciple. It can and should be the daily practice of Christians in their quest to learn to see rightly, and in its light come to understand whatever value is to be accorded to law and judgment.

---

46 Ibid.

47 "Faith becomes genuine obedience when in its work the issue is not ourselves but gratitude and the manifestation of achieved freedom." See Kasemann, *Commentary*, p. 281.

48 Koester states: "Sin in John's gospel is first of all a relational concept. It is unbelief or alienation from God and therefore the antithesis of faith." See *Word*, p. 65.

49 Illich, *Rivers*, pp. 50–51.

Judge Not

To speak of sin leads naturally to speak of judgment. The opponent of God, whether as the tempter or Satan, appears at the beginning of the Bible and at its end, not to mention often in between, especially in the New Testament. The etymology of the term, Satan, reveals that the demon is variously a legalist, an adversary, or the prosecuting attorney of humanity.[50] These roles are depicted in the book of Zechariah, where the "accuser" who stands at the right side of the high priest is reproved by God for amplifying the mistakes of the people whom God loves (Zech 3: 1–2). In the story of Job, Satan argues that Job's model comportment reveals neither loyalty nor love but fear and self-seeking (Job 1: 9–11; 2: 4–5); and in the Book of Revelation, the full extent of Satanic intent is revealed in the cry of the victorious angels: "[N]ow has the accuser been cast out, he who accused them night and day before God" (Rev 12: 10).

Christ, on the other hand, is the redeemer. The term *ga-al* in Hebrew carries the meaning of both redeemer and the defender of the accused.[51] Christ lives to intercede for humanity, not to be its judge (Jn 12: 47). Both Matthew and Luke place the primary teachings concerning judging others within the context of the Sermon on the Mount. Here Jesus admonishes those who judge to mind the log in their own eye before pointing out the speck in the eye of another (Mt 7: 3–5; Lk 6: 41–42), and recasts the urge to bring a negative evaluation on the conduct of others with the assurance that the same evaluation will be brought against the accuser by God (Mt: 7: 2; Lk 6: 38). Matthew also places the counsel on how to pray within the Sermon, containing the same parallelism between granting forgiveness and receiving it from God (Mt 6: 12).[52] That conceptual dyad is found once again in the parable of the unforgiving servant (Mt 18: 23–35). All of this suggests that judgment, like the forgiveness of sin, can only be done rightly by God.

What Jesus suggests for his followers is not "reflection" on harm done or, worse, a retributive response, but what Theissen calls "paradoxical intervention." The Christian is to turn the other cheek (Lk 6: 29) and risk safety, possessions, and even the consequences of being a lawbreaker to come to the aid of an enemy (Lk 10: 30–37). St Paul continues the same theme: "Bless those who persecute you;

---

[50] Peggy L. Day, *An Adversary in Heaven: Satan in the Hebrew Bible* (Atlanta: Scholars Press, 1988), p. 15. The Hebrew word *ha-satan* is normally translated as "adversary." See Stephen F. Noll, "Doctrine of Angels," in *Dictionary for Theological Interpretation*, ed. Kevin Van Hoozer (London: Society for Promoting Christian Knowledge, 2005), p. 46.

[51] See Jens Soering, *The Convict Christ* (Maryknoll, NY: Orbis, 2006), pp. 78–79.

[52] Norman Perrin is among the Scripture scholars (Bultmann, Jeremias, Kasemann) who sought to discover those scripture passages that most probably contain the *ipsissima vox Jesu* (the very voice of Jesus). He concluded that aside from some of the parables, and the concept of the Kingdom of God, the authentic words of Christ are found in the Lord's Prayer. See *Rediscovering the Teaching of Jesus* (New York: Harper & Row, 1967), pp. 38–47.

bless them and do curse them … Do not repay evil for evil … If your enemy is hungry feed him; and if thirsty, give him something to drink; in this way you will make him feel shame" (Rom 12: 14, 17, 20).[53]

Still, there are many passages in the New Testament that do sanction judgment. It is Christ who judges humanity at the end of time (Mt 25: 31–46). It is Christ who states that all sin can be forgiven save the sin against the Holy Spirit (Mt 12: 31), and it is Christ who provides both the power to judge and the direction on how to judge to the apostles (Mt 16: 19; 18: 15–17; Jn 20: 23). St Paul and the authors of the other canonical letters also provide a similar warrant to "hand over to Satan" those who belligerently refuse to seek pardon for their disruptive conduct (I Cor 5: 5; I Tim 1: 20).

It has been noted that there is an eschatological expectation that runs throughout the New Testament. The vision has its time, says the prophet (Hab 2: 3), but that time has now arrived (II Cor. 6: 2; Lk 9: 59–60; Mt 8: 21–22). The passages above do not dilute or contravene the normative teachings on law and judgment, but place them in a framework wherein the hearer of the word must make an immediate determination as to their veracity and necessity. The word spoken by Christ, and the word present as Christ in the holiness of each moment, becomes the judge. One who abides in the moment knows not only the difficulty of the invitation to love, but also the pain of neglecting that invitation. He or she also knows that repentance is required not to appease an angry God, but as a necessary element in the effort to overcome the alienation caused by sin. The gospels remind us that, for many, passing through this "narrow gate" (Lk 14: 24) of enduring the internal judgment of not meeting the word with reverence requires too much humility and self-sacrifice: "This teaching is very difficult to accept. Who can respect it?" (Jn 6: 60; cf. Jn 4: 44; 7: 15; 8: 13; 9: 39).[54]

To repeat, sin breaks relationships—with God, with creation, and with one's true self. To reject the word of God is not to violate a moral code but to bring harm into the concentric circles of creational relatedness (Jn 7: 7; 15: 22–24).[55] People sin; they sinned long before Christ came into the world as they do now, but, as Koester suggests, Jesus brings into plain view the underlying fracture in the human relation to God and neighbor and the gentle and compassionate way to mend it (Jn 4: 4–42).[56]

The task of the Christian is first and foremost to love, not judge; to be fully and consciously with the other in the moment and not in a detached mental space of comparison or evaluation. That is why Jesus insists that the preliminary response to what appears to be sinful conduct is to establish relationship, and where the initial attempt fails, to enlist others in the attempt to come to common accord (Mt 18: 15–17). The "handing over to Satan" is not a rejection. Not only do the

53 Theissen, *Fortress*, p. 20.

54 Bultmann, *Theology*, II, p. 39.

55 Koester, *Word*, pp. 65–66.

56 Ibid., pp. 66–67.

gospels make it clear that all sins can be forgiven, the early church, as we will see in the next chapter, could do no other than come to the same conclusion.[57] Recommending that the assembled believers dismiss the destructive sinner is the final attempt to allow the isolated and lonely offender to come to repentance, even as it invites the chastened penitent to rejoin the community.[58] St Paul is always careful to place the "excommunication" of the errant Christian in a context of humility and charity: "Brothers, if you see someone has fallen into sin, you who are spiritual should help and correct him. But do it gently" (Gal 6: 1). He also says to "single out" and "ostracize" the one who "will not obey our injunction" but never "treat him like an enemy, rather, correct him as you would a brother" (II Thes 3: 14–15). Furthermore, the words of Christ that the obstinate offender should be treated as a pagan or tax collector is itself ironic since it was precisely to "sinners" such as these that the Kingdom of God is given (Mt 21: 32).

All of this is corroborated in subsequent Christian history, in the evolution of penance and, perhaps more cogently, in the refashioning of the meaning of confinement where, particularly in early monastic communities, the pattern for Western penal philosophy was established. There, it was firmly believed that punishment was not an external imposition upon the sinner; instead, isolation, silence, and spiritual counsel created the conditions for the offender to come to repentance, often a painful one, on his or her own. The "coming to oneself at last" (Lk 15: 17), stimulated by this penitential isolation and self-chastisement, is followed by a re-welcoming to full life within the fellowship.[59] St Paul tells the Christians at Corinth that his criticism of their licentious behavior had no other purpose than to allow them to return to God: "You bore the sadness in a way that pleased God, thus we did not cause you any damage; for sorrow that is endured in a way pleasing to God, leads to a conversion that gives salvation as its fruit, and no one can lament that" (II Cor 7: 9–10). Sanders writes that despite Paul's at times fiery denunciations of licentious and divisive conduct among members

57 Joseph Favazza, *The Order of Penitents* (Collegeville, MN: Liturgical Press, 1988), pp. 70–71. Bornkamm proposes that the sin against the Holy Spirit is only intelligible when seen in terms of the division of salvation history into epochs. Jesus as the lowly and poor Son of Man dwells in the period before the exaltation, while with the arrival of the Holy Spirit the new age comes to fruition where all are one in Christ. See Bornkamm, "End Expectation," p. 34.

58 The term "hand over to Satan" (in Greek, *paradounai to satana*) is "almost a technical term … to connote an isolation of the offender from the community so that such a one might be led to repentance … [I]f it is possible to maintain that Paul's words are first and foremost directed to the community rather than to the sinner, and that it is the repentance of the sinner that is the primary purpose of the action, then the description in I Cor 5: 1–13 is an example of what we have designated as an indirect coercive penance of isolation." Favazza, *Order*, pp. 77–79.

59 See Andrew Skotnicki, "Foundations Once Destroyed: The Catholic Church and Criminal Justice," *Theological Studies* 65 (2004), pp. 804–05; *Criminal Justice and the Catholic Church*, ch. 3.

of the communities he founded, "we are still in quest of an instance in which a sinful *deed* is unmistakably said by Paul to lead to permanent exclusion or condemnation."[60]

Summary

Marcel Gauchet analyzes the relation between Christ and the church in terms of the progressive "disenchantment" of a world where the God who was once immanent has slowly and inexorably been relegated to a distant and unbridgeable transcendence; God's once intimate presence in the material domain now replaced by the law, the power of the state, and the self-sustained individual. He writes: "Where the prince of the Apocalypse would have called for war, Jesus preached love. In other words, the law to which he bore witness had nothing to do with the cardinal imperatives of power in this world. True faith's victory … would be the complete reversal of what used to be the universal code for all humans."[61]

The victory of true faith is still a long way off. For us as individual persons and for the communities with which we ally ourselves, law and punitive judgment continue to set not only our behavioral limits but also, often, the limits of our moral imagination.

The law and its judicial extension serve many purposes but two principally bear relevance to our study: they can exist either as reminders that we can and should honor the sacredness of others better than we do, or as justifications to humble others while we often simultaneously exalt ourselves. I believe Jesus would have drawn the options no differently. His words were not commands, just lively and compelling portraits of the future reality that is mysteriously present to the childlike and the simple. They are words to be pondered. The conclusions then as now are left to the one who ponders. Unanimity in interpretation is never suggested, only love and forbearance with those who see and act differently than we would have them do.

---

60 Sanders, *Paul*, p. 110.

61 Gauchet, *Disenchantment*, p. 120.

Chapter 3
Law and Judgment in the Early Christian Community

When they said farewell to Jesus for the final time, the apostles had the task of creating something new in human history. They were to go to men and women of all nations announcing what they had seen and heard, enrolling them by baptism into the movement that Jesus had begun (Mk 16: 15, 20; Mt 28: 19–20). For the first time, a completely heterogeneous people is created with no tie to land, blood relation, or a set of laws, a community founded on nothing more than belief in the transforming and saving life of its founder.[1]

We can surmise from the centuries-long process of establishing a consistent regimen for the adjudication of grievances and the correction of fault that the naiveté of first infatuation was very much in evidence. The early Christians were, quite simply, dismayed, if not shocked, that baptism, the new life they had taken on in Christ, could not efface the irreducible human penchant for falling into sin.[2] We initially see, therefore, only ad hoc attempts in the different communities to come to grips with the weakness and malevolence of their members, relying on what they had inherited from their own cultures and, of course, what was revealed to them by Christ.[3]

From a purely Christian viewpoint, as we have seen, they had but one law to rely on: to love one another as Jesus had loved them. Jesus was, as Lactantius writes, their only law, "a living law."[4] Justin Martyr attests that Christ is "an

---

[1] Brague, *Law*, p. 66.

[2] "For the primitive church, the occurrence of sin after baptism was unexpected. Since baptism and Eucharist joined persons to Christ and made them partakers of the reign of God, there could be no possibility of sin. Yet sin was an existential reality." Favazza, *Order*, p. 70.

[3] Luke Timothy Johnson notes the non-systematic character of these early attempts at communal correction: "They arose spontaneously, either through the need to address a practical problem or as the application of the memory of Jesus to their common life, and in no manner represent a legal system in the proper sense." See "Law in Early Christianity," in Witte and Alexander, *Christianity and Law*, p. 64.

[4] God sent "His Ambassador and Messenger to teach mankind the precepts of His justice … For when there was no justice on earth, He sent a teacher, a living law." Lactantius, *The Divine Institutes*, trans. Sister Mary Francis McDonald, O.P. (Washington: Catholic University of America Press, 1964), IV, 5.

everlasting and final law … after which there shall be no law, or commandment, or precept."[5]

The first communities, however, were also struggling to locate their identity within an inherited language, a prevailing and very invasive legal system, and a set of cultural practices largely inimical to their own. Therefore, the recurrent tension evident in the extant writings is precisely how much should Christians stand aloof from the world around them, and how much could they replicate what they already knew from that world and still remain faithful to Christ.[6] Added to this ambivalence was an imposing apocalyptic awareness, aided by periods of fierce persecution that retarded or deflected the impulse to organize a consistent set of communal and correctional directives.[7]

The liturgical rites of Baptism and Eucharist, and the concomitant underscoring of a novel set of moral imperatives, emphasized irreversible boundaries between Christians and the pagan world in which they lived. Yet the pressure of ongoing and interdependent social relations, not to mention the need for evangelization and the work of charity, made some level of compromise with parallel social and legal institutions inevitable. For Augustine, and later for Gregory I, involvement in the civic arena was a combination of political shrewdness and active intervention for the sake of those being crushed by the weight of judicial reprisal.[8] "I would prefer, of course, that the African Church did not find itself in the midst of these afflictions so that it needed the help of any earthly power," Augustine writes, in an appeal to the proconsul of Africa to spare the lives of the very heretics he had asked the government to suppress![9] Gregory tells his representative to communicate "diligently" the code of instruction to be imparted to the bishops of Sicily "so that the greatest care may be taken … lest they mix themselves up in secular causes so far as the necessity of defending the poor compels them."[10]

---

5 Saint Justin Martyr, "Dialogue with Trypho," in *Writings of St. Justin Martyr*, ed. Thomas B. Falls (New York: Christian Heritage, 1948), ch. 11.

6 Wayne A. Meeks, *The Origins of Christian Morality* (New Haven: Yale University Press, 1993), pp. 10, 37.

7 Ibid., p. 188. See also, H. Richard Niebuhr, *Christ and Culture* (New York: Harper & Row, 1951), pp. 45–82.

8 The very act of verbal intervention, coupled with a rhetoric of persuasion, in itself reveals the level to which Christians and their contemporaries shared the same language and could by means of that language discuss areas of ambiguity and appeal to commonly held values. See Averil Cameron, *Christianity and the Rhetoric of Empire* (Berkeley: University of California Press, 1991), pp. 129–30.

9 St Augustine, "Letters," in *The Works of St. Augustine*, ed. Boniface Ramsey, trans. Roland Teske, S.J. (4 vols., Hyde Park, NY: New City Press, 2004), vol. 2, letter 100.

10 Gregory the Great, "Epistles," in *A Select Library of Nicene and Post-Nicene Fathers of the Christian Church*, Philip Schaff and Henry Wade (eds), trans. Rev. James Barmby (Grand Rapids, MI: William B. Eerdmans, 1956), Vol. XII, Bk. I, no. 36.

Augustine was always fighting a rearguard action against his own past as a Manichaean and neo-Platonist. The dualist inclinations inherent in those doctrines often led him on one hand to revile the earthly city and its rulers and, on the other, to magnify the virtues of the church. Yet, at other times, he manifests a longing for unity and a fervent desire to absorb all of human society within the embrace of the church: "nothing is so rent by discord than this human race, in its flawed state; though nothing was so plainly intended by its Creator for living together."[11]

It was finally this latter conviction of a shared human condition and a shared hope, aided immeasurably by the teaching of St Paul, that would, for good or ill, overcome cultic and sectarian urges for separation and difference and lead the church first to utilize and then guardedly to defend repressive measures of social control by the secular power.

Two ongoing crises in the early Christian experience swayed the church in the direction of such a compromise. The first was the consolidation of doctrine in the face of repeated heretical movements; the second was the sporadic but nonetheless devastating outbreak of persecution. Both would color the conversation over law and judgment. In both, the church confronted threats to its very existence. In many respects, Christians demonstrated that they were less concerned with physical survival than with the survival of what they perceived to be a truthful narrative of who Jesus was. Where legalism and judgment arose, it was often in this regard. But the most striking legacy passed on by these early believers, at least for the purpose of this study, was their inability to see sin, no matter how grave, as a final rupture of the sinner or lawbreaker either from God or from the community of faith. This stance owes much of its vibrancy to the thoughts of St Paul, which largely provided the terrain upon which early Christian concepts of law and judgment were built.[12]

Compromise and Compassion in St Paul

As suggested in the last chapter, St Paul's thoughts on law and judgment must be understood primarily not in terms of the revelation to Moses or any other statutory decrees, but with a focus upon faith and the indwelling Spirit (Rom 2: 14–15).[13] Augustine expresses this belief that law is internal and only made explicit due to human intransigence: "Because men and women were so avid for external things

[11] St Augustine, *City of God*, trans. Henry Bettenson (Harmondsworth, UK: Penguin, 1972), XII, 28. See also Peter Brown, *Augustine of Hippo* (New York: Dorset Press, 1986), p. 224.

[12] Brague, *Law*, p. 87.

[13] "For the apostle does not restrict the Torah to the moral law and thereby dilute it. For him everything depends on the fact that the Gentiles also experience the transcendent claim of the divine will and thus become, not *the* law or *a* law, but law to themselves." Kasemann, *Commentary*, p. 64. See also Luke Timothy Johnson, *Reading Romans*, p. 38.

that they had become estranged from themselves, a written law was given. This did not imply that its provisions were not already inscribed in human hearts."[14] St Ambrose captures this conviction and its importance for the early church: "Paul says, 'through the law I died to the law that I might live to God' (Gal 2: 16, 19); which is to say that through the spiritual law he is dead to the material interpretation of the law. Let us, too, by the law of our Lord Jesus Christ die to this law which gives authority to treacherous decrees! Faith in Christ, not law, founded the church."[15] One author, in summing up the thoughts of Jerome, Ambrose, and Augustine on judicial ethics, stated that for these early theologians law was a way of "making war on the world."[16]

This Pauline emphasis on faith rather than law, as noted, had to live side by side with another teaching of St Paul, that believers must accept whatever political arrangement in which they find themselves (Rom 13: 1–2). However reluctantly, the various churches to a large extent not only accepted this counsel but also erected a theological justification for it. Paul does indeed state that "law entered so that sin might abound" (Rom 5: 20) and that for those who dwell in Christ all things are licit (I Cor 10: 23), but he also stresses that law provides both a restraint to the malevolent and a negative reminder of comportment inimical to the ethical guidelines inscribed upon the heart (Rom 13: 3–5).

Although Christ redeemed humanity from the "curse of the law" by dying under its curse (Gal 3: 13), many writers concluded that law makes it possible for the believers to conduct their affairs honorably and with a degree of independence in spite of the dishonor surrounding them. Augustine could write "love and do what you want" to his congregation even while insisting that law reminds them of "what righteousness they have already received" and "what righteousness is still lacking to them."[17]

All of the vices of secular regimes notwithstanding, Clement of Rome orchestrates "the social and political ideals of Greek and Roman elites" in his repeated calls to the church in Corinth to live in peace and concord.[18] Augustine proposes that when the earthly city "is condemned to the final punishment, it will no longer be a city," but at the same time it "has its good in this world, and rejoices to participate in it."[19]

Blood is thicker than water and, all too often, theology is thicker than blood. Providing for the restraint of those who fail to heed the inner prompting to live

---

14 St Augustine, "Expositions of Psalms," in *The Works of St. Augustine*, ed. John E. Rotelle, trans. Maria Boulding, O.S.B. (Hyde Park, NY: New City Press, 2004), XVII, 57, 1.

15 Ambrose, "Sermon against Auxentius," 24.

16 Whitman, *Origins*, p. 30.

17 Augustine, "Letters," 157, 6; Brague, *Law*, pp. 91–92.

18 Meeks, *Origins*, p. 178; St Clement of Rome, "The Letter to the Corinthians," in *The Apostolic Fathers*, vol. I, trans. Francis X. Glimm (New York: Christian Heritage, 1947), ch. 37.

19 Augustine, *City*, XV, 4.

peaceably is one thing; their torture and murder by the "earthly city" is quite another. A community whose founder was assaulted and executed under the Roman judicial system at times found itself explicitly defending these very practices. Clement of Alexandria writes that law "trains to piety" and "restrains each one from sins ... But when it sees one in such a condition as to appear incurable ... then in its solicitude for the rest ... it condemns such a one to death, as the course most conducive to health."[20] Ambrose states that in God are found two powers: "There is the power that forgives and the power which punishes ... See to it that Christ is infused into the act of slaying an impious man and that satisfaction accompany and be part of your attempt to abolish what is abominable."[21]

Augustine attempts to steer a course faithful to Christian non-violence that also recognizes the inevitable bloodshed that accompanies earthly conceptions of legal justice. He argues that Christians who assent to the divine sanction of established authority become a tool or "sword" in the hand of that power. Presuming that they did not will personally the harm being done to another, the "commandment forbidding killing was not broken" when, "representing the authority of the state," they "imposed the death penalty on criminals."[22]

In the case of torture, Augustine wrote that the Christian could only lament the terrible justice of society in its "judicial capacity" and beg that God be merciful to those trapped in "necessity": "Here we have what I call the wretchedness of man's situation." All that is left for the judge or executioner is that "he hates that necessity in his own actions."[23]

The pact with political powers was made at a great price. All subsequent Christian history has had to reconsider the terms of that agreement, or whether it should be abrogated altogether. The one law of love cannot accommodate the need for order and the repression of the lawless without itself undergoing fundamental revision. Augustine's attempts to shield the Christian conscience through a dualist partition between the pure will of the actor and the sordidness of the action rent the simple and profound harmony of the peaceful presence of Christ who breathed forgiveness and reconciliation. Christians were then no longer simply living in the same cultural space as their contemporaries; they were allowing the story of who they were to be shaded consciously by imperial notions of law as well as Roman values of honor and shame.

---

[20] Clement of Alexandria, "The Stromata," in *The Ante-Nicene Fathers*, vol. II, eds Rev. Alexander Roberts and James Donaldson (New York: Charles Scribner's Sons, 1925), I, 27.

[21] Saint Ambrose, "Cain and Abel," in *The Fathers of the Church*, vol. 42, trans. John J. Savage (New York: Fathers of the Church, 1961), II, 4, 15.

[22] Augustine, *City*, I, 21.

[23] Ibid., XIX, 6.

Law, Judgment, and Punishment in Rome

It has been noted that for all of the contempt that Augustine at times heaped upon Rome as the paradigm of the doomed earthly city, he "took the survival of the Roman Empire for granted. For him it was 'the world' in which he had grown … He could accept the mortality of all human institutions. But his whole perspective implied a belief in the resilience of the Empire as a whole."[24]

Extant Christian source material from the period reveals that most shared Augustine's perspective and viewed peace with Rome as a necessity. It was, to be sure, not a principal focus and its justification required both ethical and theological reflection, as should any implicit or explicit support of the state by Christians. Still, leading voices such as Clement of Rome, Clement of Alexandria, Origen, and even Tertullian took pains not only to accommodate their theology to the existence of the Empire, but also to offer a restrained praise for its task of world maintenance and prayers for its continued survival.[25]

One need not have read Weber to know that the principal focus of any political community is its internal and external security, its material prosperity, and, to accomplish those objectives, its monopoly on the use of force.[26] The internal order to be protected in Rome was rigidly class based. The Romans were in many respects a people deeply concerned with moral ideas such as *humanitas*, a civic virtue inspired by the Greeks that embraced both philanthropic and educational endeavors.[27] These, however, were interpreted within a social context in which the upper classes (the *honestiores*) were given concerted preference over those in the lower rungs of the social ladder, known as *humiliores*.[28] Nowhere was this stratification more evident than in areas pertaining to law, judgment, and punishment. A legal manual from 300 AD has this provision with obvious resonance for Christians: "Those who commit capital crimes are, if from the upper classes, decapitated or exiled; those from the lower classes are crucified, burnt alive or thrown to 'beasts'."[29]

---

[24] Brown, *Augustine*, p. 294; Augustine, *City*, IV, 7.

[25] See Clement of Rome, "Corinthians," ch. 37, 1–4; Clement of Alexandria, "Stromata," I, 27; "The Instructor," in Roberts and Donaldson, *The Ante-Nicene Fathers*, I, 8; Origen, *Contra Celsum*, trans. Henry Chadwick (Cambridge: Cambridge University Press, 1953), VIII, 73. Tertullian writes: "[W]e are ever making intercession for all the Emperors. We pray for them a long life, a safe home, brave armies, a faithful Senate, a quiet world—and everything for which a man and a Caesar can pray." See *Apology*, trans. T.R. Glover (Cambridge, MA: Harvard University Press, 1960).

[26] Max Weber, *Economy and Society*, vol. II, trans. Guenther Roth and Hans Wittich (Berkeley: University of California Press, 1978), pp. 901–02.

[27] Richard A. Bauman, *Crime and Punishment in Ancient Rome* (London and New York: Routledge, 1996), pp. 13–14.

[28] Ibid., p. 7.

[29] Ibid., p. 1.

Violent punishment raised little concern in Roman society. What *was* important was law. In 193 AD, for instance, a proconsul decapitated a Gallic prisoner purely for the entertainment of his mistress. The official was punished, not, said the judicial scholars, because there was something wrong with a beheading conducted under the rubric of law, say "for the purpose of inspiring terror at the might of the empire;" it was unacceptable because it was done "at the whim of a courtesan."[30]

Intimately tied to the classification of punishment according to social standing were the emphases upon honor and shame. Philanthropic tendencies aside, honor was the highest value in Roman society; shame the lowest.[31] These concepts dominated Roman judicial procedure in which protecting the honor of elite citizens was scrupulously maintained. Imprisonment and even capital punishment were almost exclusively reserved for the poor, for slaves, and for laborers. The practices of *libera custodia* (a form of house arrest) or banishment to another civic jurisdiction were the most common punishments for even capital crimes if one possessed wealth or high rank.[32] Julius Caesar, for example, ordered that Lentulus and other members of a seditious conspiracy be transported to Italian towns where they were to spend the rest of their lives.[33] On the other hand, the less influential citizen who committed parricide was "sewn into a leather sack in company with a dog, a monkey, a snake and a rooster, and was thrown into the sea or a river."[34]

Shame was indelible. Once a free citizen was found guilty of a serious offense, he or she normally saved their lives, never their reputation. The practice of *infamia*, later reproduced in the Middle Ages, permanently stigmatized the offender. Rather than a sign branded on the forehead, as in the Code of Hammurabi, the indelible nature of illegality was represented by a mark placed beside one's name on the census list. The bearer was subsequently deprived of certain legal rights, especially in matters of litigation.[35] Worse still, rules of status convention dictated that the individual now would "reciprocate naturally," assuming a posture of what Goffman terms "phantom acceptance."[36]

Honor and shame are swords that tear into the fabric of Christian ethics. They are tools of judgment that divide and alienate "the mystery" revealed in Christ: "to

---

30 Ibid., p. 19.

31 Meeks notes that the society "was ruled by honor and its opposite, shame." See *Origins*, pp. 39–41. See also Peter Garnsey, *Social Status and Legal Privilege in the Roman Empire* (Oxford: Clarendon, 1970), pp. 1–5.

32 "Of the penalties recognized and prescribed by the late-Republican laws, the death penalty … was the most serious. There is little evidence, however, that it was actually inflicted on members of the citizen population, or, at any rate, on members of the higher orders." See Garnsey, *Social Status*, p. 105.

33 Ibid., p. 148.

34 Bauman, *Crime*, p. 30.

35 Shlomo Shoham, *The Mark of Cain* (Jerusalem: Israel Universities Press, 1970), p. 12.

36 Erving Goffman, *Stigma* (Englewood Cliffs, NJ: Prentice Hall, 1963), p. 122.

bring all things into one in him in the heavens and on the earth" (Eph 1: 10; cf. Col 1: 20). Early Christians would have been deeply cognizant of these cultural values, whether or not they awarded them explicit recognition. Meeks notes that in the close quarters of the Mediterranean city "common expectations of the way public honor and shame were awarded would be very strong."[37] Despite the example of Christ who decisively overturned the honor/shame system in his deliberate choice of poverty and in his equally deliberate elevation of the *humiliores* to the highest place in the reign of God, it was a difficult teaching for his followers to adopt. Paul scolds the factions evident in the Eucharistic gatherings of the church at Corinth in which "some go hungry while others get drunk" (I Cor 11: 17–22). St James castigates his own congregation for its quickness to award places of honor in the Eucharist to the wealthy while relegating the poor to the rear of the assembly, reminding his hearers that God has chosen the very ones that they humiliate (James 2: 1–9).

Neither could Roman concepts of order, with some of the concomitant judgmental prejudices, fail to embed themselves into the very structures of the early church. Ullmann states that when the Bible was translated into Latin by the turn of the fourth century, it "was suffused with notions, ideas and quite specific linguistic expressions which had been taken from the Roman constitutions and law."[38] Another author suggests that even the organization of penitents, despite its aims of pardon and full reconciliation of the offender, revealed notions of *infamia* and the general class-consciousness of the surrounding social milieu.[39] Ambrose gives a stark reminder of the influence of Roman legal metaphors in his otherwise earnest exhortation to Christians to confess their sins so as to avoid divine censure: "Hence, in the civil courts, those who deny their guilt are put on the rack, whereas an admission of guilt tends to mercy on the part of the judge. To confess his guilt … indicates that the sinner humbly awaits his sentence. Admission of guilt placates the judge, whereas denial rouses his suspicion."[40]

One could rightfully conclude that the first Christians, by and large, had theological resources sufficient to resist the type of explicit legalism to which some members of the Jewish community were subject. Those resources, however, were not as readily available to resist fully the incorporation of Roman principles into their own understanding of law and judgment.

The irony in all of this can be found in regard to heresy. The church gave so much attention to combating theological errors that it, perhaps, hardly noticed the incursion of Roman values into its organizational life. This oversight was immeasurably aided by the fact that peace with Rome often provided the benefit of police power to rid certain jurisdictions of heretical influence. Pollock notes that

---

[37] Meeks, *Origins*, p. 43.

[38] Walter Ullmann, *Law and Politics in the Middle Ages* (Ithaca: Cornell University Press, 1975), p. 42.

[39] Favazza, *Order*, pp. 65, 234–35.

[40] Ambrose, "Cain and Abel," II, 9, 27.

after the conversion of Constantine, "the 'confessor' of yesterday was frequently the persecutor of today: [by] about 350 a pagan sacrifice was by the letter of the law a capital crime."[41] Christian emperors like Theodosius inscribed numerous security measures into the law to protect the hegemony of the church in matters of religious belief. An entire section of the Theodosian Code is entitled *de Hereticis* (Concerning Heretics), the statutes of which according to one author "are too many and too long to be recited."[42] Here those possessing unorthodox opinions are deprived of commerce with Christians and the right to hold civil office. A general tone of infamy runs through them all.[43]

Augustine liberally utilized the power of the state to suppress the Donatists and, responding to the criticism of the latter, then found himself in the difficult position of having to defend the sovereign rights of Rome to executive coercion.[44] Gregory the Great, writing to the exarch of Africa over the continued Donatist presence in that region, was placed in a similar circumstance: "[L]et your eminence suppress their attempts, and subdue their proud necks to the yoke of rectitude."[45]

Not only the limited tactical concerns of the church were at stake here; theological understanding also had to be amended to sanction such a strategy. Irenaeus concludes: "Earthly rule, therefore, has been appointed by God for the benefit of the nations … so that under the fear of it men might not eat each other up like fishes; but that, by means of the establishment of laws, they might keep down the great wickedness of the nations."[46] Ambrose, commenting on Isaac's blessing of the clever Jacob over his older brother Esau, remarks in similar fashion that "the wise" are put in command "to control the wayward populace with their special capacity to establish control with a show of power."[47] In the life of Constantine by Eusebius, the emperor "assumes a role in the divine dispensation akin to Moses, if not Christ himself."[48] Augustine's position was to suggest that it is the duty of the church to punish sin and the duty of the state to punish crime: "If we see some great and good man, obeying the call of honor and duty, allow his body to be burned with fire, we do not call this a penalty for sin, but a proof of courage

---

41 Frederick Pollock, *The History of English Law Before the Time of Edward I* (Cambridge: Cambridge University Press, 1968), I, 3.

42 Joseph Bingham, *Antiquities of the Christian Church* (London: William Straker, 1844), VI, 95.

43 Concerning commerce, see Leg. 17, 18, 36, 40, 48; concerning office-holding see Leg. 9, 25, 29, 42, 58, 61, 65; concerning infamy see Leg. 7, 13, 54. Jill Harries and Ian Wood (eds), *The Theodosian Code* (Ithaca: Cornell University Press, 1993).

44 Peter Brown, "Religious Coercion in the Later Roman Empire," *History* 48 (1963), p. 300.

45 Gregory the Great, "Epistles," I, 54.

46 Irenaeus of Lyons, "Against Heresies," in O'Donovan, *From Irenaeus to Grotius*, V, 24.

47 Ambrose, "Letter 7," in *From Irenaeus to Grotius*, 8.

48 Cameron, *Christianity*, pp. 53–54.

and endurance … When, however, we see the body of a cruel robber consumed as a punishment in the same way, we approve the 'lawful' enforcement of public order. Both men make these sufferings honorable, but one does so by his virtue, the other by his sin."[49]

The compromises made by the church cannot be denied. There is a permeable boundary between espousing the duty of the emperor to quell lawlessness and exploiting a favored relation with the sovereign to advance private gain or personal vendetta, as in the execution of a Spanish heretic in 385 AD for "magic and obscene practices." There was a swelling of public anger against the incident "largely because the death made plain how easy it might be for unscrupulous bishops and authoritarian officials to make a permanent breach in the wall of principle."[50]

The purpose here is not to entertain or look aghast at the sins of our ancestors in the faith, but to emphasize that each generation of Christians at best must translate the gospel message for untutored ears; at worst, allow parochial and sinful concerns to twist its meaning.[51] The important idea for our purposes is that the church, in spite of its awkward peace with the Empire and the stain of blood upon its conscience, was willing to suffer the consequences of making peace with Babylon, as Augustine termed it, knowing in the end that Christian judgment must yield to mercy and law must yield to love.

Merciful Justice and Pardon for Sin

If it was, in the main, legitimate for the state to judge and punish the offender, most Christian sources emphasize an equal or greater legitimacy for the church to both practice and plead for leniency and forgiveness. Some of the most eloquent Christian appeals for clemency and mildness in the exercise of penal justice by the ruling authorities are found among the "fathers" of the early church. A moving example of this can be found in a letter from Augustine to the imperial commissioner of Africa after members of the Circumcellion and Donatist sects murdered one priest and tore out the eye and cut off the finger of another: "We still do not want the sufferings of the servants of God to be avenged by punishments equal to those sufferings, as by the law requiring an eye for an eye." Augustine pleads that "no part of the body be mutilated," rather that "they be taken from their mad restlessness and steered to the peace of good health by the restraints of the law or that they be assigned to some useful work."[52] In another instance, he states that if in the Old Testament punishments "were levied against the wicked

---

[49] St Augustine, *The Problem of Free Choice* (*De Libero Arbitrio*), trans. Dom Mark Pontifex (Westminster, MD: Newman Press, 1955), III, 28.

[50] Brown, "Religious Coercion," p. 300.

[51] Ernst Troeltsch, *The Social Teaching of the Christian Churches*, trans. Olive Wyon (2 vols, Chicago: University of Chicago Press, 1960), vol. 1, pp. 27–30.

[52] St Augustine, "Letters," II, 133.

for a good purpose," then in the New Testament "we are urged to pardon offenders with mercy, either as a saving remedy by which our own sins may be pardoned, or as a means of commending gentleness, so that truth, when preached by those who pardon, may not be so much feared as loved."[53] Ambrose writes: "Once the crime is admitted ... then the divine law of mercy should be extended." He notes that God drove Cain into exile, preferring "the correction rather than the death of a sinner," and "did not desire that a homicide be punished by the exaction of another act of homicide."[54] Gregory argued that dissenters from Christian doctrine should be called to the "unity of faith by gentleness, kindness, admonition, [and] persuasion."[55] A sweeping call for forgiveness was decreed at the Council of Sardica: "[S]ince it often happens that those who are suffering from injustice or who are condemned for their offences to deportation or banishment to an island, or, in short, have received some sentence or another, seek refuge with the mercy of the church, such persons should be succored and pardon be begged for them without hesitation."[56]

If St Paul was instrumental in providing a bridge between Christian ethics and political order, he was similarly influential in providing encouragement toward forbearance and trust in God's justice over that of human beings (Rom 12: 17–21). Paul suggests that if Christians examined their own conduct, they would have little cause to fret over the conduct of others (I Cor 11: 27–32), an exhortation certainly not lost on Augustine: "Men are hopeless creatures, and the less they concentrate on their own sins, the more interested they become in the sins of others."[57] Meeks notes that the teaching led early Christians "to use belief in the ultimate judgment of God in order to relativize or to restrain judgments."[58]

Aside from the threat of heresy, the other great defining event in the early centuries of Christianity was persecution; and the companion theme of persecution was imprisonment. Not only were Christ and many of the apostles incarcerated, but a lengthy martyrology and a vibrant literary corpus emerged in the early church testifying to the nobility of imprisonment: "[W]e were brought to the procurator ... Ah, what a joyous day! The glory of being in bonds! The chains that were the object of all our prayers! Iron more noble and precious to us than the finest gold!"[59] In the same vein, Cyprian writes: "Blessed is the prison which

---

53 St Augustine, "Letter from Augustine to Macedonius, Provincial Governor of Africa," in O'Donovan, *From Irenaeus to Grotius*, 153, 16.

54 Ambrose, "Cain and Abel," II, 9, 38.

55 Gregory the Great, "Epistles," I, 35.

56 Henry R. Percival, "The Seven Ecumenical Councils of the Early Church," in Philip Schaff and Henry Wace (eds), *A Select Library of Nicene and Post-Nicene Fathers*, Vol. XIV, c. vii.

57 St Augustine, "Sermons," 19, 2.

58 Meeks, *Origins*, p. 188.

59 "The Martyrdom of Sts. Montanus and Lucius," in Herbert Musurillo (trans.), *The Acts of the Christian Martyrs* (Oxford: Clarendon, 1972), p. 219.

your presence filled with light; blessed is the prison that sends men of God to heaven. I hail the darkness which outshines the sun itself."[60] This theme would extend well into the Middle Ages where divine favor for prisoners is obtained not only through God's endless compassion for the suffering but because Christ identifies himself with all prisoners, regardless of the cause of their confinement (Mt 25: 39–40).[61] Christopher Dawson suggests that the "church grew under the shadow of the executioner's rods and axes, and every Christian lived in the peril of torture and death. The thought of martyrdom colored the whole outlook of early Christianity."[62]

The primal sense of identity with lawbreakers is in the marrow of the gospel and the ancient Christian experience. This sense of solidarity tended to overcome, not without degrees of difficulty, and certainly not without some expression of contrition, the stain of sin, any sin.[63] The preeminent expression of the gospel call to repentance, forgiveness, and full reinstatement to the community is found in the sacrament of penance.

Most early Christians probably did not require the stern advice of both Jesus and St Paul to avoid having their disputes settled in civil courts (Lk 12: 57–59; Mt 5: 25–26; I Cor 6: 1–8), but what the scriptures did provide them was the legitimacy of communal intervention in the questionable practices of believers, along with a divinely approved methodology for doing so. Christ imparted to Peter the keys of the Kingdom with the power to bind and to loose (Mt 16: 18–19) and commissioned the disciples to forgive sin (Jn 20: 23). He also taught that the resolution of all offenses must be guided by peaceful dialogue, first between the affected parties, then, in the absence of reconciliation, with the aid of several others and, finally, before the entire congregation (Mt 18: 15–18). It can be inferred that, harmonious with his insistence that his followers not judge others, Christ was saying that initial conclusions concerning the conduct of others possess neither moral nor spiritual certitude. Polycarp, the bishop of Smyrna, in a letter to the

[60] St Cyprian, *The Letters of Cyprian of Carthage*, trans. G.W. Clark (2 vols, New York: Newman Press, 1984), vol. 1, 6, 1–2.

[61] Many saints and the Virgin Mary were engaged in the liberation of the imprisoned. See "S. Quintino Martyre," in *Acta Sanctorum*, 31 Octobris (Paris, 1883), Tomus XIII; "Sanctus Leonardus," in *Acta Sanctorum*, 6 Novembris (Brussels, 1910), Tomus III; *The Miracles of Our Lady of Rocamadour*, trans. Marcus Bell (Woodbridge, UK: Boydell Press, 1999); *The Book of Sainte Foy*, trans. Pamela Sheingorn (Philadelphia: University of Pennsylvania Press, 1995). Cameron notes that as a "story religion," the growth of Christianity was aided immeasurably by a narrative dominated by biographies and "acts." See *Christianity*, p. 89.

[62] Christopher Dawson, *The Making of Europe* (New York: Meridian, 1958), p. 45.

[63] "The overwhelming evidence of the New Testament confirms the willingness of the Church to offer the possibility of penance and reconciliation to all sinners." Favazza, *Order*, pp. 70–71.

Philippians counsels them: "be not quick to believe anything against any man, not hasty in judgment, knowing that we are all under the debt of sin."[64]

From these sources and their own internal desire to build a Christian alternative to the worldly view of justice, the believers constructed an elaborate and lasting system of healing moral weakness first by communal, later by private confession. The institutional rudiments would provide the basis for the entire Western penal system, while the spiritual guidelines would institute a comprehensive method of forgiveness and reconciliation.[65]

Human nature from an early Christian perspective is inherently good and perpetually graced. Augustine states that nothing in nature is evil: "There can be no doubt that the fault of wickedness supervenes upon a faultless natural state. Evil is contrary to nature; in fact it can only do harm to nature."[66] Despite this, all willingly do harm to their good nature. "All have sinned," states St Paul (Rom 3: 9); and Christ deflects the flattery offered by the rich young man: "Why do you call me good?" (Mk 10: 18). Even more to the point, Christ repeatedly insists that the precondition for acceptance of the gospel is repentance (Mk 1: 15; Mt 4: 17). He even undergoes John's baptism, based upon cleansing its initiates from the stain of sin (Mk 1: 4, 9).

Forgiveness was available, repentance was mandatory, and reconciliation was required. The earliest non-biblical documents we possess stress these principles. In the Didache we hear, "reprove one another, not irately, but peaceably, as you have it in the gospel; and let no one speak to any person who has wronged another … until he repents."[67] The author of the Shepherd of Hermas provides the words of an angel claiming that "for the heathen repentance is open until the last day."[68]

Pope Stephen I and Cyprian exchanged letters in the mid-third century over how best to proceed with regard to Christians who had renounced their faith during the Decian persecution and who now sought reinstatement into the community. The dialogue was never whether the lapsed Christians should be forgiven and reintegrated into the church, only over what degree of repentance was required to atone for their fall.[69] Stephen writes: "If therefore any come to you from any

64 St Polycarp, "Letter to the Philippians," in *The Apostolic Fathers*, vol. I, 6, 1.

65 On the impact of penance on Western disciplinary practice, see Skotnicki, "Foundations," pp. 801–04; *Criminal Justice and the Catholic Church*, pp. 74–81.

66 Augustine, *City*, XI, 17, 22.

67 *Didache*, trans. Robert A. Kraft (New York and Toronto: Thomas Nelson & Sons, 1965), 15, 3.

68 "The Shepherd of Hermas," in *The Apostolic Fathers*, vol. II, trans. Kirsopp Lake (London: William Heinemann, 1959), Vision II, ii, 5.

69 The "conversation" was in other matters much more heated. Stephen and Cyprian disputed whether those baptized by Novatian heretics who sought admission into the church had to be re-baptized. Cyprian said yes, Stephen no. There was no final resolution as Stephen died in the midst of the conflict. See Frend, *Rise of Christianity*, pp. 351–56.

heresy, whatsoever, let nothing be renewed except what has been transmitted, so that the hand is placed upon them for repentance."[70]

Cyprian's own view in the matter reveals much of the theological basis often employed in understanding repentance, including the use of temporal exclusion as a means to both inspire and express that repentance. He writes with deep frustration: "a deceptive readmission to communion is being granted, a reconciliation that is null and void."[71] Cyprian is arguing not that those who fail need to be punished; he is arguing in full accord with the scripture that sin is death (Rom 6: 23). To betray one's faith, to find it acceptable to trade one's eternal salvation for a few meager years of life, is, in the eyes of Cyprian, to have fallen beneath the weight of pride or what Boethius would later call "the ruthless chains of the deceiving passions."[72] The only answer Cyprian offers is "the slow, painful road to recovery," "the genuine cure through satisfaction done." Reinstatement without some form of "excommunication" would be no more than a "covering up" of "the wounds they are dying of."[73]

This approach to penance and "criminal justice" repudiates the efficacy of punishment as such but pines for a moral and spiritual renewal within the offender which is internal to him or her and, because it implies the death of the sinful impulse, painful.[74] Repentance cannot be imposed, but the history of penance, and later that of imprisonment, suggests that for the early Christians it can be summoned. It is a holy rite aimed at creating the conditions for a purely private confrontation, a moment of truth between the errant human and the God who dwells within.

The only true understanding of punishment, as the ancient writers often taught, is the price God asks of each sinner to buy back his or her full humanity and eternal peace. Clement of Alexandria states: "I will grant that [God] punishes the disobedient (for punishment is for the good and advantage of him who is punished)

---

70 Henry Denziger, *The Sources of Catholic Dogma*, trans. Roy J. DeFerari (St Louis: B. Herder, 1957), 22. Clement writes: "Even those were leaders of rebellion and schism must look to the common hope." "Therefore, let us also intercede for those who fall into any transgression ... so that they may yield not to us but to God's will. For in this way there will be for them a fruitful, perfect, and compassionate remembrance with God and the saints." "Corinthians," chs. 51, 56.

71 St Cyprian, *The Lapsed*, trans. Maurice Bevenot, S.J. (Westminster, MD: Newman Press, 1957), ch. 15.

72 Boethius, *The Consolation of Philosophy*, trans. W.V. Cooper (New York: The Modern Library, 1943), 64.

73 Cyprian, *The Lapsed*, ch. 15.

74 Cyril Vogel notes that numerous texts reveal that excommunication, not punishment and certainly not permanent exclusion, was understood as "the supreme attempt to bring back certain recalcitrant sinners to repentance." See "Sin and Penance," in Philippe Delhaye et al., *Pastoral Treatment of Sin* (New York: Desclee, 1968), pp. 193–94.

... but I will not grant that He wishes to take vengeance."[75] Origen maintains: "if Scripture says that God inflicts pains ... in order to convert and heal those who are in need of such punishment, there can be no ground for objection to what the Bible says."[76] Tertullian, who wrote the first penitential handbook, writes that the process casts down the sinner but "raises him up all the more; when it makes him sordid, it cleanses him all the more; when it accuses, it excuses; when it condemns, it absolves."[77] I believe Augustine has this internal dynamic in mind when he writes: "Now the voluntary state where sin is committed is a shameful state. Therefore to this is applied a penal state, to set it where such may fitly be, and to make it harmonize with the beauty of the whole, so that sin's punishment may make up for its shamefulness."[78] Finally, a contemporary criminologist, Graeme Newman, reveals both the wisdom of the ancient practice, its initial impact on the Western penal system, and its necessary retrieval in modern penology. He states that the Christian approach understood guilt in a fully moral way, "which is to say that the offender has a guilty mind, and that only by a series of ritually purgative functions can this guilt be assuaged." So to the murderer who hypothetically says, "I can't bring the victim back, so what else can I do?" Newman replies, echoing Cyprian's words after nearly two millennia, that "murderers should suffer the long journey towards contrition." He then adds, "Unfortunately, penologists have lost sight of this important function of retribution, so that they have allowed punishments to destroy souls rather than save them."[79]

The penitential journey was always a holy journey, a pilgrimage. Bear in mind, one did not become a public penitent and bear the pains of separation for minor offenses; these latter foibles were purged by what was termed *exomologesis*, a public statement of fault and personal acts of piety and self-denial.[80] Public penance involved the laying on of hands, the ancient biblical practice of election done under the guidance of the Holy Spirit (Acts 6: 6), and the symbolic gesture so often used by Christ to bring healing to the sick (Mk 5: 23; 6: 5). Recall Pope Stephen's words: "the hand is placed upon them for repentance."[81]

Like Simon of Cyrene and the women who watched with Jesus to the end, Christians bearing the penitential cross were to be accompanied by members of the community who were to offer encouragement and prayer.[82] Ignatius of

---

75 Clement of Alexandria, "The Instructor," I, 8.

76 Origen, *Celsum*, VI, 56.

77 Tertullian, *On Penitence*, trans. Maurice Bevenot, S.J. (Westminster, MD: Newman Press, 1957), ch. 9.

78 Augustine, *Free Choice*, III, 26.

79 Graeme Newman, *Just and Painful* (New York: Harrow and Heston, 1995), p. 82.

80 John T. McNeill and Helena M. Gamer, *Medieval Handbooks of Penance* (New York: Columbia University Press, 1938), p. 6; Vogel, "Sin," p. 202.

81 Denziger, *Sources*, 22.

82 Bernhard Poschmann, *Penance and the Anointing of the Sick*, trans. Francis Courtney, S.J. (New York: Herder & Herder, 1964), pp. 86–87; Vogel, "Sin," p. 193.

Antioch counsels the Christians at Ephesus to engage in unceasing oration for the penitents, to give them the "chance to be instructed" and never fail to "hope of their conversion."[83] Following the period of exclusion, the offender was then called back to the assembly, the hand of healing was extended, and full communion was restored.[84]

So what seems clear from this brief survey is that in early Christian theology, judgments are never given validity on face value, only by the full assembly and its head after at least three remedial interchanges. The sentence of excommunication from the community is not an imposition of punishment but an invitation to engage in an internal struggle to reclaim the true spiritual dignity of the sinner. The community is charged to help and pray for penitents, neither reviling nor abandoning those who have failed; and, at the conclusion of the ascetic regimen, forgiveness is total, binding, and fully restores the "lost sheep" to full stature.

The ideal need not recoil nor suffer loss of prestige due to violations of the above commitments. It was easy then, as it is easy now, to condemn the actions of others rather than one's own. Fear of heresy and perhaps just human self-righteousness led to severe penitential conditions that often stayed in force after the sin was remitted.[85] The general rule in the West in the early centuries was that one could only receive the sacrament once in a lifetime.[86] Some sins, however, were deemed so severe that, on rare occasions, the penitent was deprived of the sacrament even at the point of death.[87] The era of canonical penance, overseen by directives from church councils beginning in the fourth century, and lasting until the advent of private confession at the turn of the seventh century, was dominated by rigorous attempts to defend theological boundaries and widespread accusation and condemnation of heretical opinion. The Council of Toledo (400 AD) begins with the words: "[Here] begin the rules of the Catholic faith against all heresies."[88] The beginning of the Athanasian Creed states: "Whoever wishes to be saved, needs above all to hold the Catholic faith; unless each one preserves this whole and inviolate, he will without doubt perish in eternity."[89]

These examples serve to remind us that even as the rudiments of the penitential ritual were being formalized, even with the triumph of the theological position

---

83 St Ignatius of Antioch, "To the Ephesians," in *The Apostolic Fathers*, vol. I, trans. Gerald G. Walsh, S.J., ch. 10.

84 "Concilium Toletanum I," in Johannes Dominicus Mansi, *Sacrorum Conciliorum* (Paris and Leipzig, 1901), III, c. 2.

85 Favazza, *Order*, pp. 247–48; Vogel, "Sin," p. 239.

86 Karl Rahner, "Penance in the Early Church," *Theological Investigations*, vol. XV, trans. Lionel Swain (New York: Crossroad, 1982), pp. 4–5.

87 One such sin so condemned by the Council of Illiberit was sex with children: "Stupratoribus puerorum nec in fine dandam esse communionem." See Mansi, *Sacrorum Conciliorum*, c. lxxi.

88 Denziger, *Sources*, 12.

89 Ibid., 15.

that law, judgment, and punishment were to be interpreted under the light of the gospel's gentle call to love and forgiveness, there was a constant temptation to capitulate to fear and to inflict punishment on the threatening and the sinful. The latter position was not the rule, however, but its exception. This same tension between the noble aspiration and the base application can be found in the origins of penal confinement, once again related to penance and located most influentially in the monasteries.

Monastery as Prison; Prison as Monastery

What emerges from the monastic experience is a confirmation of the transformational efficacy of silence, solitude, prayer, fasting, meaningful labor, and spiritual counsel. Imprisonment as a widespread reformative practice in the West began because monks were already prisoners, having taken a binding vow of stability that confined them in the monastic enclosure until death.[90]

The normal practice of penance in the wider church would have been replicated in the monasteries. This is revealed in the earliest monastic rule, that of Pachomius, and reproduced in the rules of Sts Basil and Benedict, among others. Those in violation of ecclesiastical and communal norms of behavior were approached on a series of occasions, and only after repeated resistance were they brought before the abbot and given a penance.[91] The noteworthy innovation was that the resistant brother was placed in isolation, later almost universally in a cell, with the firm belief that the foundational disciplines of the monastic life would guide the journey of repentance to forgiveness and reconciliation.[92]

[90] Among the general introductions to imprisonment in the West that testify to the monastic influence, see Norman Johnston, *Forms of Constraint* (Urbana, IL: University of Illinois Press, 2000); Karl Krauss, *Im Kerker* (Freiburg and Leipzig, 1895); Thorsten Sellin, "Dom Jean Mabillon: A Prison Reformer of the Seventeenth Century," *Journal of the Institute of Criminal Law and Criminology* 17 (1927), pp. 581–602. Bear in mind that prior to its transformation by the church, prison was rarely employed. Death, mutilation, and fines were the time-honored means of expressing criminal justice. See Jean Dunbabin, *Captivity and Imprisonment in Medieval Europe, 1000–1300* (Houndmills, UK: Palgrave Macmillan, 2002), p. 3. See also my own work: *Criminal Justice and the Catholic Church*; "God's Prisoners: Penal Confinement and the Creation of Purgatory," *Modern Theology* 22 (2006), pp. 85–110.

[91] St Benedict, *Benedict's Rule*, trans. Terrence G. Kardong (Collegeville, MN: Liturgical Press, 1996), ch. 23; St Pachomius, "Precepts and Judgments," in *Pachomian Koinonia*, trans. Armand Veilleux (2 vols, Kalamazoo: Cistercian Publications, 1981), vol. 2, 4.

[92] St Basil, "The Long Rules," in *St. Basil: Ascetical Works*, trans. Sister M. Monica Wagner (New York: Fathers of the Church, 1950) Q. 51; St Benedict, *Rule*, chs. 24–25; Pachomius, "Precepts and Judgments," vol. 2, 1.

Contemplative prayer is based in the theological conviction that all of nature is graced, that awareness of the present moment is awareness of God. In this light, as Scripture says, we see light (Ps 36: 9). The person of faith receives no more revelation than does the nonbeliever, no more than rain distinguishes upon whom it falls (Mt 5: 45). The early Christians, especially the monks, simply translated this awareness into a correctional formula. Those entrenched in habits of self-preoccupation and self-indulgence, even those who commit the most horrific acts, can be reformed. Basil used the metaphor of encrusted wax that had to be melted before it could again be written upon and then added "solitude provides us with the greatest help toward this achievement, quieting our passions" and providing the time "to uproot them completely from the soul."[93] Augustine encourages a friend anxious to advance in prayer to imitate the mantric chants of the "monks in Egypt" who are said "to offer frequent prayers, but these are very short and hurled like swift javelins. Otherwise their watchful attention, a very necessary quality for one at prayer, could be dulled and could disappear through protracted delays."[94]

To repeat the idea that introduces this section, just as the monk is by definition a prisoner; the prisoner, at least in the initial understanding, is a monk. The veracity of the method of temporal exclusion in a contemplative framework such as the one described above is equal to the veracity of two thousand years of penitential and monastic practice. It echoes Jesus' own contemplative stance, nurtured with long nights "absorbed in prayer" (Mk 1: 35; Mt 14: 23) and expressed in a focused, peaceful, and forgiving manner of breathing (Jn 20: 22).

Whatever evidence we have of sadistic treatment by monks of their wayward brothers, and there is certainly evidence, must be measured against what should be considered the most humane innovation in the history of correction until that time, and perhaps into our own.[95] Incarcerated offenders are to be loved and encouraged, insists Benedict. He makes it mandatory that wise spiritual guides visit them frequently lest, referencing St Paul, their self-chastisement further their sense of loneliness and sorrow (II Cor 2: 7).[96]

Clearly, in the Rule of Benedict and commonly in other monastic literature, the emphasis is on neither judgment nor punishment, certainly not on the sanctity of the law as such, but on the effort to bring a brother who has alienated himself from the community, and by extension from himself and God, into harmony with the divine order of creation. Benedict writes that the abbot "should focus all his

---

93 St Basil, *Letters*, trans. Sister Agnes Clare Way, O.P. (Washington, DC: Catholic University of America Press, 1951), I, 2.

94 Augustine, *Letters*, 130.

95 The Benedictine historian, Dom Jean Mabillon, writes of a meeting of Benedictine abbots in 817 at Aix la Chapelle to discuss ways to correct abuses of prisoners by their brother monks. See Sellin, "Mabillon," p. 584.

96 Benedict, *Rule*, ch. 27.

attention on the care of the wayward brother … [and] should use all the means that a wise physician would."[97]

We have spoken of the communal practice of encouraging and ministering to penitents, either in the monastery or in the wider church. Those who presumably apprised the community of aberrant conduct by other Christians were also required to aid them on their journey to spiritual health. St John Climacus performed this function at a monastery in Egypt in the late sixth century, living for a period of time in the prison constructed near the monastery. His experience inspired this reflection: "Having stayed thirty days in the prison … I returned to the great monastery and the great shepherd … 'Well, Father John, did you see the struggles of those who labor at their task?' I replied: 'I saw them, Father, and I was amazed; and I consider those fallen mourners more blessed than those who have not fallen and are not mourning over themselves, because as a result of their fall, they have risen by a sure resurrection'."[98]

The degree to which this monastic approach was translated into the wider church is a matter of debate.[99] There is clear evidence that laypersons and clergy were remanded to monasteries as a penitential discipline.[100] It is also certain that confinement was practiced as part of the penitential experience of the wider church.[101] In light of the conflicting evidence throughout the entire first millennium, one can only conclude that, to the degree a correctional framework reflected the need for order and control, the detainee was apt to suffer not only punitive judgment but an incarceration in which privation and pain were externally imposed; to the degree it reflected a belief in the healing power of prayer, penance, and solitude, it often effected many a "sure resurrection."

The approach employed in matters of legal and moral failure would also have been affected by the fact that clergy were often placed in judicial positions, from the Fall of Rome at least until the eleventh century.[102] The temptation to allow law, judgment, and punishment to overrule a gospel-centered approach would probably have been pronounced. Both torture and capital punishment were frequently

---

[97] Ibid., 27.

[98] St John Climacus, *The Ladder of Divine Ascent*, trans. Archimandrite Lazarus Moore (London: Faber and Faber, 1959), 5, 26.

[99] I borrow this idea from Stanley Hauerwas. See "Punishing Christians," in *Performing the Faith* (Grand Rapids, MI: Brazos, 2004), pp. 185–200.

[100] Dunbabin, *Captivity*, p. 25; R.I. Moore, *The Formation of a Persecuting Society* (London: Basil Blackwell, 1987), p. 24; Pieter Spierenburg, *The Prison Experience* (New Brunswick, NJ: Rutgers University Press, 1991), p. 14.

[101] Poschmann, *Penance*, pp. 136–37. A canon of the Council of Matison orders that clergy guilty of indecency or seditious conduct be confined on bread and water for 30 days. See Mansi, *Sacrorum Conciliorum*, IX, c. 5.

[102] Manlio Bellomo, *The Common Legal Past of Europe*, trans. Lydia G. Cochrane (Washington, DC: Catholic University of America Press, 1995), p. 47; Dawson, *Europe*, p. 49; Robert W. Shaffern, *Law and Justice*, p. 88.

given sanction throughout the first millennium by church leaders.[103] Although the prohibition against the shedding of blood by Christians traces to the origins of the church, and judges were perceived as shedders of blood, we have already noted that the efforts of secular judges to create a peaceful environment for Christian religious practice led to the principle of the two aspects of judicial identity, the person and the instrument in the hands of the law.[104] Such justifications survived Christian antiquity and would find their way into the Middle Ages, and even into the age of Christian monarchy with the concept of the two bodies of the king.[105]

Summary

The understanding of law and judgment in the early Christian community was destined to have lasting effects on the history of both concepts. Early alliances were formed with the ruling powers in order to offset fear of persecution, the threat of heresy, and, to some degree, with the hope that the gospel could be preached to and embraced by all humankind. There was a widespread acceptance, especially in the period before the fourth century, that compromises were being made, in other words that law was not a given and that punitive judgments needed far more justification than a simple acknowledgment that offenders violated the law and therefore got what they deserved.[106]

Currents of cruelty, torture, and political opportunism were flanked by two institutional developments that provided a renewed hearkening to gospel directives concerning the goodness of creation and the beneficence of divine grace; they were the sacrament of penance and the development of the monastic tradition. These also provided a methodology of correction, to a large degree without repercussion.

The influence of shame and honor codes so central to the ethic of Roman society, coupled with the practice of permanent stigmatization by way of the mark of *infamia*, can be located in certain apologetic and politically opportunistic Christian texts but are also paralleled by a still vibrant sense of evangelical witness. The call to forgive all sin and to reconcile all sinners was made by figures such as Ignatius of Antioch, Polycarp, and Cyprian, whose words were hallowed in the blood they shed for those convictions. In addition, in contrast to what was to occur in the

---

[103] Francesco Compagnoni, "Capital Punishment and Torture in the Tradition of the Catholic Church," in Franz Bockle and Jacques Pohier (eds), *The Death Penalty and Torture* (New York: Seabury, 1979), pp. 41–42.

[104] Whitman, *Origins*, pp. 30–39; Augustine, *City*, I, 21.

[105] Ernst Kantorowicz, *The King's Two Bodies* (Princeton, NJ: Princeton University Press, 1957).

[106] Cameron states that the themes of "convergence and accommodation" in early Christian experience "not only failed to drive underground paradoxical elements inherent in Christian discourse since its inception but actually encouraged their parallel development." See *Christianity*, p. 155.

Middle Ages, crime was not yet distinct from sin. Both were viewed primarily as violations against God and one's neighbor, not as violations of law. Certainly the continued survival of the vendetta, where the family of the accused, not the state, hunts down and punishes the villain who failed to make the prescribed amends, reveals that law, even in strictly secular matters, had much more to do with persons than with the independent validity of particular statutes.[107]

Edward Peters concludes that in the early Church the gospel ideal of love and forgiveness, coupled with a revilement of "terrestrial" justice, "grew up side by side" with "a spiritual universe of judgment, fear, and torment," a troubled relationship that would continue unabated into the Middle Ages.[108] Perhaps no one embodied this tension more than Augustine, whose writing shaped so much of the deeply evangelical and shrewdly pragmatic approach to law and judgment in the early church, and whose influence upon later generations of Christian theologians on these matters would be unprecedented. A reference to Augustine is thus an appropriate way to sum up the evidence in this chapter and its relevance to the overall theme of the book. For all of his attempts to maintain the purity of the gospel by seeking protection beneath the Roman legal edifice, he lived to see the Vandal invasions destroy not only Rome's power but also much of his life's work in Africa, a poignant reminder for Christians that whatever security life and law afford can only be found in the shadow of the cross.[109]

---

107 Dawson, *Europe*, p. 74. Julius Goebel, Jr., *Felony and Misdemeanor* (Philadelphia: University of Pennsylvania Press, 1976), p. 89.

108 Edward Peters, "Destruction of the Flesh—Salvation of the Spirit: The Paradoxes of Torture in Medieval Christian Society," in Alberto Ferreiro (ed.), *The Devil, Heresy, and Witchcraft in the Middle Ages* (Leiden: Brill, 1998), p. 134.

109 Brown, *Augustine*, p. 425.

Chapter 4
Law and Judgment Prior to the Enlightenment

The period in Christian history beginning with the pontificate of Gregory VII (1073 AD) and ending with the Enlightenment was of the utmost importance in reshaping how Christians came to think about law and punitive judgment. Just as the early church found itself torn between the inspiration of the gospel and the needs of order and security, the medieval church would not only reproduce this tension but seek to ameliorate it, if not eliminate it, by placing law within God's plan of salvation and viewing law as a reflection of God's own mind. The initial gospel ethic of love, shading in the direction of antinomianism, was thus formally conjoined to an ethic of order, shading in the direction of legalism. In this new formulation, crime for the first time became an independent social and theological concept, a public defiance of law rather than an offence against God and neighbor. People were no longer simply sinners who needed to repent; some were criminals who needed to be punished not only for their sins but also, and especially, for violations of the law.

This chapter will discuss how law and the judgments imposed upon its ecclesiastical and secular subjects rose to a position of spiritual and political prominence among Christians. It will survey some of the principal figures and movements that expressed in varying ways this new legal culture, among them proponents of natural law, nominalism, and the Reformation. It will also speak of those Christians who, in the midst of centralization of authority and preoccupation with security, continued to embody the still-vibrant strands of memory that urged Christians to judge no one and to see and love the image of God in every creature. The chapter will conclude with summary observations concerning the Christian understanding of law and judgment prior to the Enlightenment.

Apotheosis of Law in Church and State

For the Greeks, law enshrined timeless moral precepts because its statutes derived their meaning and legitimacy from a natural law.[1] This natural law, as the theologian Francisco de Vitoria expressed it, referencing Aristotle, "springs from things themselves, and what springs from things themselves is necessary

[1] Aristotle, *Ethics*, V, vii.

… [I]t is that which is properly and of itself right."[2] In Christian Europe prior to the late eleventh century, however, law's moral relevance had little to do with the fact that it was in some fashion eternal. It was authoritative because it expressed "what we do around here," the old ways that had proven themselves true; and even then, writers such as Bernard of Clairvaux argued that law was not to be accorded validity in and of itself, only when measured against what was "advantageous" and what was "suitable."[3] As if to underscore its somewhat redundant nature in relation to lived communal experience, law was rarely written down; nor was there anything reminiscent of what we today know as a professional judiciary, trained lawyers, legal literature, or a even a legal system. Simply put, the idea of a separate Christian legal system in such an environment would have been unthinkable.[4]

Just as unthinkable would have been the concept of the state. Joseph Strayer relates that early in the second millennium there was no such thing as national identity; it was the one "without a family or a lord, without membership in a local community or a dominant religious group, who had no security and no opportunity, who could survive only by becoming a servant or a slave."[5] Related to this, and echoed in the developments described in the previous two chapters, was the still-robust teaching of the early Christian church, though somewhat tattered by compromise, that both law and human security are fulfilled in Jesus alone. Thus, despite the unquestioned legitimacy of local ordinances and the obedience they rightly claimed, such human formulations were widely held to be of small value when compared to the law of God, which alone could save one from the perils of damnation.[6]

All of this changed dramatically with the pontificate of Gregory VII (1073–1085). A long period of conflict with secular rulers exercising influence on the appointment of bishops and, through the latter, upon the affairs of the church,

---

2 Quoted in Bernice Hamilton, *Political Thought in Sixteenth Century Spain* (Oxford: Clarendon Press, 1963), p. 12.

3 Bernard of Clairvaux, "On Consideration," in O'Donovan, *From Irenaeus to Grotius*, 275.

4 In the period of the Jurists (before the formation of canon law beginning in the late eleventh century), the divine element in law was understood as the quality of mercy and equity the judge would bring to the case. Ivo of Chartres writes concerning the teaching of the popes: "In quo prudentem lectorem praemonere congruum duximus ut, si forte quae legerit, non ad plenum intellexerit, vel sibi invicem adversari existimaverit, non statem reprehendat; sed quid secundum rigorem, quid secundum moderationem, quid secundum judicium, quid secundum misericordiam dicatur, diligenter attendat; quae inter se dissentire non sentiebat, qui dicebat: *Misericordiam et judicium cantobo tibi, Domine*." Later, the commands of law themselves would be seen as divine. See Ivo of Chartres, "Decretum," in J.P. Migne, *Patrologiae Cursus Completus* (Paris: 1844), vol. 161, col. 47; Brague, *Law*, p. 220.

5 Joseph Strayer, *On the Medieval Origins of the Modern State* (Princeton, NJ: Princeton University Press, 1970), p. 3.

6 Berman, *Law and Revolution*, p. 83.

formally known as the Investiture Controversy, led to Gregory's momentous decree in 1075 that established the Catholic Church as a social and spiritual entity independent of outside political control.[7] As a result of this development, what Berman sees as perhaps the most influential revolution in Western history, the church became the first institution in the world both to will and call itself a state; and law, in like fashion, took on a significance in both church and state unknown both to Christian antiquity and to the modern age.[8]

In every country wherein the church resided, there began to appear "professional courts, a body of legislation, a legal profession, a legal literature, and a 'science of law'."[9] With the creation of canon law, the Greek juridical ideal was recaptured. Law achieved transcendent power and respect inasmuch as it surpassed its practical and local function and became synonymous with religion itself.[10] Indeed, as Ullmann states, Gregory VII viewed the Catholic Church with the pope at its head as the very embodiment of *justitia*, "and hence the pope alone

---

[7] Gregory thus fulfilled a dream of ecclesiastical independence dating back at least to Pope Gelasius who, in a letter in 494, expressed his concept of the two swords of authority: church and imperium. Each complements the other, but the latter must concede ultimate authority to the church due its supernatural nature. See Gabriel LeBras, "Canon Law," in C.G. Crump and E.F. Jacobs (eds), *The Legacy of the Middle Ages* (Oxford: Clarendon Press, 1926), p. 337.

[8] Brague, *Law*, p. 136; Pollock, *English Law*, vol. 1, p. 111; Ullmann, *Law and Politics*, p. 28.

[9] Berman, *Law and Revolution*, p. 50.

[10] The formation of the first code of canon law is a fascinating study in itself. After the decree of Gregory VII, church canonists hurriedly began to comb through and revise the massive reservoir of papal decrees (or decretals), legislation from church councils, other ecclesiastical rulings, and apocryphal decisions. Furthermore, the discovery in an Italian library of the *Digest* of the Emperor Justinian provided the early compilers with an authoritative source in attempting to answer problems in specifically secular areas of legal interest, e.g., marriage, contracts, and crime. Several noteworthy attempts at systematization had been achieved by the end of the eleventh century by figures such as Ivo of Chartres and Burchard of Worms, but it was the Bolognese monk, Gratian, who, shortly after 1140, devised the definitive collection of past rulings arranged in a dialectical format that enabled him to reconcile "discordant" canons. His work, *Concordantia Discordantia Canonum* (Concord of Discordant Canons), formed the basis of the first code of canon law. The corpus grew as the result of a number of church councils called to complete the system: Third (1179) and Fourth Lateran (1215); First (1245) and Second Lyons (1274); and Vienne (1311). Two popes trained as lawyers, Gregory IX (1234) and Boniface XIII (1298), added to the collection. With only several short additions, the body of law created, the *Corpus Iuris Canonici*, had full doctrinal force and governed the affairs of the Catholic Church until a revision was ordered in 1917. See Brague, *Law*, pp. 105–07; R.H. Helmholz, "Western Canon Law," in Witte and Alexander, *Christianity and the Law*, pp. 71–87; LeBras, "Canon Law," pp. 321–361; Ullmann, *Law and Politics*, pp. 119–145; Constant Van De Wiel, *History of Canon Law* (Louvain: Peeters, 1991).

… is entitled to issue on the basis of *justitia* concrete and detailed laws which bind everyone, without exception."[11]

The revolutionary aspect of these events was not simply the creation of the world's first "modern" political institution and the world's first legal system. Perhaps of even greater significance was the necessary creation, and by inference divine legitimation, of the state as a discrete legal and social entity. Here we see the real beginning of secularization, not a movement emanating from a disbelieving world intent on banishing religion from public life, but a measured and calculated decision by the church itself to guarantee its full independence from secular rule.[12] This was a far greater bestowal of honor upon the terrestrial domain than Augustine's rather begrudging neo-Platonic inference that political authority has its part to play in the divine scheme simply, and finally, in its ability to use force to keep the peace.[13] It also refashions Augustine's largely soteriological vision of the two cities—the glorious city of God and the spiritually doomed earthly city—in that the latter is now accorded both political significance and, as we will see with the flowering of natural law thinking, an explicit theological warrant, one in which human salvation, and not simply human security, is aided immeasurably by the governing power.[14] As a result, just as the church created law and a judicial framework, expressive of God's own will, and castigated those in violation of that law, so the state then began to reproduce not only the right to judge and punish legal infractions, but also to do so with the express consent and blessing of the church.[15]

Natural Law

The natural law has in some fashion always found a place in Christian theological and political thought. Not only were many Patristic writers influenced by Greek thought, wherein the idea originates, but scripture itself, notably the writing of St Paul, also contains explicit reference to the natural law. In one notable passage, Paul acknowledges that among the reasons why Gentiles are free of the constraints imposed by the Mosaic law is that the necessary guidelines for proper behavior are already inscribed by God upon their hearts (Rom 2: 14–15).

Natural law argues that human moral decisions as well as legal statutes attain legitimacy only to the degree that they reflect those timeless truths to which St Paul is referring; truths that are part of the very fabric of the universe. Medieval

---

11 Walter Ullmann, *The Growth of Papal Government in the Middle Ages* (London: Methuen & Co., 1955), p. 275.

12 Taylor, *Secular*, pp. 265–66.

13 Augustine, *City*, XV, 4; Chana Kasachkoff Poupko, "The Religious Basis of the Retributive Approach to Punishment," *The Thomist* 39 (1975), p. 532.

14 Alasdair MacIntyre, *Whose Justice? Which Rationality?* (Notre Dame, IN: University of Notre Dame Press, 1988), pp. 161–62.

15 Poupko, "Retributive Approach to Punishment," p. 528.

Christian theology, particularly with the discovery of the thought of Aristotle, refashioned and magnified this belief in ways germane to the mission of the church. Even before this occurred, however, Christian writers and theologians had utilized the concept and contended that the natural law revealed to all humans the basic thrust of the biblical ethic. Thus Gratian, the influential author of the foundational volume of canon law, begins the *Decretum* (c. 1140) not only with a reference to the natural law but also equates it with a portion of the Great Commandment: "The human race is ruled by two [means] namely natural law and by usages. Natural law is what is contained in the Law and the Gospel by which each is commanded to do to another what he wants done to himself."[16] Shortly afterwards (c. 1157), Rufinus the Canonist produced the first commentary on Gratian's seminal work. His gloss on the above passage states that natural law is "a kind of natural propulsion, implanted by nature in each person, to do good and avoid evil."[17] Rufinus also anticipates later commentators, among them the Protestant reformers, in asserting that the natural law is expressed in the Ten Commandments, and even more perfectly in the gospels, "in which natural law was restored entirely, and so, perfected."[18]

The reader hardly needs to be reminded of the towering achievements of St Thomas Aquinas, but one among them has had a lasting impact, namely the construction of a system of law that relies in part on the sources just mentioned. It was a schema that, at the high point of the development of the Catholic Church as a universal, rather than simply a regional, phenomenon, provided a parallel justification for that development with an equally universal, transcendent, and binding structure of legal authority.

In many ways, the medieval mind was poised to embrace this juridical turn due in part to theological speculation, a theme of which was a fascination with the faultless order of the cosmos whose design provided unimpeachable proof of God's existence.[19] There was "singularly unanimous agreement" that the perfect

---

16 "Humanum genus duobus regitur, naturale videlicet et iure, moribus. Ius naturale est, quod in lege Evangelio continetur." Gratian, "Decretum Gratiani," in *Corpus Iuris Canonici* (Lyon, 1616), Distintcio Prima; Brian Tierney, *The Idea of Natural Rights* (Atlanta: Scholars Press, 1997), p. 58.

17 Rufinus the Canonist, "Summa Decretum," in O'Donovan, *From Irenaeus to Grotius*, I, I.

18 Ibid.

19 Aquinas states: "The fifth [proof of the existence of God] is taken from the governance of the world. We see that things which lack intelligence, such as natural bodies, act for an end, and this is evident from their acting always, or nearly always, in the same way, so as to obtain the best result. Hence it is plain that not fortuitously, but designedly, do they achieve their end. Now whatever lacks intelligence cannot move towards an end, unless it be directed by some being endowed with knowledge and intelligence; as the arrow is shot to its mark by the archer. Therefore some intelligent being exists by whom all natural things are directed to their end; and this being we call God." *Summa Theologica*, (*ST*), I, Q. 2, a. 3.

laws of a perfect Creator were manifested in this natural beauty and harmony and it was thus "natural" to assume that human laws patterned on this design would produce similarly sublime effects.[20] In like fashion, St Thomas, like Gratian and Anselm before him, exemplified the dialectical method of thought and intellectual inquiry. As R.W. Southern notes, the love of dialectic was more than a "literary affectation—it was the expression of a deep intellectual need for order and balance, and of sharpness of vision in which there were no blurred edges."[21] Finally, and perhaps most ironically, one of the reasons paving the way for this enchantment with the law may have been sacred scripture itself. One can infer not only the obvious influence of the First Testament in affecting this transformation but, as noted in the last chapter, the entire Latin translation of the Bible by St Jerome, the Vulgate, was suffused with Roman legal concepts: "If the educated classes had not been familiar with the Vulgate and therefore had not absorbed its Roman jurisprudential wealth, this reception would not have been so quick … Roman law was so to speak transmitted under the cover of the Bible."[22]

The union of heaven and earth under the rule of law envisioned by Aquinas was thus a union of scriptural interpretation, Christian theology, and Greek philosophy. On one hand, St Thomas was well-versed in the faith tradition he had inherited, one in which the harmony of the natural law with fundamental biblical precepts had already been given voice; on the other hand, he was deeply indebted to the thought of Aristotle—so much so that the latter was never referred to by name, only by the supreme encomium, "the philosopher."

Although Aristotle posited a natural law, he did not delve deeply into its specific contours. St Thomas, however, both embraced and expanded the range of the concept. Building upon the thought of his theological and philosophical forebears, among them his tutor, Albert the Great, he proposed that natural law is a reflection in the human mind of the very mind of God. It is an imprint of what Aquinas and others called the "eternal law," an indelible orientation that, aside from conferring ontological dignity and sacredness upon the human person, enables him or her to proceed according to clear guidelines oriented to social health and personal salvation.[23]

The natural law, echoing the perfect truth of God, consists of one basic principle with three applications. This normative centerpiece is expressed in the phrase utilized by Rufinus, "do good and avoid evil."[24] One must seek to do the good in those inclinations one shares with all creation, namely, to preserve life and resist death. Second, one must choose the good in those activities one has in common with all animals. Here, Aquinas, following the Roman jurist, Ulpian, postulated

---

20 Ullmann, *Law and Politics*, p. 46.

21 R.W. Southern, *Saint Anselm And His Biographer* (Cambridge, UK: Cambridge University Press, 1963), p. 45.

22 Ullmann, *Law and Politics*, pp. 45–46.

23 Aquinas, *ST*, I-II, Q. 91, a. 1–2.

24 Ibid., I-II, Q. 94, a. 2.

that all animals are oriented to the union of male and female and the mutual care of offspring. Finally, one must do what the good demands in the behavioral patterns one shares with all rational creatures: to live in society, to seek the truth, and to worship God.[25]

Law, in the Thomist formulation, functions in a descending hierarchy of privilege and jurisdiction infused with an organic unity. Just as the human person possessing the natural law participates in but neither encloses nor supersedes God (the bearer of eternal law), so does human statutory law depend upon coherence with the natural law to achieve its legitimacy and binding force. Human laws echo the natural law in the same way the latter echoes the eternal law.[26] As such, Thomas thoroughly believed that there cannot be an unjust law so long as the pattern above holds true.[27]

Aside from the need for positive law to cohere fully with these timeless principles, St Thomas stated that for each legal statute to retain its validity, it must be "promulgated," not whimsically decreed by a ruler with the power to ensure compliance, and it must always be directed to the common good.[28] This latter concept has been a principal commitment of Catholic social thought throughout its history, but understandably began to assume a position of greater prominence in the legal age about which we are speaking. Peter Abelard, a century before Aquinas, wrote that the standard by which punishments are meted out for injury done to others should be determined by the common good: "For whatever can redound to the common ruin or public detriment should be punished with greater correction, and what causes greater wrong deserves among us a heavier penalty."[29] For his part, St Thomas orchestrated the centrality of the common good throughout his written corpus. In several early works, he stated that the common good is not only superior but also "more divine" than the good of any individual person.[30] The concept is equally vital to his mature expression of law.[31] Erasmus would later

---

25 Ibid.

26 Ibid., II-II, Q. 91, a.3.

27 Ibid., II-II, Q. 95, a. 2; II-II, Q. 96, a. 4.

28 Ibid., I-II, Q. 90, a. 4; Q. 96, a. 1–5. We will see that Thomas' own commitment to reason as the basis of legal promulgation will be challenged not only by the Protestant reformers but by some Franciscan and Jesuit writers for whom the will and, by extension, power was the principal motivation for legislation.

29 Abelard, *Ethics*, p. 43.

30 See *On the Governance of Rulers*, trans. Gerald B. Phelan (London: Sheed & Ward, 1938), I, 1, 9; *On the Truth of the Catholic Faith (Summa Contra Gentiles)*, trans. Vernon J. Burke (Garden City, NY: Image Books, 1956), III, 147, 5.

31 "Now laws are said to be just … when, to wit, they are ordained to the common good—and from their author, that is to say, when the law that is made does not exceed the power of the lawgiver—and from their form, when, to wit, burdens are laid on the subjects, according to an equality of proportion and with a view to the common good." *ST*, I-II, Q. 94, a. 1.

state, fully in line with much of the tradition preceding him, that it is "royalty's duty to know nothing of personal inclinations and to judge everything by the common good."[32]

Aquinas embraced more than Aristotle's concept of a natural law, he adopted Aristotle's teleological system, making it the theoretical basis of his entire theological project. As the acorn has but one end or *telos*, that of becoming an oak tree, humans have but one end, the attainment of union with God and all of God's creation in the beatific vision.[33] Thomas, however, reasoned that the attainment of the principal end was contingent upon a secondary requirement, that of living in a just and virtuous society guided by law.[34]

The role of virtue and of the ruling authority in providing one of the primary means to sanctification is paramount. One must develop virtues in order to respond to the dictates of the natural law.[35] Once again, St Thomas found in Greek philosophy an intellectual resource, emphasizing, as had many before him, the classic "cardinal virtues," prudence, justice, fortitude, and temperance, as necessary components of the moral life. They were disciplines that every person had to learn by way of membership and participation within primary communities, each of which finds its place within the natural law: family, state, and church. It was the responsibility of political authority through the promulgation of laws harmonious with God's donation to human beings to preserve and support these communal pillars so essential to the inculcation and reproduction of virtuous action.[36]

Finally, to complete the system, Aquinas posited a fourth set of laws, the divine, that are not in themselves natural. These are located only within the church and find their expression in the theological virtues of faith, hope, and charity. These gracious gifts of God are bestowed upon the faithful Christian through participation in the liturgy and the sacraments. Thus, just as the eternal law stands above the natural in goodness, knowledge, and privilege, so does the church stand above the state. Since the church, through the virtues specially imparted to it, participates in the life of God in a way greater than normal human participation, it

---

32 Erasmus, "The Complaint of Peace," in O'Donovan, *From Irenaeus to Grotius*, 579.

33 Aquinas, *ST*, I, Q. 12, a. 8; I, Q. 44, a. 4. The act/potency distinction is discussed often in Aristotle. See, e.g., *Metaphysics*, trans. John Warrington (London: Dent, 1956), Alpha, 12.

34 Aquinas, *ST*, I-II, Q. 95, a.1; *On the Governance of Rulers*, ch. 1; *On the Truth of the Catholic Faith*, III, c. 141, 6. "As the Philosopher says (Phys. ii, 2), the end is twofold—the end 'for which' and the end 'by which'; viz. the thing itself in which is found the aspect of good, and the use or acquisition of that thing." *ST*, I-II, Q. 1, a. 8.

35 For St Thomas, the cardinal virtues were aided by another virtue that gave one the ability to know and apply the dictates of the virtues correctly. This was the virtue he called *synderesis*. See *Truth*, trans. James V. McGlynn, S.J. (2 vols, Chicago: Henry Regnery, 1953), vol. 1, Q. 16, a. 1–3.

36 On the cardinal and theological virtues, see *ST*, I-II, Q. 61, Q. 62. On the role of the political community in promoting the cardinal virtues, see *ST*, I-II, Q. 96.

is incumbent upon the church to insure that the ruling authority and the legislation enacted by that authority are harmonious with the natural law and directed to the common good.[37]

Contact with law, for the first time in Christian history, now puts humans in contact with God.[38] The divine canopy that had been spread over ecclesiastical and secular statutes was given further credence by the conviction that the entire juridical and hierarchical edifice is fully rational. Nicholas of Kues in the fourteenth century not only recalls his predecessors in avowing that no law can be valid that does not reflect natural law principles; he also reminds his readers that since those principles are "naturally based in reason … those better endowed with reason are the natural lords and masters of the others."[39]

The project undertaken by Aquinas to provide a theory of law and society grounded in divine benediction and serving the internal and external designs of the Catholic Church cannot be accused of either political absolutism or strict legalism. The brilliant Dominican was often at odds with ecclesiastical officials, especially in his reliance on "pagan" philosophers such as Aristotle and, to some extent, the Muslim scholars who introduced Aristotle to the West, Avicenna and Averroes.[40] Additionally, just as steadfastly as he contended that all legislative decrees were binding since, as an articulation of natural law, they were at the same time just, he asserted that deformations of law—statutes promulgated for sinful motives—had no inherent moral authority.[41] Nor was this caveat unique to St Thomas. Abelard suggested a similar resistance to obeying unjust laws, especially those enacted by the church, referencing both Origen and Gregory the Great in so doing.[42] And even

---

37 Ibid. I-II, Q. 91, a. 4. In this triumphal logic, Aquinas echoes a sentiment tracing back to Pope Gelasius I in the late fifth century. See also, Bernard of Clairvaux, "On Consideration," in O'Donovan, *From Irenaeus to Grotius*, IV, 3; John of Salisbury, *The Statesman's Book of John of Salisbury* (*Policraticus*), trans. John Dickinson (New York: Russell & Russell, 1963), IV, 3.

38 Brague, *Law*, p. 219.

39 This is not an affirmation of political absolutism, however, since legitimate political power relies not only upon the common good but, in a phrase that prefigures other developments of immense significance, upon "the election and consent of the others." Nicholas of Kues, "The Catholic Concordance," in O'Donovan, *From Irenaeus to Grotius*, 544.

40 M.C. D'Arcy, S.J., *St. Thomas Aquinas* (Westminster, MD: Newman, 1955), pp. 32–37.

41 On law and justice, see *ST*, II-II, 57, 1. On the right to resist unjust laws, see *ST*, I-II, 96, 4; "Commentary on the Sentences," in O'Donovan, *From Irenaeus to Grotius*, II, 44, 2. Aquinas did argue, however, that the primacy of the common good modified the right to refuse compliance with unjust laws. If the discord and other ill-effects of a principled disobedience result in greater harm than the good such resistance might bring, then political subjects are required to obey, not out of respect for authority but out of love for those who might be harmed in the ensuing conflict. See *ST*, I-II, Q. 96, a. 4.

42 Abelard, *Ethics*, pp. 117–19.

as staunch a defender of political authority as John of Salisbury asserted that the solider was not bound to follow unjust commands: "Some things are so necessary that they require no command; others so detestable that no command will possibly justify them."[43]

In similar fashion, the Thomist system, like virtually all others in this period, is marked by a flexible, intuitive approach, not a strict, deductive one with regard to the meaning of the rules enacted. It is important to remember that natural law is not law per se, only the moral conditions necessary for the creation of law. Thomas and others provided broad latitude in the determination of how the primary formulations were to be expressed in secondary legal statutes, conforming to the specific needs of the common good as ascertained in each unique social environment. In this, St Thomas again reveals the influence of both Aristotle and Albert the Great. Aristotle, unlike Plato, saw derivations from the legal norm as the means to improve law, since no law could fittingly be applied to the multiple shades of meaning in human actions, not to mention how those actions are interpreted in different social networks.[44] Albert stated: "[O]ne must respect the continuing variability of the real, and not attempt to locate all human actions under one and the same universal rule. The real must not be bent to the rule; it is the rule which must be adapted to the real."[45] This attitude was also generally embraced within the new law of the church that was, according to Gabriel LeBras, characterized not "by the dogmatism that one might expect" since "the rules of Canon law were formulated and applied with a remarkable absence of rigidity."[46]

By way of summary, I am reminded of a professor of ethics in a class I once took who remarked that people have been trying to bury the natural law for well over two millennia; and it has ended up burying every one of its undertakers. His remark is worth heeding. The high principles invoked by the doctrine concerning the organic unity of creation and the ontological sacredness of the person, safeguarded and promoted in social institutions, are ensured a permanent place in both theological and philosophical conversation. Similarly, it is only proper to assume that advocates of natural law seek to further ends prompted by a commitment to communal flourishing as well as spiritual fulfillment. Finally, it is clear that the understanding of law in this system is much more formal than material. As one writer remarked, natural law is more akin to establishing curbs on the road than minute directions on how to drive.[47]

---

43 John of Salisbury, *Statesman's Book*, VI, 12.

44 John Mahoney, *The Making of Moral Theology* (Oxford: Clarendon, 1987), pp. 235–36.

45 Quoted in Mahoney, *Moral Theology*, p. 237.

46 LeBras, "Canon Law," p. 328.

47 Columba P. Ryan, OP, "The Traditional Concept of Natural Law: An Interpretation," in Ronald Hamel and Kenneth Himes (eds), *Introduction to Christian Ethics* (Ramsey, NJ: Paulist Press, 1989), pp. 419–20.

Having said that, the problems many find with the natural law are just as indelible as its virtues. The theory, at least in its classic scholastic exposition, is beset with a methodological duality that leads to troubling conclusions.[48] The primary applications of the precept "do good and avoid evil" have often been translated into legal statutes with punishment inflicted and justified for violation of those statutes.[49] In like manner, the utilization of the doctrine has been instrumental in enabling the church to turn judicial decrees, and the corresponding judgments made for their infringement, into a distinct source of truth that is often in tension with the great commandment of unconditional love that the church is compelled to honor and to preach. Furthermore, this ideological aura surrounding the legislative process, and the violent punishments often sanctioned under its aegis, were quickly reproduced by the emerging European states, which were not constrained by the task of having to provide a theological justification for the infliction of suffering.

But of all the challenges posed by the medieval legal revolution in general, and the natural law in particular, to the simple New Testament ethic of a loving, non-judgmental presence to the other, perhaps none was more instrumental in building the theological justification for a harsh justice toward legal infractions, then and now, than when human error in the public sphere lost its appellation as a "relational" offense and became a crime.[50]

Criminal Sin, Criminal Punishment

Many authors have remarked that people in the Middle Ages were just as poised to render, and even take delight in, brutal punishment for legal infractions as they were to honor the moral constraints placed upon law by its divine origin. Delumeau has tracked extensively the sea change in social psychology that characterized the period in which the horror of sin and the obsessive fear of damnation pervaded the cultural landscape. In this milieu, some chose what has been termed the *fuga*

---

48 The methodological duality consists in an inductive understanding of the ethical implications of the first and third applications (protection of life on one hand, the role of institutions in promotion of the common good on the other), and a deductive approach to the second (union of male and female). Regarding the latter, sexual activity that does not approximate the union of male and female is more culpable morally than actions that do. Thus masturbation would be viewed as more culpable than rape. See Charles Curran, *Directions in Fundamental Moral Theology* (Notre Dame: University of Notre Dame Press, 1985), pp. 125–37; Jeffrey Stout, *Ethics After Babel* (Boston: Beacon Press, 1988), pp. 158–59.

49 The connection between the natural law and violence has been explored by Stanley Hauerwas. See *The Peaceable Kingdom* (Notre Dame: University of Notre Dame Press, 1983), p. 61.

50 Prior to the systematization of law of which we have been speaking, sin and crime were virtually interchangeable concepts. Adultery was as much a crime as usury was a sin. See Berman, *Law and Revolution*, p. 73; LeBras, "Canon Law," p. 356.

mundi (flight from the world) ethos of monasticism for the purpose of spiritual deliverance from evil; most, however, in Delumeau's interpretation, succumbed to a *contemptus mundi* (hatred of the world), a neo-Gnostic or Stoic scorn for the world that could not but result in a deep-seated antipathy for humankind and initiate a macabre theater of sanguinary punishment.[51] In this latter perspective, as Norbert Elias contends, "rapine, battle, [and] the hunting of men and animals" were perceived not only as acceptable but also as "vital necessities" and "natural" expressions of human emotion.[52]

Since the Catholic Church as a monolithic, worldwide religious organization did not exist prior to the pontificate of Gregory VII, all politics in the early Middle Ages was, in effect, local. The punitive judgments one finds throughout the first millennium, usually decided upon in church councils and, most often, against heretics, were invariably penitential sentences imposed under the confessional rubric of contrition, ascetic practice, forgiveness, and reinstatement.[53]

Canon law, however, developed the concept of "criminal sin" to punish, for the first time, public offenses against law itself, not simply against persons or communities. In this new taxonomy of fault, a strict division was drawn between what were termed the internal forum and the external forum. The former is the domain of priest and penitent, the area of conscience and personal failing, of confession, penance, and absolution. The latter took shape as an attempt to reprove publicly actions detrimental to the church or actions that would be severely penalized under civil or royal decree. Such acts were not only sins; they were also crimes.[54] As transgressions of legal statutes, they were perceived to emanate

---

51 Delumeau, *Sin and Fear*, pp. 4, 9–14.

52 Norbert Elias, *The Civilizing Process*, trans. Edmund Jephcott (2 vols, New York: Urizon, 1978), vol. 1, pp. 193–94. See also Peters, "Destruction of the Flesh," p. 147. Huizinga emphasizes the dualism of the medieval mind between piety and violence. As to the latter, he writes that "revenge" and a "primitive barbarism" were present to an unprecedented degree. See J. Huizinga, *Waning of the Middle Ages* (New York: Doubleday, 1954), pp. 23–24.

53 Most sins in the Eastern Church were remitted by means of a four-tiered classification of gravity with accompanying public penances required of the offender. In the West, penitents were either given the ascetic disciplines discussed in the last chapter, overseen by members of the congregation, or remanded to a monastery. After the seventh century, the era of private penance began. Here the penitential cure was determined between priest and penitent. Grave offenses were often met with the assignment of a pilgrimage for a period of time, sometimes years. For examples of early penitential discipline and the differences between penance in the Eastern and Western churches, see Percival, "Ecumenical Councils," pp. 24–26; Poschmann, *Penance*, pp. 87–91; Vogel, "Sin," pp. 228–29. On the penitentials, see McNeill and Gamer, *Medieval Handbooks*. On the use of pilgrimage, see Jonathan Sumption, *Pilgrimage: An Image of Medieval Religion* (London: Faber & Faber, 1975).

54 The list of offenses required to be prosecuted publicly by the English church was quite large. It included not only civil offenses but also "spiritual crimes" such as adultery,

from internal corruption; hence they existed in the mind as sins before they were enacted.[55] Given this dual level of guilt, the simple absolution by the priest was only sufficient to amend the inner defect leading to the external offense. The assault upon law required the culprit to stand trial before an ecclesiastical judge.[56] In a memorable phrase, Gratian writes in the *Decretum* that "all crime is seen to be public according to the canons."[57] John of Paris, writing in the late thirteenth century, gives evangelical justification for the new legal culture in his claim that among the six powers given by Christ to the apostles was the power to judge: "The fourth power is judicial; that power to coerce in the external forum by which sins are corrected through fear of punishment, especially sins in scandal to the church." He concludes with an affirmation that "priests have full power of priestly rule over the community of the faithful."[58]

Significant theological developments had prepared the way for thinkers like John of Paris to emphasize that priests were not only pastors leading the faithful to Christ but judges with both legal and punitive authority. Part of this justification was provided in the determination that sin not only emanated from internal corruption but also initiated multiple layers of harm. St Anselm (1033–1109), for example, wrote one of the most influential treatises on the atonement, seeking to answer a question that has always vexed and inspired Christian theologians: why did Christ have to suffer? The answer he suggested assumed, among other things, that the death of Christ removed the guilt humankind bears for its sinful state: the urges of the flesh toward violence, greed, self-indulgence, and what Abelard called "contempt of the Creator."[59] He insisted, however, that although the sacrifice of Christ makes eternal salvation open to each, the actual sins humans commit must be atoned for. As Berman notes, referencing Anselm: "God accepts man as he is. But this very absolution imposes an added responsibility on each individual not to choose voluntarily to do those things that are prohibited. If he does so choose, he is punished for it—not destroyed, not hated, but made to pay a price commensurate with the offense, that is, with illegality."[60] Aquinas, following Anselm, argued similarly but extended the level of guilt even further. There were three levels of

blasphemy, usury, and illicit gaming. See R.H. Helmholz, "The Early History of the Grand Jury and the Canon Law," *University of Chicago Law Review* 50 (1983), p. 618.

55 Recall the influence of Abelard in positing that God judges the internal state of the person more than the action itself. See Abelard, *Ethics*, pp. 13–29. See also Berman, *Law and Revolution*, pp. 185–86; Durham, "Religion and Criminal Law," pp. 224–25.

56 Peters, "Destruction of the Flesh," pp. 140–41; Ullmann, *Papal Government*, p. 374.

57 "*quia omne crimen videtur secundum canones esse publicum.*" Gratian, "Decretum," C. 2, q. 3, c. 8.

58 John of Paris, "On Royal and Papal Power," in O'Donovan *From Irenaeus to Grotius*, ch. 12.

59 Abelard, *Ethics*, pp. 6–7; St Anselm of Canterbury, *Why God Became Man*, trans. Joseph Colleran (Albany: Magi Books, 1969), I, 9.

60 Berman, *Law and Revolution*, p. 183; Anselm, *Why God*, I, 11.

culpability to a sinful act: the first was personal—the internal sinful decision; the second was divine—the offense against the order of creation (natural law); and the third was political—the violation of laws meant to insure the well-being of all.[61]

Sin, in other words, was no longer a betrayal of love; it came to be understood more and more as breaking the law—law that had become, in the words of John of Salisbury, "passionless."[62] The Second Lateran Council declared in 1215 that the sacrament of confession was now binding upon each Catholic. He or she must confess at least once a year to a priest or be guilty of mortal sin.[63] One could incur damnation not as a result of cruelty to others or abject denial of God but simply by failure to honor a law.

Similarly, illegality was no longer related mainly to the action committed, it began to define the person who committed it. It was not only a designation indicating wrong as opposed to right action; it also began to indicate an evil as opposed to a good person. St Raymond of Penyafort, one of the first great scholars of canon law, said in the *Summa de Penitentia* that it was permissible to kill if "keeping to the order of law."[64] In effect, the new legal variable, even presuming the best of intentions of its proponents, called into formal question the essential link in Christian revelation between fault and forgiveness.[65]

Perhaps of even greater note in these developments was the modification of the benevolent Christian anthropology in which being is graced with the divine presence prior to the choices humans make and cannot be eradicated regardless of what evil one causes as a result of those choices. According to the natural law, the very first moral guideline God placed within human reason was to defend life and resist death, an indication that each life is immeasurably and inviolably sacred.[66] Thus, in order to construct a justification for capital punishment, theologians working from a natural law perspective were compelled either to reject unconditionally the killing of another or to argue that the actions of the criminal offender revealed the incapability of rational deliberation. He or she was not human but a "beast." St Thomas, for example, strictly maintained the first application of the natural law against the willful taking of human life. He reasoned, however, that this moral prohibition does not extend to animals: "By sinning man departs from the order of reason, and consequently falls away from the dignity of his manhood … and he falls into the slavish state of the beasts … Hence, although it be evil in itself to kill

---

[61] "Accordingly, man can be punished with a threefold punishment corresponding to the three orders to which the human will is subject … one inflicted by himself, viz. remorse of conscience; another, inflicted by man; and a third, inflicted by God." *ST*, I-II, Q. 87, a. 1.

[62] John of Salisbury, *Statesman's Book*, IV, 2.

[63] Lateran IV, c. 21, http://fordham.edu/halsall/basis/lateran4.asp.

[64] Quoted in Whitman, *Origins*, p. 48.

[65] Delumeau, *Sin and Fear*, p. 4.

[66] Aquinas, *ST*, I-II, Q. 94, a. 2.

a man so long as he preserves his dignity, yet it may be good to kill a man who has sinned, even as it is to kill a beast."[67]

Recall the ancient Roman practice of infamy, the perpetual stigma of shame placed upon those in violation of law. Recall also that as the early canonists constructed the complex dimensions of church law, they relied on the legal codes of the Emperor Justinian to address areas of concern related to civil conduct that had not previously been addressed by papal decree or church councils. Infamy once again appears; this time in canon law, especially in regard to heresy.[68] Beginning in the thirteenth century, punishments ordered by the Inquisition, particularly in France and Spain, frequently required even repentant heretics to wear yellow crosses "as a mark of infamy." Known as the "San Benito," these symbols were to be placed on their outward garments at all times.[69] The influential legal code of Alfonso X (1221–1284) reveals that aside from a "scapulary," a public penitent could also be forced to "wear about his neck a stick a cubit in length … or wear an iron bound upon his arm, or about his neck, or go naked, or in his undergarments."[70] Often accompanying vestigial humiliation was public flagellation. Henry Kamen notes that flogging as a criminal punishment "was very severe, carrying with it the stigma of degradation and shame. It could be used only against those of low social status."[71]

The point here is not to judge the actions of revered scholars and saints. It is to reveal what happens to people in general, and Christians in particular, when law competes with the gospel as a source of spiritual value and moral analysis. Inevitably, the line between what is true and what is commanded becomes permeable. Such a fracture in the relevance of the gospel to provide the means to address all human dilemmas also inevitably leads to some form of violence and, more often than not, violence justified with little or no remorse for those upon whom it falls. In the words of Rene Girard: "Legal societies build the threat of violence into the fabric of social life." In such societies the judicial system "has the monopoly on revenge … is fully independent of everyone … and is universally respected."[72]

---

67 Ibid., II-II, 64, 2. The support of law and political authority, coupled with its belief in the common good over the individual, led Catholic theologians to accept the legitimacy of capital punishment, even if they did not necessarily comply with St Thomas in the specifics of their reasoning. See Compagnoni, "Capital Punishment," pp. 39–53.

68 Goebel, *Felony and Misdemeanor*, p. 71, n. 17.

69 Henry Kamen, *The Spanish Inquisition: A Historical Revision* (New Haven: Yale University Press, 1997), p. 200. See also James B. Given, *Inquisition and Medieval Society* (Ithaca: Cornell University Press, 1997) pp. 68–69; Shoham, *Mark of Cain*, p. 14.

70 Alfonso X, *Las Siete Partidas*, ed. Robert I. Burns, S.J., trans. Samuel Parsons Scott (Philadelphia: University of Pennsylvania Press, 2001), I, iv, xx.

71 Kamen, *Inquisition*, p. 202.

72 Rene Girard, *Violence and the Sacred*, trans. Patrick Gregory (Baltimore: Johns Hopkins University Press, 1977), pp. 20, 23.

Law, Punishment, and the State

The papal revolution whereby the church became a legally independent institution ultimately resulted in the creation of the state as an autonomous legal entity. There continued to be frequent interchanges, compromises, and no small amount of intrigue between the two but, nevertheless, the creation of canon law and its claim of full jurisdiction over all affairs of the church led to the parallel development and aim of civil law. Just as the church solidified its internal affairs by legal means, the state was born when political power came to be defined less by the goal of extensiveness, seen in the strategy of conquest, and more by the focus upon intensive internal order and supervision.[73]

In like manner, as the church usurped the role of secular authority and took upon itself the right to punish clerics guilty of crime, so the state strengthened its own authority in establishing legal justification to punish its unruly citizens.[74] This was aided immeasurably by the fact that early secular legal codes borrowed liberally from canon law.[75] In the earliest utterance of English law, for example, one finds the Greek words for "bishop, priest, and deacon."[76] The laws written by St Louis of France were often copied and are considered trustworthy evidence of thirteenth-century customs. Here we find decrees such as, "he who harbors murderers shall be hanged like a murderer." The king then quotes canon law (the decretal "Quia questium" of Gregory IX), "those who go along are punished like perpetrators."[77] Gratian, in a number of places, provides explicit consent for secular retributive practice: "If holy men and public powers waging wars are not transgressors of that mandate: 'Thou shalt not kill,' although they kill some criminals worthy of death … if it is not shedding blood to punish murderers and

---

73 "The lively and relevant legislative activity of the papacy most effectively imprinted the idea of the rule of law upon society." Ullmann, *Law and Politics*, p. 141. See also Berman, *Law and Revolution*, pp. 165–198.

74 The so-called "privilegium fori" was given much support in Canon Law, most notably in the *Decretum* of Gratian. It protected the clergy from prosecution in secular courts and was a focus of attention and no small amount of consternation between church and state, particularly when clerics were accused of crimes such as murder. See William M. Bowsky, *A Medieval Italian Commune: Siena Under the Nine* (Berkeley: University of California Press, 1981), pp. 110–11; Trevor Dean, *Crime in Medieval Europe* (Harlow, UK: Longman, 2001), p. 109.

75 R.H. Helmholz notes, for example, that the origin of the grand jury in twelfth-century England relied on the practice in canon law wherein an inquest of sworn testimony witnesses stated whether there was public fame sufficient to bring an indictment. See "Early History," p. 622.

76 Frederick Pollock, *English Law*, vol. 1, p. 1.

77 Saint Louis, *The Etablissements de Saint Louis*, ed. and trans. F.R.P. Akehurst (Philadelphia: University of Pennsylvania Press, 1996), xii, I, 36.

prisoners, but the ministry of laws … it is obvious that it is permitted not only to whip the evil, but also to kill them."[78]

The long tradition of ecclesiastical refusal to allow clergy to participate in the shedding of blood was one area of cooperation between church and state that served the ends of both.[79] Heretics who refused to repent, or those whose sins were particularly reprehensible, were a burden to the orderly concerns of both jurisdictions. Therefore, those found guilty of such crimes in an ecclesiastical court were often relegated to what was called "the secular arm." There they would be put to death without transgressing the law forbidding blood contamination. St Louis decrees the fate of such a person excommunicated by the church, once again quoting Pope Gregory: "If someone is suspected of heresy, the judge shall arrest him and send him to the bishop; and if he is convicted, he should be burned."[80]

As the Council of Trent (1545–1563), recapitulating the intent of Gregory VII, declared the church a "perfect society" claiming certitude in law and legitimacy in retributive judgment within its realm, the aura of perfection was easily transferred to the decrees of the secular magistrate and to the frequently severe penalties for their violation.[81] Thus, the crime of felony was broadened to include an ever-increasing array of offenses, all punishable by death. Originating from the Latin verb *fallere* (to fail), felony is found initially in Norman France, where it was considered "the most heinous of all crimes"—the betrayal of one's lord. As law, however, increasingly became associated with the person of the king and, like him, assumed a transcendent validity and authority, what had been common offenses suddenly became acts of treason. Maitland notes, for instance, that in the laws of Henry II (1166), felony retains its more restricted definition, but by the end of the twelfth century, "every crime of great gravity became a capital offense."[82] A quote from John of Salisbury reveals the reverence owed to the sovereign and the price

[78] Quoted in Stanley Chodorow, *Christian Political Theory and Church Politics in the Mid-Twelfth Century* (Berkeley: University of California Press, 1972), p. 236.

[79] Gratian references a canon from the Council of Toledo (675 AD) concerning the prohibition of bloodshed: "His, a quibus Domini sacramenta tractanda sunt, iudicium sanguinis agitare non licet." See "Decretum," C. 23, q. 8, c. 30; see also Chodorow, *Christian Political Theory*, p. 227.

[80] *Etablissements*, Bk. I, 90; see also Bk. I, 127. The Constitutions of medieval religious orders give evidence of the practice of excommunicating and releasing the "rebellious who refuse to adhere to the discipline of the Order on account of their contumacious and obstinate behavior … to the secular arm" ("brachum seculare"): "Illi, quoque, qui Ordinis disciplinae tam sunt rebelles, ut propter suam contumaciam, et obstinationem, vel excommunicare debeant, vel ad eos coercendos oportet adhibere brachum seculare." See "Statua Ordinis Praemonstratensis," in Lucas Holstenius, *Codex Regularum Monasticarum et Canonicarum* (Graz: Akademische Druck—U. Verlagsanstalt, 1957), V. Dist. III, Caput IX, 3.

[81] Ivan Illich, *Rivers*, pp. 92–93.

[82] F.W. Maitland, *The Constitutional History of England* (Cambridge: Cambridge University Press, 1968), p. 110.

for its neglect: “Even to presume aught [anything] against the inanimate statue of the prince at any time whatever is to commit the crime of lese majeste and merits punishment, as the ancients taught, by the most cruel death.”[83]

Fear of Judgment and the Paradox of Medieval Christianity

One might think from the evidence thus far presented in this chapter that there is little left to prove in the quest to find where in Christian history the New Testament ethic of a radical acceptance of sinful humanity ceded priority to one based upon law, judgment, and punishment. That is not the case, however. Alongside—sometimes literally alongside—a culture steeped in violence, there existed an equally fervent belief in the unmitigated benevolence and mercy of God, in God’s identification with the lowest, especially those imprisoned and doomed to die, and a near phobia against passing judgment upon sinners and criminals, regardless of the transparency of their guilt.

The bloodthirsty mobs so often alluded to by historians were at the same time unwilling to provide evidence to prove the guilt of their contemporaries and, even in the midst of executions, often sought reasons to believe in God’s prodigal favor and the salvation of the victim, who was at times transposed into a martyr. Huizinga corroborates this anxious relation between cruelty and exceptional piety. He provides an eyewitness account of an execution in France in 1411 in which the hangman, as was the custom, knelt before the condemned asking for his forgiveness. The victim not only forgives him “with all his heart,” he “then begs the executioner to embrace him. There was a great multitude of people, who nearly all wept hot tears.”[84]

Instances such as the one just narrated abound in this tumultuous period. It was tumultuous not simply due to revolutions in church and state, the birth of humanism and the Renaissance, and deep theological rifts prefiguring the Reformation, but also because the mind of the age kept both the high vision of the gospel and the practical ethos of a “passionless” legal justice, less in an unbreachable duality as in an uncomfortable and unpredictable tension. Such a strange juxtaposition of ethical opposites “tended to produce that perpetual oscillation between despair and distracted joy, between cruelty and pious tendencies which characterize life in the Middle Ages.”[85] Side by side one finds riotous merriment at public displays of torture and painful death, accompanied by cries of jubilation at the yearly lottery in numerous cities where on feast days condemned prisoners upon whom the gracious lot fell would immediately be released and carried in triumph throughout

83 John of Salisbury, *Statesman’s Book*, VI, 26.

84 Huizinga, *Waning*, pp. 11–12.

85 Ibid., p. 10.

the city.[86] As one historian of the period remarked, it was a cause of joy for people to be reminded of how God's mercy makes the justice practiced by civil and ecclesiastical courts, with their elaborate displays of formality and righteousness, appear ineffectual and foolish. Such demonstrations of benevolence were a vivid and celebrated reminder that "at least for one day" people could celebrate a justice "that firmly put divine love above human law."[87]

Samuel Edgerton analyzes the function and effects of public art in Florence to provide similar evidence of a generous Christian empathy thwarting civil and ecclesiastical attempts to insert a punitive legalism into the gospel. He narrates how secular authorities liberally utilized artistic renditions of biblical pericopes such as the Last Judgment in adorning courts of justice. Florentine criminal practice at that time was "uncompromising, harsh, and eschatologically anchored to the proposition that just as the sinner's immortal soul will suffer forever in hell, so his living body must be punished on earth."[88] The works produced, however, often triggered a reaction among the populace diametrically opposite to the one sought. Images of the passion of Christ and the bloody torments of saintly victims engineered to steer public sentiment against perpetrators of "evil" often, though quite unintentionally, began to subvert the very assumptions upon which punitive judgments were based. "By comparing the plight of the poor on the scaffold with vividly realistic portrayals of martyred saints and Jesus' suffering, Christians slowly became aware of their own inhumanity in the practice."[89]

We saw in the last chapter how in the early church a full choir of saints devoted their heavenly power to the liberation of captives. Their number swelled in the Middle Ages. Ste Foy, Leonard of Noblat, Dominic of Silos, Mary Magdalene, the Virgin of Rocamadour, St Adalbert, and St Wenceslaus all received abundant ritual devotion. Some, such as Ste Foy and St Leonard, had shrines erected in their honor—filled with the chains of prisoners they had miraculously freed, many of them rescued from captivity for no other reason than that their cries of sorrow stirred heavenly compassion.[90] The capriciousness of the saints was at times hard to fathom for some Christians of that time. Bernard of Angers remarked concerning Ste Foy: "It makes no difference whether a person is held in prison justly or unjustly … Those whom arrogance had once lured into crime come forward from confinement into the light, reformed."[91]

Even more pronounced than the overturning of human justice by the emissaries of a Savior once crushed under the weight of judicial reprisal was the fervent and widespread unwillingness of Christians to be party to legal accusation. In the early

86 Dunbabin, *Captivity*, p. 138–39; Samuel Edgerton, *Pictures and Punishment* (Ithaca: Cornell University Press, 1985), pp. 78–79.

87 Dunbabin, *Captivity*, p. 139.

88 Edgerton, *Pictures and Punishment*, p. 13.

89 Ibid., p. 14.

90 Dunbabin, *Captivity*, pp. 133–34.

91 Ibid., p. 134.

Middle Ages, a guilty verdict required the testimony of reliable witnesses. Yet, despite intimate knowledge of the circumstances of a given offense, including the culpable agent, it was the common practice of onlookers to refuse to testify.[92] Although theological speculation tracing back at least to Origen and Ambrose, and recapitulated by Gratian, had opened the way for Christians to act as judges by deftly bifurcating the magistrate as person from the public role as an agent of justice, the weight of anxiety over the infliction of suffering or death by one sinner upon another effectively stymied the prosecution of cases. Writers of the period reveal the intensity of cultural awareness of and reverence for the teaching of Christ that the measure used to measure the conduct of others will be measured back to the one standing in judgment (Lk 6: 38). Vincent of Beauvais was fond of describing the horrible fate of judges. His work entitled *The Mirror of History* relates tales of ancient magistrates who, duped by demons, condemned others only then to be consumed by bolts of lightning or other violent forms of death.[93]

The widespread breakdown of the judicial process based on the fear of passing judgment was a principal reason for the origin of the ordeal, a dramatic ritual in which God provided definitive proof of guilt or innocence, exculpating in the process those overseeing the execution of sentence.

Specifically, God's verdict was determined in a church setting, preceded by special orations. The accused would normally retrieve a ring from a cauldron of boiling water or be forced to carry a red-hot iron for several paces. The wound was then bandaged. After several days, the defendant returned to the sanctuary and the dressings were removed. If the hand was found to be infected, he or she was guilty of the misdeed; if the hand had begun to heal, he or she was innocent.[94]

To bolster further the prevalent attitude of unwillingness to assist in judgments bringing harm upon others, the process of the ordeal invariably found the culprit innocent—even in cases where there was little public doubt concerning culpability. Like the example of the condemned prisoners freed on festival days, such signs of divine justice provided for many certain proof of the strange and wonderful ways of God and the uncertainty and pretentiousness of human justice. Some, however, were not as serene. King William Rufus of

---

[92] One reason for this reluctance was the sacred overtones of the process. Oaths were given in church under precise circumstances where every word was essential and where the slightest moral equivocation was laced with eternal consequences. See Maitland, *Constitutional History*, pp. 115–18.

[93] Whitman, *Origins*, p. 93.

[94] See "King Ethelstan's Laws Ecclesiastical," in John Johnson (ed. and trans.) *A Collection of the Laws and Canons of the Church of England* (Oxford: John Henry Parker, 1850), pp. 341–47; Robert Bartlett, *Trial by Fire and Water* (Oxford: Clarendon, 1986); Thomas Head, "Saints, Heretics, and the Fire: Finding Meaning through the Ordeal," in Sharon Farmer and Barbara H. Rosenwein (eds) *Monks and Nuns, Saints and Outcasts* (Ithaca: Cornell University Press, 2000), pp. 200–34.

England is quoted as saying that God was not a just judge since He was in the habit of acquitting those known to be guilty.[95]

In brief, the ordeal, as James Whitman observes, was not instituted in order to get the facts straight about the incident in question, but in order to "spare human beings the responsibility of judgment."[96]

After the ordeal was banned by the Fourth Lateran Council in 1215, the inauguration of what is known as the inquisitorial system—a trained judiciary, the ability of the defendant to cross-examine witnesses, the establishment of legal precedent—did little to resolve the problem. As in the story of Jesus liberating the adulterous woman from the sentence of death (Jn 8: 1–12), those summoned to corroborate the accusation were still reluctant to cast the first stone knowing full well their own sinfulness. The result, whether on the continent or in England, was the concerted effort by officials to compel people under threat of punishment to testify against their neighbors. Thus, as Whitman argues, the reason behind revered judicial innovations such as trial by jury was neither democratic reform nor improvement of legal procedure, but a way for rulers and magistrates to avoid the awesome burden of judgment and to pass the guilt to be incurred for such patent violations of Christian ethics upon someone else.[97]

There is much evidence to further the contention that neither law nor judgment provided any certain moral or spiritual assurance for the conscientious Christian. We have already noted the justification for judgment and the contention of theologians, particularly those embracing a social ethic grounded in the natural law, that the state in its structure as well as in its judgments was an expression of divine truth when its decrees coincided with natural law. Yet even these forceful defenses of social order and legal justice were accompanied by frequent injunctions to the practice of equity in legal matters and often to mercy and benevolence toward those found guilty under the law.[98] Aside from his belief, following Aristotle, that "particular justice," a focus on the unique circumstances in each case, is superior to strict "legal justice," St Thomas also provided a treatment of the evangelical law or the law of the Holy Spirit that he believed was far superior to the pragmatic deductions typical of the application of natural and human Law.[99] In fact, Aquinas insisted that all laws, including those of the church, are secondary, and could even lead to harm if the individual legal interpreter lacked an internal experience of

---

95 Whitman, *Origins*, p. 63.

96 Ibid., p. 56.

97 Ibid., p. 95.

98 John of Salisbury states that the prince "must ceaselessly mediate wisdom, that by its aid he may do justice, without the law of mercy being ever absent from his tongue." *Statesman's Book*, IV, 8.

99 On particular justice, see *ST*, II-II, Q. 58, a. 7. On the evangelical law, see *ST*, I-II, Q. 106.

the presence of God: "Wherefore the letter, even of the Gospel, would kill, unless there were the inward presence of the healing grace of faith."[100]

The Prison

In our treatment of the early church, it was noted that a truly evangelical and humane innovation took place when the first Christians saw in penance and monastic asceticism the true path to human perfection. Sinners were invited to embark on an inner penitential journey, prompted not by a need to suffer the vitriol of those whose expectations or demands they had failed, but by faith in a God whose power shines most clearly in human weakness (II Cor 12: 9), and by what Aquinas would call the "gnawings of conscience."[101] Flanked by communal elders committed to assist them, their internal battle to rediscover their own inner freedom and holiness was complemented by the graces of forgiveness and reconciliation. Despite episodes of cruelty and intolerance, the method of criminal correction was largely informed by the evangelical belief that Christ was somehow bound to those confined not only in monastic prisons but likewise in those administered by secular authority.

Recall that imprisonment was at this time an infrequent method of punitive expression. Fines and some form of blood vengeance were the invariable means by which the guilty were required to make amends.[102] As noted earlier, with the promulgation of the first legal codes and the identification of crime with treason, sanguinary and capital penalties grew in significance and extent. At the same time, the church normalized the prison as the means to express its penitential ethos and, in quick succession, virtually all secular polities began to expand their own use of incarceration, often incorporating the moral and theological concepts practiced in the monastic and ecclesiastical venues.[103] One begins to find in civil jurisdictions not only an expansion of pardons using "the vocabulary of penance," but also "a growing interest in inmate well-being and a proliferation of charitable bequests earmarked for aiding prisoners."[104] Inmates in Venice, for instance, were exempted from the fees the confined were normally charged for their entry, exit, and upkeep, and some form of legal aid was available throughout the late thirteenth and fourteenth centuries.[105] One study sums up the evidence concerning the medieval prison by insisting that the popular assumption of the "hell hole …

100 Ibid., I-II, Q. 106, a. 2.

101 Ibid., II-II, Q. 25, a. 7.

102 Dunbabin, *Captivity*, p. 23; George Ives, *A History of Penal Methods* (Montclair, NJ: Patterson Smith, 1970), p. 7; Ralph B. Pugh, *Imprisonment in Medieval England* (Cambridge: Cambridge University Press, 1970), p. 2.

103 Dean, *Crime*, p. 121; G. Geltner, *The Medieval Prison* (Princeton: Princeton University Press, 2008), p. 28.

104 Dean, *Crime*, pp. 134–35; Geltner, *Medieval Prison*, p. 15.

105 Ibid.

is simply untenable."[106] The author states that "incarceration … meant much more than neutral, sterile sequestering. Prison walls, rather than severing the inmate community from the outside world, actually helped structure prisoners' interaction with various members of the free society."[107] The constraints caused by poverty and social class also became a visible cause of public concern due to the efforts of confraternities committed to the care of the poor, notably prisoners, and a still-vibrant sense of God's favor for the rejected and the vulnerable.

We conclude this section aware then that a troubling paradox invaded and perplexed Christians in this period. They were often violent and at the same time often susceptible to an exaggerated benevolence, predicated on the tension between legal formality and human care. This was the climate in which the next great movement of medieval Christian thought arose. We now investigate accounts of law and judgment in the nominalist school and among Spanish thinkers of the Second Scholasticism. Their innovations provided not only some of the foundation for the Reformation and the Enlightenment but also for the positivist legal philosophy still in vogue in many contemporary jurisdictions.

Free Will, Human Rights, and the Inscrutable God

The natural law system sought to bind the human, the social, and the divine into a harmonious and organic union. It was, however, hierarchical. The church, as moral custodian of the legitimacy of human law and the channel of the special graces provided to believers by way of the divine law, was above the "earthly city" in the same way that the supernatural took preeminence over the natural.

This same two-tiered approach marked the difference between clergy and laity. The higher road of evangelical perfection was the path of priests and members of religious orders whose vows of poverty, chastity, and obedience bore witness to the highest aspirations of the Christian ethic, while the necessary, albeit lower, order of Christian witness belonged to those engaged in the mundane activities that comprise the lives of most men and women.

Despite these formal distinctions, the acute sense of sin and the uncommon anxiety over salvation that shadowed the otherwise raucous tenor of the age stimulated amongst many lay people a quest for perfectionism and, at the very least, a deep concern for personal sanctity.[108] This was a contributing factor in the doctrinal declaration of the concept of Purgatory.

Long a current running at the core of the Christian imagination, Purgatory reminded each person of the passage of time and the weight of personal decisions

---

106 Ibid., p. 101.

107 Ibid., p. 106.

108 Francis Oakley, *The Western Church in the Later Middle Ages* (Ithaca: Cornell University Press, 1979), pp. 232–33.

in an extraordinary way.[109] For Purgatory not only transformed the geography of the afterlife, now home to something very much akin to a divine prison, it also extended earthly time into the eternal dimension.[110] Moreover, with the introduction of All Soul's Day, the day of the dead, into the calendar of revered Christian feasts, the living and dead were further conjoined in a synchronic relation. One's sins on earth were weighed in temporal terms, and if not amended by earthly penance would be satisfied in penitential time served in the hereafter. Also, one's prayers for the departed could aid them in securing an earlier redemption from otherworldly confinement and hasten their day of eternal beatitude.[111]

The effects of this doctrinal development for our story are twofold, one psychological and one structural, although they tended to influence one another. The first effect of Purgatory was a profound sense of individuation. Medieval Christians experienced a much keener sense of personal time, of responsibility for its wise usage, and its continuation in a world of punitive remorse.[112] Structurally, as the moral imagination was engaged in a more intense drama over personal salvation, the medieval synthesis of redemptive virtue gained by faithful participation in a hierarchical ordering of natural institutions began to undergo substantial criticism.

We have noted already some of the objections to the natural law, but the legal framework that was in many ways its sustaining element and that was also the foundation of the "universal" church and the emerging state came under scrutiny on several fronts. Conciliarists such as Marsilius of Padua were adamant that the church could not stay loyal to Christ if engaged in the manufacture of law and the punishment for its disobedience; nominalists such as William of Ockham questioned the very legitimacy of moral universals and, to a significant degree, the political and ecclesiastical regimes that enforce them; and Neo-Scholastics, such as the Spanish Jesuit, Francisco Suarez, with his concept of purely penal law, removed the divine aura surrounding political legislation, insisting in most cases that it is based on will and power rather than reason and moral coherence. Variously, these new perspectives, among others, would elevate the substance and intensity of questions concerning natural rights, the locus of authority, and the moral legitimacy of both political and ecclesiastical judgment and would, in turn, stimulate both the Reformation and the Enlightenment.

---

109 Richard Fenn, *The Persistence of Purgatory* (Cambridge: Cambridge University Press, 1995), pp. 1–4.

110 Jacques LeGoff, *The Birth of Purgatory*, trans. Arthur Goldhammer (Chicago: University of Chicago Press, 1981), pp. 1–2; Skotnicki, "God's Prisoners," pp. 85–110.

111 Berman, *Law and Revolution*, p. 171; LeGoff, *Birth of Purgatory*, p. 128; L.M. Smith, *Cluny in the Eleventh and Twelfth Centuries* (London: Philip Allen, 1930), p. xvi.

112 Fenn, *Persistence*, p. 55.

Medieval Synthesis in Question

It may seem strange to begin this summary of the critique of orthodox Catholic legal theory with St Francis of Assisi but, perhaps more than anyone, this saintly man inspired a movement that confronted the papacy on the question of the nature of human rights and, in doing so, opened the way to theological and social perspectives on law and judgment that would influence Christianity as well as modern political theory. Francis was inspired to embrace his life of holy austerity and to found the Order of Friars Minor on hearing the passage from Matthew's gospel in which Christ counseled his disciples to carry neither sandals nor coin, neither clothing nor cane on their missionary sojourns (Mt 10: 9–10). In the words of St Bonaventure, Francis "immediately took off his shoes from his feet, put aside his staff, cast away his wallet and money as if accursed, was content with one tunic and exchanged his leather belt for a piece of rope."[113]

The brotherhood he inspired, dedicated to "holy poverty," was supported by Pope Innocent III, and its rule of life endorsed again by Honorius III. The Franciscan ethos was reconfirmed by Gregory IX, author of one of the texts of canon law, in his bull "Quo elongate" (1230), and in the bull "Exiit" by Nicholas III (1279).[114] In the latter documents, the popes assented to the order's evangelical witness as summarized by Bonaventure: "Because they possessed nothing that belonged to the world, they were attached to nothing and feared nothing. They were safe everywhere, not held back by fear, nor distracted by care."[115] The pontiffs also agreed with the claim that, similar to Christ and his disciples, the followers of Francis were meant to own nothing. Gregory stated that the brothers simply used goods with no proprietary claims over them, while Nicholas indicated that the mendicant lifestyle was defined by "simple use of fact" (*simplex usus facti*).[116]

It was these papal claims that were subsequently challenged by Pope John XXII in a series of documents issued in the 1320s, triggering an eruption of controversy. He argued, in opposition to Franciscan claims of a fully non-possessive poverty, of the incongruence of the Holy See owning "an egg, a piece of cheese, or a loaf of bread" while the Franciscans merely used them. He then stated that Jesus and his disciples *did* have earthly possessions and that it was fundamentally unjust to separate the right of use from ownership.[117]

The shift in papal policy might have remained a mere historical footnote had not one of the most brilliant thinkers of the age, the Franciscan William of Ockham, taken issue with the decree and in the process initiated a very loud

113 St Bonaventure, "The Life of St. Francis," in *Bonaventure*, trans. Ewert Cousins (Mahwah, NJ: Paulist, 1978), 3: 1–2.

114 Ibid., 4: 10; 6: 5. Tierney, *Natural Rights*, pp. 94–95.

115 Bonaventure, "St. Francis," 3: 7.

116 Tierney, *Natural Rights*, pp. 94–95.

117 Pope John XXII, "Cum inter nonnullos," in Denziger, *Sources*, pp. 193–94; Tierney, *Natural Rights*, p. 96.

exchange of ideas that surfaced both philosophical and theological tensions over the primacy of reason, the place of the will in the moral life, and the very authenticity of positive law as opposed to internal freedom and the rights of the individual associated with it.

That the public debate over the nature of human rights began in the wake of St Francis is, in retrospect, not hard to fathom. As one legal theorist claims, the Franciscans were a "cradle" of rights doctrines stemming from the radically personalist character of their founder's life in which the eternal was to be loved and embraced in each particular aspect of creation.[118] Francis sought and found God and an uncompromised dignity in those creatures ignored, exploited, and in varying degrees proscribed by common consent. He spoke to and loved animals, lived with and shared the misery of the abandoned, and not only embraced the lepers he encountered, he sought out the hidden places to which they were consigned and "washed their feet, bandaged their ulcers, drew the pus from their wounds and washed out the diseased matter; he even kissed their ulcerous wounds."[119]

Bonaventure had earlier argued against philosophical naturalism, legalism, and, by inference, Aquinas, positing instead a fully Christocentric doctrine based upon faith.[120] Ockham deepened the rift with his reappropriation of Augustine's emphasis on the will, positing that law, whether civil or ecclesiastical, cannot naturally express the divine will since God's designs are ineffable and can neither be grasped nor comprehended by human reason. The individual political subject may take the utterance of the sovereign or the pope to be true but "nothing more is asserted than that on the basis of the proposition's being uttered and the habit that persists in the listener's memory … that things are in reality as they are signified by the proposition."[121]

Ockham thus called into question not only the entire classical and scholastic philosophical traditions, extending from Plato and Aristotle through Aquinas, with their belief in universals and fixed essences that could be comprehended rationally; he also dismissed the entire hierarchical schema of a descending order

---

118 Michel Villey is quoted in Tierney, *Natural Rights*, p. 35.

119 Bonaventure, "St. Francis," 1: 5–6; 2: 6.

120 Bonaventure was directly addressing a pamphlet written by a cleric, and possibly a university administrator, who charged that the mendicants, especially the Franciscans, had misinterpreted Christ's teaching in the radical nature of their lifestyle: "This reasoning has no weight whatsoever; it proceeds from a thought deeply disordered. No one indeed would reason in this way without at the same time committing the distasteful lapse of associating … argumentative litigation with the condescension of divine sweetness that consisted in assuming our infirmities." See St Bonaventure, "Defense of the Mendicants," in *The Works of Bonaventure*, trans. Jose de Vinck (4 vols, Paterson, NJ: St. Anthony Guild, 1966), vol. 2, 9.

121 William of Ockham, *Quodlibetical Questions*, trans. Alfred J. Freddos and Francis E. Kelley (New Haven: Yale University Press, 1991), III, 13.

of legal power that characterized the reforms of Gregory VII.[122] He insisted, instead, that the love of God is the only purely and necessarily virtuous act and therefore "no [other] act is necessarily virtuous."[123] In fact, he contended that God's unfathomable will could just as easily have created a universe in which lying, stealing, and adultery were licit behaviors.[124]

For Ockham, human will mirrors the "unfettered" will of the Creator. In this schema, based on an unimpeachable inner freedom, law, rather than an expression of the divine mind, becomes an imposition, and compliance is determined not by "slavish obedience" but by the subject's own conscience.[125] For Christ, "who instituted the papal principate, deprived no man of his rights and liberties in completing the task which his Father had given him to perform."[126]

We cannot enter deeply into the subtleties of Ockham's thought, but he was by no means a pure antinomian. True, there was no descending order of power, but neither was there an ascending one. Those in positions of authority, especially when their authority has been granted them by common consent, cannot be deposed arbitrarily. God granted humans dominion over creation and, after the fall, the natural right to organize politically and establish rulers.[127] Law, while lacking legitimacy simply through promulgation, must be obeyed if its mandates accord with the divine commands contained in Scripture or, especially, if they are conformable to right reason. The latter is a prudent judgment based upon the nature of things as evidenced in human experience.[128] Here, then, is a novel theory of human autonomy in which a right is a power inherent to humans that is based in reason but also grounded in those New Testament texts announcing that, for the Christian, the only law is the law of liberty.[129]

---

122 "But just as Christ did not give Saint Peter such a plenitude of power in temporals, so neither did he grant him such a plenitude of power in spirituals. For … the evangelical law is a law of lesser servitude than that of Moses." William of Ockham, *On the Power of Emperors and Popes*, trans. Annabel S. Brett (Bristol, UK: Thoemms, 1998), ch. 4. "But no divine revelation establishes that God assigned any particular temporalities to the empire or supreme lay power as its property, nor that he gave specific orders to that effect. In sum, there is no ground in revelation for thinking that the empire has its property from God alone." William of Ockham, "Eight Questions on Papal Power," in O'Donovan, *From Irenaeus to Grotius*, ch. 6.

123 Ockham, *Quodlibetical Questions*, III, 14.

124 Tierney, *Natural Rights*, p. 98.

125 Ockham, *Quodlibetical Questions*, I, 1; Marilyn McCord Adams, "The Structure of Ockham's Moral Theory," *Franciscan Studies* 46 (1986), p. 16; Mahoney, *Moral Theology*, pp. 228–29.

126 Ockham, *Emperors and Popes*, ch. 4.

127 McGrade, *Ockham*, pp. 105–06.

128 David W. Clark, "Voluntarism and Rationalism in the Ethics of Ockham," *Franciscan Studies* 31 (1971), p. 76; Tierney, *Natural Rights*, p. 130.

129 Brian Tierney, "Natural Law and Natural Rights," in Witte and Alexander, *Christianity and Law*, p. 97.

Ockham was not alone in upholding rights as internal safeguards that determine the veracity of law and its judgments. Leading thinkers of the day such as Jean Gerson and John Wycliffe held similar views.[130] Nor was he without allies in his rejection of ecclesiastical power, especially under the guise of law. Marsilius of Padua also dismissed the legitimacy of papal claims to temporal sovereignty, although for different reasons. He was a fervent Aristotelian and an early and very influential advocate of government by common consent. He argued that the gospel exercises a gentle dominion of healing and instruction that is inimical both to the exercise of power and to the provenance of any law save the divine: "Christ, in his purposes or intentions, words, and deeds, wished to exclude and did exclude himself and the apostles from every office of rulership, contentious jurisdiction, government, or coercive judgment in this world."[131]

Although their theological and philosophical systems are different, Ockham and Marsilius, as well as Wycliffe, understood law primarily as the maintenance of order grounded in power.[132] They preserve on one hand the capacity of the church to remove itself from legal and administrative concerns but, on the other, help foster an attitude among Christians that moral questions related to civic affairs and criminal justice lie outside the domain of Christian ethics.[133]

Suarez and the Second Scholasticism

Francisco Suarez, writing two centuries after Ockham, became familiar with the lines of thought discussed above as a student of philosophy and canon law at Salamanca. The curriculum there was dominated by a movement begun by Francisco de Vitoria that came to be known as the Second Scholasticism and that changed the foundation of post-medieval theological discourse. Prior to this, the principal text of study—one in which, for instance, both Aquinas and Ockham

130 Right is "a proximate faculty or power which belongs to some subject as prescribed by primary justice. This prescription is called *law*, since law is a rule in conformity with what right reason prescribes." Jean Gerson, "On Church Power and the Origin of Law and Right," in O'Donovan, *From Irenaeus to Grotius*, 13. John Wycliffe posits a "natural lordship" in which "every righteous man is lord of the whole sense-perceptible world." See "Civil Lordship," in O'Donovan, *From Irenaeus to Grotius*, I, 7.

131 Marsilius of Padua, *The Defender of Peace (Defensor Pacis)*, trans. Alan Gewirth (New York: Columbia University Press, 1956), II, iv, 4.

132 Wycliffe states: "What, then, is civil and human law in its aspect as a form of justice? It is the law which contains the appropriate orders to secure temporal resources for the welfare of the state, to restrain willful attempt to overthrow it, and to administer them farsightedly in times of scarcity." See "Civil Lordship," I, 18.

133 Marsilius states that "we ought to be subject to Caesar in all things, so long as they are not contrary to piety." See *Peace*, II, iv, 9. Ockham writes: "For law and the ruler seem to be most principally instituted for the same things. The law, however, is not instituted because of the good, but for correcting and punishing the bad." Quoted in McGrade, *Ockham*, p. 115. Wycliffe writes: "Civil lordship is occasioned by sins … It is not capable of being shared or communicated." See "Civil Lordship," I, 18.

would have been tutored—was the *Sentences* of Peter Lombard. As Michael Buckley notes, this work provided medieval theology with a common language that allowed differences in interpretation to be made intelligible. Vitoria, however, began the custom of making the *Summa Theologica* of St Thomas the fundamental work upon which theological inquiry was to be based.[134] Suarez identified himself as a faithful Thomist but was also influenced by the thought of his predecessors, among them Ockham. It was his goal to reconcile these different perspectives. Whether or not he did so is a matter of opinion, but his ideas have had an impact on legal thought and Christian ethics that endure to our own day.

In his influential treatise on law, Suarez, as befitting his debt to Aquinas, began with the natural law: "[T]he Catholic faith teaches not only how far we must obey God when he commands in the supernatural order; it teaches also what nature forbids, commands, or permits."[135] As he proceeds, however, one notices a markedly different approach to the understanding of natural law. Whereas St Thomas stressed that the doctrine and the human directives patterned upon it proceed directly from the mind of God, Suarez viewed it as an application of theology wherein the "goodness and rectitude" of human laws are judged by "principles of faith" and "the obligations of conscience."[136] He goes on to state that "only that which is a right and virtuous rule can be called a law."[137]

This "negative" rendition of natural law is due in large part to the influence of some of the thought we have just discussed on the nature of rights as subjective powers that determine the legitimacy of the statutes enacted by secular authority. Recall that for Ockham, Gerson, and others, including Vitoria, there was a distinction between written law (*lex*) and *ius*—the power that binds in conformity

---

134 Michael Buckley, S.J., *At the Origins of Modern Atheism* (New Haven: Yale University Press, 1987), p. 43.

135 Francisco Suarez, S.J., "On Laws and God the Lawgiver," in *Selections From Three Works of Francisco Suarez, S.J.*, trans. Gwladys L. Williams, Ammi Brown, and John Waldron (Oxford: Clarendon, 1944), Preface.

136 Aquinas, *ST*, I-II, Q. 90; Suarez, "Laws," Preface.

137 Suarez, "Laws," I, I, 6. Aquinas did frequently stress that statutes not coherent with natural law were not law but rather its deformity. These abuses of law, and especially disobedience to them, were still to be judged against primary commitments to the community. If resistance to bad law leads to more disharmony than that caused by the law itself, then subjects ought to obey. See *ST*, II-II, Q. 42, 2; "Commentary on the Sentences," II, 44, 2. St Thomas also upheld the principle of *epikeia* whereby in questions of the binding power of a law in an ambiguous situation, the questioner is permitted to interpret the mind of the legislator. By placing the measure of legal effectiveness within each person's conscience as opposed to the common good, however, Suarez establishes an inherent and ongoing tension between law and those whose behavior it seeks to control: "[I]t behooves us to distinguish between the interpretation of a law and true *epikeia*, or equity. For 'interpretation of law' is a term much broader that *epikeia*; inasmuch as the relationship between the two is that of a superior to an inferior." "Laws," II, XVI, 4.

to right reason.[138] Suarez followed this logic, noting that natural law (*ius naturale*) is less linked to the inherent validity of statutory law as with the internal power, i.e. right, to determine the binding nature of legal enactments: *Ius* is "a certain moral power which every man has, either over his own property or with respect to that which is due to him. For it is thus that the owner of a thing is said to have a right (*ius*) to that thing." He goes on to affirm that this right (*ius*) "appears to be the true object of justice."[139]

Suarez not only adopted the notion of rights as internal powers from his theological predecessors, he also took interest in, if not complete agreement with, the priority of will in determining the limits of ethical obligation.[140] While he was too much in debt to Aquinas to adopt Ockham's posture of the unfettered freedom of the divine will and, to a large extent, the human will, he revolutionized legal theory by inserting will into the psychological process whereby legal statutes are promulgated.[141] The result was his theory of purely penal law.

The crux of his idea is that a person who determines that a law is not binding in conscience may be punished "without guilt but not without cause."[142] Suarez, again steering a middle ground between natural law and voluntarism, argues that civil authority is a divinely sanctioned necessity: "the authority of all laws must ultimately be ascribed to [God]."[143] He also stands in the shadow of Aquinas in noting that the goal of all law is the common good: "[L]aw, in so far as it is externally imposed upon the subjects, is a species of means for securing their welfare and peace or happiness."[144] But he then attests that the will of the lawmaker is an inescapable and mitigating factor in the legislative process: "it is certain, to begin with, that both the intellect and the will intervene in the making of law."[145] And,

---

138 Tierney, *Natural Rights*, p. 68.

139 Suarez, "Laws," I, II, 5.

140 In his location of freedom not in the political process but in the will, Suarez references the thought of a number of theologians, among them Bonaventure, Duns Scotus, and Ockham. Ibid., I, V, 8.

141 Sir William Blackstone argued that purely penal law, a forerunner of legal positivism, entered legal history with Suarez. See *Commentaries on the Laws of England (1765–1769)* (4 vols, Oxford: Clarendon Press), vol. 1, pp. 57–58.

142 The phrase "*sine culpa sed non sine causa*" can be found in Catholic thought as early as Gregory the Great. See David Cowan Bayne, *Conscience, Obligation, and the Law* (Chicago: Loyola University Press, 1966), pp. 45–46.

143 Suarez, "Laws," Preface. He later states: "For [public promulgation] is essential, since if he did not do so, the will of the prince could not be binding upon his subject, inasmuch as it would not be made known … It is clear, moreover, that this [act of promulgation] suffices, since the will of the prince is itself efficacious. For that will is derived from a sufficient authority and is, so we assume, accompanied by an absolute and binding decree; consequently, if the said will is adequately revealed to the subject, it effects that which is willed; hence, it establishes an obligation." "Laws," I, IV, 12.

144 Ibid., I, IV, 6.

145 Ibid.

again, "the precepts of positive law, whether divine or human, are characterized not by an intrinsic necessity, existing in themselves, but by a necessity resulting from an extrinsic will."[146] Whatever the intent of the lawmaker in creating a statute, the resulting provision is binding upon all subjects and penalties are attached for its violation.[147] Speaking of the law of nations (*ius gentium*) and its relation to natural law, Suarez notes in an illustrative phrase: "From the standpoint of human reason, then, the *ius gentium* is not so much indicative of what is [inherently] evil, as it is constitutive of evil. Thus it does not forbid evil acts on the grounds that they are evil, but renders [certain] acts evil by prohibiting them."[148] It is in this way that Suarez both defends the integrity of civil law, its relation to a natural order intended by God for human social organization, and, at the same time, the "right" of each person to determine whether or not the law is in accord with right reason and should be obeyed. The violation, according to Suarez, is just as legitimate as the punishment to which the negligent person must submit morally. We thus have the rudiments of purely penal law, or how the lawbreaker is punished "without guilt but not without cause."

Suarez thus fosters a mentality in which personal piety and self-determination exist on a different moral plane than the affairs of men and women in the world. Ironically, this demystification of law, rather than weakening its grip in the face of those intent on orchestrating its diminished spiritual authority, provided the context for the conviction, seen in the contemporary prominence of legal positivism, that law should not be evaluated in moral terms at all but only in its effectiveness as an instrument of power.

Summary

The authors mentioned in this section are to be commended for clouding the theological and moral aura that the natural law imparted to legal systems. It can be said that they aided the church of their day, and perhaps ours today, in the insistence that Christianity is not, or at least should not be, a religion based upon the rule of law.

They also, perhaps more than any other coterie of thinkers, established the theological and philosophical presuppositions necessary for both the Reformation and the Enlightenment. They did this by centering questions of faith and morality within the knowing and willing subject, emphasizing the right of human beings to determine by use of their own conscience the proper relation to be assumed with regard to directives of the state and, perhaps of greater note for the Reformation, those of the church.

It may not have been their intention, but central figures such as Ockham, Wycliffe, and Suarez (however much their theories and methods differ) helped

146 Ibid., III, Introduction.

147 Ibid., I, IV, 7–8.

148 Ibid., II, XIX, 2.

pave the way for what authors such as Taylor and Gauchet, echoing Weber, have called the desacralization of the world. This was encouraged not as a result of the critique of natural law, but in leaving matters of faith and morality in large part to the unfettered will of the individual; and, without my own endorsement of the rationalism and barren Christology of the natural law, these authors contributed to a political philosophy in which social control for the purpose of order replaced intervention in the life of the "criminal" for the purpose of sanctification. In so doing, a worldview in which God was removed more and more from intimate contact with creation was given substantial reinforcement.[149]

The conversation initiated by the thinkers we have discussed is philosophically profound but lacks the single element that matters most to the existence of the church and to the believing Christian: the centrality of Christ and the message of the gospel.[150] Law is not an end in itself, nor is it simply the exercise of power and control. For the Christian, law, like all other elements of human life, must be measured by the call to bear the cross of Christ, to suffer without judging or seeking revenge, to transform violence through a loving forbearance, and to intervene in the lives of the self and socially destructive for their sake, not our own. Ockham laudably notes an ontological dignity that graces human life and that often relegates law to the morally redundant or the superficial, but he was so embroiled in political controversy and his running battle with the papacy that he spent little time invoking either the humility and egalitarianism of the Franciscan charism, or that of its founder, both of which he dearly cherished.[151]

There is thus something of the "right thing for the wrong reason" in some of the systematic critiques of church and secular law that we have been discussing. It is not the frequent antinomian tenor of the argument or its rejection of ecclesiastical power that gives the respectful observer pause, but the improper theological assumptions at its base: either that God is absent from personal contact with the world or, in the case of Marsilius, that the social ends of civil peace

149 Taylor, for instance, draws a direct line between Ockham's endorsement of an instrumental reason that rejects all final causes and the Reformation, then to Francis Bacon and the scientific revolution, and finally to a disenchanted world and an absent God. See *Secular*, pp. 97–98. David Clark states: "the determiner of moral obligation [for Ockham] is the prudent judgment of Right Reason … therefore, the obligation to obey the will of God is a secondary obligation since prudence or Right Reason must first judge that everything pleasing to God is to be done." See Clark, "Voluntarism," p. 76.

150 Buckley, *Atheism*, p. 33.

151 On the organic unity that precedes the state, see McGrade, *Ockham*, p. 118. Ockham penned his work in defense of the Franciscans at the behest of his Franciscan superior, Michael of Cesena, and notes he wishes "to render an account before a judge of all those things which I have done, written or said, since I undertook the rule of St. Francis." *Emperors and Popes*, Prologue.

require Christians to submit wholeheartedly to the virtually infallible authority of the assembled multitude.[152]

The irony in the effort of the church to honor its own declaration of autonomy by removing itself from the secular sphere, and that of theologians to limit the authority of the state by locating true power within the individual, was to invite what Gauchet calls a "pseudo-sacralization" of law and the power of the very state they each troubled themselves to destabilize: "[W]ith the state, divine otherness is transported into the 'social sphere' and the nonhuman has been incorporated into the structure of human ties."[153] Taylor notes that the "new" natural law, one in which rights and the power of reason determine ethical conduct as much as the traditional theological sources, was far more about humans than about God.[154] The insights of these authors are hard to deny as one detects the simultaneous advance of repressive law with the noticeable retreat of gospel directives in theological literature addressing the political and legislative realms.

As God became more and more "different" as a result of the developments we have been discussing, as the cult of the saints who redeemed prisoners began to lose their charm, as the confraternities bound to minister to the "poor of Christ" began to disappear, as references to the ethics of the cross and the unconditional mandate to love and forgive gave way to the expansion of legal infractions and punishable crimes, and as persons came to see themselves as autonomous bearers of rights, a new ethic of manners, polite behavior, and "civilized" conduct came to dominate Christians in the educated classes. Elias describes the birth of attitudes of disgust and embarrassment over the coarse manners of the poor.[155] Huizinga states that etiquette and civility in the late Middle Ages took on "almost religious significance."[156] Taylor describes at length the ethos of the day where by 1400 it was a common belief that the cultured elites must embrace the duty to "civilize" the ignorant masses—more and more perceived as threats to moneyed interests—who had to be disciplined so as to be fit for military duty and taxable income. Briefly put, the prevailing judgment of the upper classes was *they* are "savages" but "we have the law."[157]

---

[152] "Objections will be made to our above statements, to the effect that the authority to make or establish laws does not belong to the whole body of citizens. The first objection is that those who for the most part are vicious and undiscerning should not make the law. For these two sins, malice and ignorance, must be excluded from the legislator … As for the first objection … this is granted. But when it is added that the whole body of citizens is such, it must be denied. For most of the citizens … are of sound mind and reason, and have a right desire for the polity and for the things necessary for it to endure, like laws and other statutes or customs." Marsilius, *Peace*, I, XIII, 1, 3.

[153] Gauchet, *Disenchantment*, pp. 35–36.

[154] Taylor, *Secular*, p. 164.

[155] Elias, *Civilizing Process*, p. 280; Taylor, *Secular*, pp. 138, 141.

[156] Huizinga, *Waning*, pp. 41–49.

[157] Taylor, *Secular*, pp. 99–103.

Law, Judgment, and the Reformation

The second great legal revolution, after that initiated by the papacy in the eleventh century, came as a result of the Protestant Reformation. Luther's attempt to free Christianity from the control of the Roman Catholic Church decisively fractured, among other things, the medieval synthesis of earth and heaven bound by legal ties. The foundation of that union had already been severely weakened by internal strife, witnessed in events such as the Great Schism, and by some of the theological challenges discussed in the previous section.[158]

Unlike the Catholic Church, however, Luther had to contend with more than theological challenges. He was forced to be equally aware of the pragmatic realities of political order and security. Whatever else may have motivated the rulers and magistrates who embraced the ideals of the Reformation, their survival in the face of violent civil unrest and threats from Roman Catholic jurisdictions was paramount. Theology and politics did not have the luxury of an extended courtship prior to their hurried union. Yet unite they did; and the changes to the legal tradition emanating from this association indelibly colored the canvas of law's meaning, content, and justification.

The Reformation ushered in substantial and lasting changes to the understanding of Christian faith, but also reproduced in many ways some of the characteristics that have been noted concerning the legal revolution in both Catholic philosophy and institutional organization. The elements reviving the spirit of the gospel can be seen in its often proper understanding that law in itself is not an evangelical good, and therefore that the moral allegiance it demands is suspect. Luther continued the assault begun by nominalist and conciliarist thinkers upon the concept of ecclesiastical jurisdiction, proclaiming that the church is not an institution based upon law. Rather, he reclaimed Augustine's spiritual sense of the church as a community bound together by the Holy Spirit and famously proclaimed that all are now priests.[159] On the other hand, one often finds among reformist theologians an exaggerated dualism in which a fully individualist account of faith coexists with a political agnosticism; the latter leading either to silence or complicity in the face of repressive tactics and violent punishments levied by the secular power. As Berman notes, Protestantism spiritualized the law at the same time that it secularized it.[160] God was freed from the hierarchical structure of Catholicism and, at the same

---

158 Between 1378 and 1410 a dispute over papal succession led eventually to three different pontiffs (in Rome, Avignon, and Pisa) claiming rightful succession to the Chair of Saint Peter.

159 "Therefore everyone who knows that he is a Christian should be fully assured that all of us alike are priests, and we all have the same authority in regard to the word and the sacraments, although no one has the right to administer them without the consent of the members of the church." Martin Luther, "Pagan Servitude of the Church," in Dillenberger, *Martin Luther: Selections from His Writings*, 6.

160 Berman, *Law and Revolution II*, p. x.

time, a nearly unquestioned sovereignty was bestowed upon the ruler and the ruler's laws—one form of magisterial hierarchy, in effect, replacing the other.

Another significant development occurred in the economic arena. In their critique of Catholic theology, the ethos of monasticism, and the obligation of charity to the poor, Luther, and especially Calvin, inverted what Weber called the "other worldly asceticism" of Catholicism, in which salvation was assured by faithful immersion in the sacramental system, and preached an inner-worldly asceticism, in which Christians were "called" by God to engage in productive activity in the economic realm as a sign of their election to grace and salvation.[161] The dark side of the equation was that the salvation seemingly bestowed upon the economically solvent and the sober-minded was invariably withheld from the economically destitute and those convicted of crime.[162]

In short, we see in the Reformation a Christian movement that often reconnected the function of law and ethics to their evangelical roots but which, at the same time, reinforced the advancing disenchantment of a world that could do no less than create in God's absence an infinite vacuum that law, power, and punishment would soon fill.

Law and Secular Authority in Luther

The hand of Augustine reached deeply into the heart of Reformation theology; both Luther and Calvin developed his thought more than any other Christian theologian, although one also sees clear signs of the influence of St Thomas Aquinas. Luther was a priest in the Augustinian order at the time of his conflict with Rome. In conceptualizing his own social ethic, he looked to Augustine's *City of God* and its structure of two parallel but alien social entities: the earthly and the heavenly cities, held together by the mutual desire for relational tranquility. He was also influenced by the "natural" communities spoken of by Aquinas. These concepts helped provide the basis for Luther's political theology, which conceived of distinct "orders of creation."[163]

---

161 "Waste of time is thus the first and in principle the deadliest of sins … Thus inactive contemplation is also valueless, or even directly reprehensible if it is at the expense of one's daily work. For it is less pleasing to God than the active performance of His will in a calling." Max Weber, *The Protestant Ethic and the Spirit of Capitalism*, trans. Talcott Parsons (New York: Charles Scribner's Sons, 1958), pp. 157–58. Luther states that monasticism "deserves to be called a worldly, harmful, and damnable station and life." See Martin Luther, "Explanation of the Psalms," in *Luther's Works*, vol. 13, trans. Daniel E. Poellot (St. Louis: Concordia, 1956), Psalm 111: 3.

162 See Snyder, *Spirit of Punishment*, pp. 11–15; Kai Erikson, *Wayward Puritans* (New York: Wiley, 1966).

163 "These divine stations and orders have been established by God that in the world there may be a stable, orderly, and peaceful life and that justice may be preserved … For if God had not Himself instituted these stations and did not daily preserve them as His work,

Luther's exegesis of the opening chapters of Genesis affirms the imprint of the divine placed upon creation in its infancy: "Even if the wise of this world did not perceive the creation of the world, they could have recognized the invisible things of God from the works of the created world, namely, by taking as Word and Scripture those works that testify to God."[164] As with St Thomas, he perceived a fundamental set of autonomous yet interdependent orders, each preserving the specificity and harmony of creation: the church, the family, and after the death of Abel, civil government.[165]

As noted above, Luther was as much a realist as a visionary. Unlike St Thomas, whose descending order of authority culminated in a divinely inspired set of human laws, Luther contended that God established the rulers of the earth and the laws they enact not to participate in the work of salvation by instilling virtue through just decrees but to restrain the violent and predatory. Civil authorities in their quest for order provide the two functions of law: to remind subjects of their sinful inclinations and actions and to repress and punish those who do not heed legislative decrees: "Since, however, no one is by nature Christian or pious, but every one sinful and evil, God places the restraints of law upon them all, so that they not dare give rein to their desires and commit outward, wicked deeds. In addition, St. Paul gives another function … It is to teach men to recognize sin, that they may be made humble unto grace and unto faith in Christ."[166]

The repressive nature of the state tends to attract political officials whose moral attributes are equal to the sordidness of their mission: "a wise prince is a rare bird indeed; still more so a pious prince. They are usually the greatest fools or the worst knaves on earth."[167] He recalls a quote from Augustine concerning a captured pirate who is condemned by the emperor for robbery upon the seas—a domain too small for the larcenous grasp of the emperor: "They are hanging the thieves and executing the robbers, and thus the big thieves act as judges of the little thieves."[168]

no particle of right would last even a moment." See Luther, "Explanation of the Psalms," Psalm 111: 3.

164 Martin Luther, "Lectures on Romans," in *Luther's Works*, vol. 25, trans. Walter G. Tillmanns (St. Louis: Concordia, 1956), Scholia 1: 20.

165 "Here [with the command concerning the tree of knowledge] we have the establishment of the church before there was any government of the home and of the state … After the church has been established, the household government is also set up. Moreover there was no government of the state before sin." Martin Luther, "Lectures on Genesis," in *Luther's Works*, vol. 1, trans. George V. Schick (St. Louis: Concordia, 1956), 2: 16. "This penal law existed from the beginning of the world. For when Cain slew his brother he was in such great terror of being in turn killed that God specially forbade it and suspended the sword for his sake … He would not have had this fear if he had not seen and heard from Adam that murderers should be slain." Martin Luther, "Secular Authority," in *Martin Luther: Selections from His Writings*, I, 1.

166 Luther, "Secular Authority," I, 3.

167 Ibid., II.

168 Luther, "Lectures on Romans," Scholia 2: 1.

In the Lutheran schema, truth and law are for the most part set at odds since the state is not a part of the eternal order but strictly a result of human sin: "Civil government is a remedy required by our corrupted nature. It is necessary for lust to be kept in check by the bonds of laws and penalties. For this reason you may correctly call civil government the rule of sin."[169] He referred to the analogy of the sheep and wolves to reinforce the foolishness of attempting to govern "wild and savage beasts" with the order established by the gospel. Such a ruler "would be like a shepherd who should place in one fold wolves, lions, eagles, and sheep together and let them freely mingle with one another." In such an arrangement the sheep "would not live long; nor would any beast keep from molesting another."[170]

In contrast to the political realm, Luther believed that the church is a spiritual body of believers built up and sustained by the word of God and by the sacrament of the Lord's Supper. His evangelical faith soundly rejected any need for law or judgment in a community nourished by faith, grace, and Scripture: "if all the world were composed of real Christians, that is, true believers, no prince, king, lord, sword, or law would be needed."[171] In like fashion, he recalled the words of Christ who forbad his followers from standing in judgment of others: "this [prohibition of judgment] must also be understood as applying to those who secretly in their hearts are judging others. Yes, they also judge them with their mouth when they denounce them, and yet they are in every respect exactly like those whom they judge."[172] Nor can Christians go to court to defend their rights or seek damages against an opponent. The committed disciple is to bear the loss of all in imitation of Christ, for he or she belongs to a kingdom "where the only regulation should be the prayer, 'Forgive us our debts as we forgive our debtors.' Here only mutual love and service should prevail, even toward those who do not love us."[173]

Despite the immunity of Christians from the restraint of law and their charge to resist casting judgment, the strict separation of the orders of creation compelled these same Christians both to support and to serve the punitive function of government in any manner in which they were capable, not out of a desire to harm, but out of a love for those being harmed by the malicious conduct of others.[174] Luther states: "Because the sword is a very great benefit and necessary to the whole world, to preserve peace, to punish and to prevent evil, [the Christian]

---

169 Luther, "Lectures on Genesis," 2: 16.

170 Luther, "Secular Authority," I, 4.

171 Ibid., I, 3.

172 Luther, "Lectures on Romans," Scholia 2: 1.

173 Luther, "Lectures on the Sermon on the Mount," in *Luther's Works*, vol. 21, trans. Jaroslav Pelikan (St. Louis: Concordia, 1956), 5: 38–40.

174 "There is not prohibition against punishment aimed at correction … But only he is competent to inflict his sort of punishment who by the greatness of his love has overcome the hatred with which those are wont to be inflamed who desire to be avenged." St Augustine, *The Lord's Sermon on the Mount*, trans. John J. Jepson (Westminster, MD: Newman, 1948), I, 20, 63.

submits most willingly to the rule of the sword, pays tax, honors those in authority, serves, helps, and does all he can to further the government."[175] The Christian "serves the State not because he needs it, but because others need it ... If he did not do it, he would be acting not as a Christian but contrary even to love."[176] Therefore, Luther maintains for the same set of reasons that "should you see that there is a lack of hangmen, beadles, judges, lords, or princes, and find that you are qualified, you should offer your services ... that necessary government may by no means be despised and become insufficient or perish."[177]

While the theology of Luther's orders of creation preserves the centrality of the message of Christ to forgo judgment, to live "outside the law," and to seek only to love and forgive the offender, it continues the strand of medieval pessimism and adds an unprecedented portrayal of fallen human nature.[178] This traces to the theological belief that, unlike the more optimistic theology of natural law, and even that of the nominalists, in which "right reason" is capable of knowing the truth and, with the aid of virtue, capable of acting upon it, human reason has been fully corrupted by sin. Without the intervention of God's grace in the life of the person of faith, Luther argues in a rebuke of Erasmus that free will "is not free at all, but is the permanent prisoner and bondslave of evil, since it cannot turn itself to good."[179]

Luther's theory of law was restated and refined by a series of influential jurists. Philip Melanchthon (1497–1560), Johann Oldendorp (ca. 1480–1567), and Johann von Schwarzenberg (1463–1528) systematized Luther's legal writing and added important modifications that would distinctively color the Western legal tradition. Melanchthon summoned several of Luther's quotes in which a third use of the law was implied, a pedagogical function in which Christians are given guidance as to the conduct appropriate for them in the civil arena "that the saints may know and have a testimony of the works which please God."[180] He then turned to Luther's own insistence that the natural law was effective in pointing out proper conduct but futile in facilitating such behavior. Melanchthon used the distinction in St Thomas between the natural law (given to all humans) and divine law (given to Christians) to shift the content of the former in a way similar to that of Suarez and the Spanish neo-Thomists. Like them, he saw in the natural law a moral pattern

---

175 Luther, "Secular Authority," I, 5.

176 Ibid.

177 Ibid., I, 6.

178 Delumeau writes that despite some eloquent testimonies to the union of spirit and flesh in Luther and Calvin, it was "in the sixteenth century, and specifically in Protestant theology, that the accusation of man and the world reached its climax in Western civilization. Never had they been so totally condemned, and never had this condemnation reached such a large audience." See *Sin and Fear*, p. 27.

179 Luther, "Bondage of the Will," in *Martin Luther: Selections from His Writings*, ix.

180 Philip Melanchthon, "Loci Communes," in O'Donovan, *From Irenaeus to Grotius*, ch. 7. See also Berman, *Law and Revolution II*, p. 76.

linked to the second table of the Decalogue, those commandments directed to ethical conduct with others. He then insisted that the state utilize the Decalogue as the basis of positive law and, with his deployment of the third legislative function, he and those theorists who followed him provided some assurance that by faithful adherence to law the final end of social life can bring salvation and not damnation to the conscientious citizen.[181]

In similar fashion, Oldendorp reconfigured the traditional Roman Catholic distinction between eternal, natural, and human law to construct a legal system consisting of a biblically based set of divine ordinances, an internal cognizance of those mandates, and their incarnation in positive law. More importantly, he expanded Melanchthon's justification for a third use of law with the contention that every application of law involves the need for equity—a concentration on the particular facts of a case as opposed to a formulaic judgment based solely upon the law.[182] Implied within his theory is a softening of the strict Lutheran anthropology of human depravity devoid of grace with the rudiments of a moral sense theory. As Berman phrases it, this legal philosophy affirms that each person has "certain moral sentiments relating to legal justice, including a respect for civil authority, for human life, for property, for family responsibilities, for fair procedures, and, in general, for the rights of oneself and others."[183]

This tripartite legal taxonomy provided the basis for an influential code of criminal law, the "Carolina," penned by Johann von Schwarzenberg and enacted in 1532. This collection emphasized the centrality of equity in legal judgment and provided the basis of many Western judicial systems with its three purposes of criminal law and punishment: the preventive or deterrent function, the punitive or retributive function, and the rehabilitative or restorative function.[184]

It is noteworthy that the emendation of Lutheran legal theory, particularly with the third function of the law developed by the jurists just discussed, modified the interpretation of the law suggested by Luther at the same time that it echoed the attempt by Roman Catholic canonists to utilize law as a source of training in the virtues and place it on a near equal footing with Christian revelation. The result, in both instances, was a retreat from the simplicity and freedom of the gospel, and at least a tacit alliance between church and state in the joint task of social control. Many of these ideas with important variations are also found in the work of John Calvin.

---

[181] Ibid., pp. 79–83. John Witte writes concerning these reformers and the three uses of the moral law: "It coerces sinners so that they can be preserved. It condemns them so that they can be justified. It counsels them so they can be sanctified." See *God's Joust, God's Justice: Law and Religion in the Western Tradition* (Grand Rapids: Eerdmans, 2006), pp. 266–67. On Schwarzenberg's influential legal codes, see Berman, *Law and Revolution II*, pp. 137–46.

[182] Ibid., p. 91.

[183] Ibid., p. 98.

[184] Witte, *God's Joust*, p. 263.

Law and Judgment in Calvin

As with many of the reformers, Calvin derived much of his theology from the writings of Sts Paul and Augustine, but he also echoes the thought of Marsilius of Padua and, despite the polemics common to virtually all writers of the time, the ideas of St Thomas Aquinas. His understanding of law and judgment would continue the dualist notions found in Luther's orders of creation but he would also, like Marsilius, lay the groundwork for democratic and constitutional systems of governance.[185]

Similar to Luther and to the internal/external forum distinction in Catholic legal theory, Calvin carefully distinguished between the interior government of the spirit and the external political regime. In the domain of faith and piety, the gospel takes precedence and Calvin is as antinomian as Paul at his most contentious or as radical as some of the Franciscan philosophers in his reflections on this inner sovereignty: "[Law] leaves no man righteous … there must then be no consideration of the law, but Christ alone must be proposed for righteousness, who exceeds all the perfection of the law."[186] Christians must, in fidelity to Christ, attend to the teaching in Galatians concerning the futility of the law: "Paul hesitates not to assert that [Christ's] death is rendered vain if we suffer our souls to be in subjection to men."[187]

Appended to this fervent encomium to the freedom of the Christian is Calvin's sense that the liberated person of faith is now subject only to divine guidance: "being liberated from the yoke of the law, they yield a voluntary obedience to the will of God."[188] The path is then cleared to return to a respect, even reverence, for the law since it *is* the will of God that the evil not prey upon the good, that human creativity and work receive their just recompense, and that law function as the instrument to punish those who defy the divinely endorsed political order.

These dual and independent jurisdictions of piety and politics "will prevent what the gospel inculcates concerning spiritual liberty from being misapplied to political regulations, as though Christians were less subject to the external government of human laws because their consciences have been set at liberty before God, as though their freedom of spirit necessarily exempted them from all

---

185 Recall that Marsilius, in his attempt to restrict the mission of the church to the preaching of the gospel, located the source of political authority within the people, a source which was largely infallible and determinative save if contrary to piety: "Let us say … that the legislator is the people or the whole body of citizens." "So, then, we ought to be subject to Caesar in all things, so long as they are not contrary to piety, that is, divine worship or commandment." *Peace*, I, 12, 3; II, 4, 9. Calvin will restate both of these principles. See John Calvin, "On Civil Government," in *Calvin: On God and Political Duty*, ed. John T. McNeill (Indianapolis: Bobbs-Merrill, 1950), VIII, XXXIII.

186 John Calvin, "On Christian Liberty," in *On God and Political Duty*, II.

187 Ibid., XIV.

188 Ibid., IV.

carnal servitude."[189] One obeys God in conscience and "inward integrity of heart" by resisting temptations to "obscenity" and "lasciviousness," but government is "preposterous" if it does not honor these claims of piety through legislation banning such actions.[190]

Lodged within this approach is a belief in natural human depravity that so marked the anthropology of the reformers generally, and Calvin particularly, for whom the human person "cannot, without sacrilege, claim for himself even a crumb of righteousness, for just so much is plucked from the glory of God's righteousness."[191] This lack of innate goodness makes each a tyrant and fully unsuited, without force, to accede to the demands of communal association: "I say that the nature of man is such that every man would be a lord and master over his neighbors and no man by his good will would be a subject."[192] With a hint of the Thomist approach, Calvin locates the content of God's moral designs for humanity in a natural instinct or "sentiment of conscience" that, as with the Lutheran scholars, coheres with the commandments in the Decalogue addressing human social behavior. However, like Luther, he also despairs that humans with their own moral resources can ever adapt their actions to these truths: "[Men and women] perversely search out God's handiwork in their own pollution, when they ought rather to have sought it in that unimpaired and uncorrupted nature of Adam. Our destruction, therefore, comes from the guilt of our flesh, not from God, inasmuch as we have perished solely because we have degenerated from our original condition."[193]

Given this fatal moral flaw, several political and legal remedies are necessarily required, fully in harmony with Christian liberty. The first is that Christians recognize political rule as "the most sacred and honorable [calling] in human life" and, as with Luther, honor the passage in Romans that declares the divine benediction on all forms of government so that "it is impossible to resist the magistrate without at the same time resisting God himself."[194]

The authority of the magistrate is not simply a curb on perverse behavior, it parallels the uses of the law proposed by the Lutheran jurists, particularly the

---

189 Ibid., XV.

190 Ibid., XIV; "Civil Government," IX.

191 Quoted in Taylor, *Secular*, p. 78.

192 Quoted in Michael Walzer, *The Revolution of the Saints* (Cambridge, MA: Harvard University Press, 1965), p. 31.

193 John Calvin, *Calvin's Institutes*, ed. Hugh T. Kerr (Louisville: Westminster/John Knox, 1989), II, 1, 10.

194 "Civil Government," IV, XXIII; "Commentaries on the Epistle to the Romans," in *Calvin: On God and Political Duty*, XIII, 1. As with Luther, and later with Hobbes, there are limits on obedience to the magistrate who, though "a living law," will also be judged on the political decisions rendered, and whose authority does not extend to the curtailment of the Christian in following the essential demands of faith. See "Civil Government," XIV, XXXII.

third, that repeated obedience to statutes produces a state wherein "every person may enjoy his property without molestation; that men may transact their business together without fraud or injustice; that integrity and modesty may be cultivated among them; in short, that there may be a public form of religion among Christians and that humanity may be constituted among men."[195]

Secondly, the state, to use Michael Walzer's words, must constitute an "order of repression."[196] Calvin reminds his readers that a political regime that "did not inflict the most exemplary vengeance upon murderers, would soon be ruined by murders and robberies."[197] Like St Thomas and Luther, the execution of murderers is understood to reflect the moral law: "all laws agree in punishing murder with death."[198] In line with a consistent tenet of Christian legal theory since the time of Augustine, Calvin sees no sin in the judge ordering the execution of the malefactor because the magistrate is not personally willing the punishment but enforcing the verdict revealed by God: "To hurt and to destroy are incompatible with the character of the godly; but to avenge the afflictions of the righteous at the command of God is neither to hurt nor to destroy."[199]

Thirdly, since the state is not a natural institution, as in Catholic legal theory and in Luther's orders of creation, and since humans lack the internal moral power to live in accord with God's decrees, it is the duty of the saints to establish the political conditions for the curbing of asocial behavior and the instillation of virtuous habits. The formation of a Christian commonwealth is the duty of those destined for salvation and a necessity for human social existence.[200]

The impact of Calvin's thought for the future of politics cannot be underestimated. Like Marsilius before him, he laid the foundations for constitutional democratic polities. For although the state was principally an order of repression, the structure of the political order was to be imposed not by brute force but by a force justified and created by the consent of the elect. It was the duty of the Christian to do more "than merely to seek and secure the salvation of his own soul." Rather, the "prime motive of his existence" was to be characterized by "zeal to show forth the glory of God."[201]

Calvin and those who were inspired by his theology also lent credence to the interiority of religious convictions, the disenchantment of the world, and, with their avowal of democracy as the best form of political organization, the ascent of human rights as independent powers relative not only to the state but also to the church.

---

195 Ibid., III.

196 Walzer, *Revolution*, p. 30.

197 Calvin, "Civil Government," XVI.

198 Ibid.

199 Ibid., X.

200 "I approve only those human constitutions which are founded upon God's authority, drawn from Scripture, and, therefore, wholly divine." Calvin, *Institutes*, IV, 10, 30. Walzer, *Revolution*, p. 28.

201 Quoted in Walzer, *Revolution*, p. 54.

Of equal importance to the theology of disenchantment was its social psychology, another area investigated by Weber. As suggested earlier, the assurance of salvation previously provided to Christians by living according to the law of the church, especially through the absolution of sin in the sacrament of penance, had to be attained in the new asceticism solely by worldly conduct: "The religious virtuoso can be placed in the world as the instrument of a God and cut off from all magical means of salvation. At the same time, it is imperative for the virtuoso that he 'prove' himself before God, as being called *solely* through the ethical quality of his conduct in this world."[202] The sense of a fallen world is thus conjoined to a world in which "methodical and rationalized routine activities of workaday life in the service of the Lord" take on an eschatological urgency.[203]

Secularization, as we noted, was given its initial impetus in the attempt by the Catholic Church to protect its own internal affairs from outside influence. In equating its law with an eternal power, independent of the teaching of Christ, Catholic leaders set a pattern to be replicated in subsequent secular legal codes. The influence of the disenchantment brought on by the Protestant reformers such as Calvin accelerated the process of liberating an entire sphere of social life, that of law and judgment, from the influence of the gospel. The need to prove oneself as chosen by God was expressed in the need to find a material analogue in terms of economic success and political obedience.[204] As Richard Fenn notes, in this serious world of work and political involvement "monastery bells became transformed into bells of the city and the workplace, and they were slowly replaced ... by clocks that spelled out the hours of work, leisure, of civic meetings and social obligations."[205]

The Other Reformations and the Law

We have discovered throughout our story the principal factors leading away from what John Howard Yoder, an heir to the Anabaptist tradition, terms the "confessing church," wherein all things, including law, judgment, and punishment are measured against the teachings of Christ. In the new moral economy, the church became increasingly content to leave important elements of both the social and internal realm to either the claims of established authority or those of the autonomous individual.[206] The Anabaptist movement and the English Reformation

---

202 Max Weber, "The Social Psychology of the World's Religions," in H.H. Gerth and C. Wright Mills, *From Max Weber* (New York: Oxford, 1946), pp. 290–91.

203 Ibid., p. 291.

204 Weber, "The Protestant Sects and the Spirit of Capitalism," in Gerth and Mills, *From Max Weber*, pp. 302–22; Walzer, *Revolution*, pp. 28–29.

205 Fenn, *Persistence*, p. 185.

206 John Howard Yoder, "A People in the World: Theological Interpretation," in *The Concept of the Believer's Church*, ed. Leo Garret, Jr. (Scottdale, PA: Herald Press, 1969), pp. 252–83.

had important parts to play in that story, but since most of the themes previously discussed are reintroduced, albeit in different forms, in each of these expressions of Christianity, I will only briefly outline their significance.

The sectarian impulse in the lives of Anabaptist leaders such as Conrad Grebel and Menno Simon was inspired in part by their correct appraisal of the shortcomings of the approach to law held by many of their Christian contemporaries. They soundly criticized the ways in which practical issues of governance for Catholics and the other Reformation movements had led to an uncoupling of the life of the church and its theology from intimate contact with the directives of the gospel.

The Schleitheim Confession, a seminal document of Anabaptist theology, presents the reader with a vivid reminder of the central commitments of early Christians to avoid civil courts, civil administration, enlistment in the military, the use of violence, and the taking of oaths.[207] Of special note, judgment of others is clearly proscribed: "it will be asked ... whether a Christian shall pass sentence in worldly disputes and strife such as unbelievers have with one another. This is our united answer. Christ did not wish to decide or pass judgment between brother and brother in the case of the inheritance, but refused to do so. Therefore we should do likewise."[208] This courageous and principled devotion earned them the hatred of many Catholics and other Protestants, and they paid dearly for their witness. One study reports that certain evidence exists for the execution of 715 Anabaptists in 123 towns in Central Europe from 1525 to 1618; reliable evidence reveals an additional 130 in 27 other locales; and there is the strong possibility that the records testifying to the execution of hundreds more have been lost.[209]

What concerns us here, however, is that the sectarian impulse tends to foster a polarity between the sacred and profane and, especially, between the elect and the damned. Augustine had a similar mentality but, as we saw, he constantly wavered in his dismissive and scornful appraisal of the "world" due not only to practical needs of security but also due to a larger vision of the unity of all things in Christ. Among the early Anabaptists, however, internal purity was often maintained with a dualism different in emphasis from the Christian churches against whom they set themselves, but nonetheless present. This stance was grounded in what sociologists suggest are the three traits of schismatic groups: antagonism, difference, and separation.[210] Evidence of these characteristics is often found in the early documents to which the following attests: "A separation shall be made from the evil and from the wickedness which the devil planted in the world; in this manner, simply that we shall not have fellowship with them (the wicked) ... For

---

207 *The Schleitheim Confession*, ed. and trans. John Howard Yoder (Scottdale PA: Herald Press, 1977).

208 Ibid., VI.

209 Claus-Peter Clasen, *Anabaptism: A Social History, 1525–1618* (Ithaca and London: Cornell University Press, 1972), pp. 370–71.

210 Rodney Stark and William Sims Bainbridge, *The Future of Religion* (Berkeley: University of California Press, 1985), pp. 21–26.

truly all creatures are in but two classes, good and bad, believing and unbelieving, darkness and light, the world and those who have come out of the world, God's temple and idols, Christ and Belial, none can have part with the other."[211]

Concerning this separatist ethos, many commentators have noted that the Anabaptists were driven into isolation; they did not choose their social marginality.[212] In sympathy with this view, Berman suggests that the movement can be considered a Protestant form of monasticism, and some of the writings, as will be seen in the next section, attest to a mystical union with God and creation. In contrast, however, their theology was often tainted by the polemics common to the age that revealed more of a *contemptus mundi* than a benign separation. Anabaptist leaders, for example, variously termed Catholic, Lutheran, and Zwinglian pastors as "false prophets and Pharisees; seducers and blasphemers; hypocrites; frauds; liars; false vipers; cursed rogues; belly preachers; barking and chasing dogs; godless, filthy perfidious villains; husbandmen of lies, foul bastards; poisonous snakes; monstrous dragons; [and] angels of Satan."[213] In such a framework, the world generally, and other Christians particularly, were to be left to their own devices; and their own wicked end is the inevitable result. One thus detects evidence of the spiritual elitism so often pointed to by Luther and Calvin in regard to the Catholic monastic orders.

The change in post-Reformation England from a monarchy unlimited in its claim of sovereignty over its subjects to one limited by a written constitution and representative government has had lasting impact on both Christianity and world politics. In this evolution, the theory of the divine right of kings was slowly replaced by a theory of natural rights. In the former, the need for the king to rival papal claims of supremacy was of the foremost importance.[214] Since the fourth century, the papacy had repeatedly sought to exert its primacy over civil rulers, never more so than after the eleventh century. Under the title of Vicar of Christ, obedience to the Pope was considered an obligation far more binding upon Christians than to a simple command from a sovereign. In divine right theory, therefore, the monarch had to be shown to be entitled to receive the same unquestioned obedience, lest the Pope find the ability to reestablish claims over a vacillating populace.[215] Robert Filmer, who devotes much of *De Patriarchia* to refuting the legal theories of

---

211 *The Schleitheim Confession*, IV.

212 Stanley Hauerwas, "Why Truthfulness Requires Forgiveness," in *Dispatches from the Front* (Durham, NC: Duke University Press, 1994), pp. 80–88.

213 Clasen, *Anabaptism*, p. 77.

214 "It was in the gradual rise of Papal claims to universal supremacy that are first put forth those notions which form the basis of all theories of Divine Right." John Neville Figgis, *The Divine Right of Kings* (New York: Harper, 1965), p. 45.

215 Ibid., p. 95.

Suarez, states that "the main and indeed the only point of Popery is the alienating and withdrawing of subjects from their obedience to their Prince."[216]

Much of the intellectual support for the movement to abolish the absolute power of the monarch and base English jurisprudence upon democratic consent was provided by Richard Hooker (1554–1600). He was steeped in Aristotelian and Thomist ideas concerning the natural law, the social nature of humans, and the role of political organization in the formation of virtue. He then used this structure to argue that the power of the king must proceed, not from divine right, but from the consent of the governed and the "law of the commonweal."[217] In this he sought to protect the church from the whims of the crown at a time when the Anglican Church was facing attacks from Presbyterian and Puritan critics as well as from Roman Catholics. However, as a child of the Reformation, he tempered his reverence for classical legal theory with the dictum that faith alone, not works, leads to salvation. The political upshot being that human nature, despite being immersed in law in an ontological sense, must be constrained by law due to human corruption.[218]

Hooker was also a leading figure in the movement to adapt natural law to what was termed the law of nature, the latter comprising moral concepts based not in theology but in human experience and known solely through the power of human reason to distinguish proper and improper forms of conduct. J.N. Figgis writes that he stands in a line of thought that "proclaims a system of politics, clear, universal, and unalterable, based not on the uncritical study of Scripture, but on what are believed to be the teachings of nature and the dictates of pure reason."[219]

Another influential Protestant figure who exemplified a similar intellectual credo, and who, like Hooker, would influence the thought of John Locke, was Hugo Grotius (1583–1645). He too reinterpreted classic natural law in terms of faith in human rationality and sociability. From this conviction, Grotius constructed a platform for rights as normative truths necessary for human society and confirmed by reason: "Since over other animals man has the advantage of possessing not only a strong bent towards social life … but also a power of discrimination which enables him to decide which things are agreeable or harmful … it is meet for the nature of man, within the limitations of human intelligence, to follow the direction of a well-tempered judgment, being neither led astray by fear or the allurement of immediate pleasure." He concludes that "whatever is clearly at variance with

---

216 Quoted in Figgis, *Divine Right*, p. 184. Suarez particularly infuriated advocates of Divine Right. His work was publicly burned at Paul's Cross in November 1613. James I said of him and his fellow Jesuit theologian, Robert Bellarmine, that in "setting up the People above their naturall King," they laid "an excellent ground in Divinitie for all rebels and rebellious people." J.P. Somerville, "From Suarez to Filmer: A Reappraisal," *Historical Journal* 25 (1982), p. 525.

217 Richard Hooker, *The Laws of Ecclesiastical Polity* (London: J.M. Dent, 1954), I, 10.

218 Ibid.

219 Figgis, *Divine Right*, p. 161.

such judgments is understood to be contrary also to the law of nature, that is, to the nature of man."[220]

The conclusion to be drawn from these remarks is that each expression of the Reformation confronted the same dilemmas as the medieval Catholic Church: how to maintain internal order, peaceful relations with the state, and some degree of coherence in its proclamation of Christ as the centerpiece of human history and the norm for human conduct. Attempts by the leaders of the various reform communities to secure their independence from external interference were surely motivated by a reverence for the evangelical call to holiness of life and fidelity to the ways of God, but these very attempts took with one hand what they gave with the other. The "divinely ordained state," to use the words of one commentator, was not only granted moral as well as political sovereignty, the laws of the state and its exertion of power could not help but shape the way Christians understood not only themselves and their civic obligations but also the teachings of Christ.

Mystical Union and the Christian Vocation

Let us begin this section with a brief comment upon Christian thought before the Enlightenment as it has thus far been presented: many Christians adhered to the belief that God's harmonious mind pervades the universe and establishes universal moral propositions upon which human laws ought to be based; other Christians expressed serious doubt as to the theological and moral efficacy of legislated decrees and, in the case of the Reformation, ecclesiastical ones. The problem for the preeminence of the gospel as the measure of a fully human life lies in the fact that the first approach confers too much moral rectitude upon law and the second too much moral authority upon the autonomous individual. Neither reflects the primacy of the relational. Neither fully honors the one law of love whose first movement is an unconditional regard for the other, an unconditional forgiveness, and a belief that penance and not punishment ends human alienation.

It is in the mystical tradition that both the unity and necessity of these truths is revealed. One philosopher, Bergson, based his thesis on morality and religion—and in many ways his entire intellectual project—upon the distinction between a restricted moral horizon and one that is limitless in scope.[221] Human sociability

---

220 Hugo Grotius, *The Law of War and Peace*, trans. Francis W. Kelsey (Indianapolis: Bobbs-Merrill, 1925), Prolegomena, 9.

221 If one focuses on the central Bergsonian concept of the *élan vital*, one finds that Bergson linked this vital force or impetus that flows through, animates, and sustains all living things to the intense immersion of mystics in the internal presence of God that liberates them from the confinement of all narrow ideologies and fills them with a divine love for all creation: "its direction is exactly that of the vital impetus; it *is* this vital impetus itself, communicated in its entirety to exceptional men who in their turn would fain impart it to all humanity." Bergson, *Two Sources*, p. 235.

always begins as a confined sociability. One learns a particular language, particular customs, and, for our purposes, a particular religion, that, unless transformed, is both narrow and exclusionary: "In a word, the social instinct which we have detected at the basis of social obligation always has in view—instinct being relatively unchangeable—a closed society, however large."[222] For Bergson, the difference between parochial, law-abiding citizens (whether to the church or the state) and those for whom no law constrains the vision of the indivisible communion of all is "one of kind and not simply one of degree."[223] The latter are those who by attending silently to the mystery within and around them have "burst the dam" that encloses and limits moral and religious commitments. They have transcended "the law which demands that the species and the individual should condition one another."[224]

The point of this short digression is that Bergson states that the most "complete" expression of this experience of being swept into the "vast current of life" is found among the Christian mystics.[225]

There are many ways to define contemplation but, as mentioned earlier, there is none more preferable than a loving and undivided attentiveness to the present moment. The God of the eternal present dwells through the act of faith in every breath, every situation, and in every element of creation. The simplicity and challenge of contemplation is no more than a personal and willful appropriation of Christ's fundamental condition for discipleship: "deny your very self, pick up your cross, and follow in my footsteps. For whoever wishes to save his life must lose it and whoever loses his life for my sake and the sake of the gospel will find it" (Mk 8: 34–35).

Early Christian mystics were therefore intent on the simple need to avoid distraction while at the same time responding lovingly to whatever and whomever they encountered. Pseudo-Dionysius, a mystic who exercised a deep influence on subsequent spiritual writers and theologians, among them Albert the Great and Thomas Aquinas, stressed this need for contemplatives to embrace the grace of each moment without venturing upward "toward an impossibly daring sight of God, one beyond what is truly granted them. Nor … tumbling downward where their own natural inclinations would take them." Rather, they are to trust the "transcendent beam" that enlightens them beyond their own vision; they are to "concentrate sightlessly and through an unknowing union on the rays

222 Ibid., p. 32.

223 Ibid.

224 Ibid., p. 230.

225 He refers to St Teresa of Avila, St Catherine of Siena, St Francis, and, by a reference to the dark night of the soul, St John of the Cross: ibid., pp. 228, 231. Paul Ricoeur similarly argues that religion is confined in fear and the hunger for consolation until it learns to wait in silence for the soundless speech of God that heals and binds the believer to the word that is Christ. See "Religion."

of 'unapproachable light'"; and they are to respond to the generous gift of the moment with "a love matching the illuminations granted them."[226]

The combination of an undivided presence to life and a loving acceptance of the present and its unfathomable spiritual richness lies at the heart of the understanding of Christian ethics in many of the contemplatives in the medieval and later periods. Francisco de Osuna, the spiritual director of Teresa of Avila, stresses that "whatever your actions, your mind must accompany them and not wander in different directions, the body being in one place and the heart in another."[227] He compares the person with "wandering thoughts" to Satan in the Book of Job who flits about from place to place. Osuna then contends that distraction "is the beginning of all evils" caused by leaving the "imagination and heart free to wander at large throughout the world."[228]

The author of *The Cloud of Unknowing* counsels that Christians imagine and then embrace a life lived between two clouds: the cloud of unknowing and the cloud of forgetting. With regard to the first, the spiritual pilgrim, aware that human reason is incapable of ascending to or comprehending the grandeur of God, forgoes speculative or evaluative thought and learns "to be at home in this darkness": "A man may know completely and ponder thoroughly every created thing and its works, yes, and God's works, too, but not God himself. Thought cannot comprehend God."[229] What the Christian must do, the author insists, is to call forth constantly all of the love within and send it up through the incomprehensible cloud. This act of willful tenderness provides all of the true knowledge one can attain in this life: "By love [God] may be touched and embraced, never by thought."[230] Secondly, the one seeking God must put everything beneath the cloud of forgetting. All "clever and subtle thought no matter how holy or valuable" is to be dismissed.[231] This includes, of course, all judgments. If one seeks to love, fixing one's presence on God with "naked desire" and a "longing stripped of all self-interest," there is no room left to reflect upon what the other has done, let alone impute or harbor negative intentions, so full is the heart with love for all that one sees.[232]

This same Christian forgetfulness is central to the thought of John of the Cross. Once again, we find a person seeking God in love, in darkness, and intent on restricting rational deliberation in favor of an instinctual longing for union. John urges his readers to center their lives on the desire to "abide in … quietude with a

---

226 Pseudo-Dionysius, "The Divine Names," in *The Complete Works*, trans. Colm Luibheid (New York and Mahwah: Paulist, 1987), 1, 2; 4, 11.

227 Francisco de Osuna, *The Third Spiritual Alphabet*, trans. by a Benedictine of Stanbrook, NY (New York: Benziger, 1931), I, 2.

228 Ibid., I, 2; IX, 2.

229 *The Cloud of Unknowing*, ed. William Johnston (New York: Image Books, 1973), chs 3, 6.

230 Ibid., ch. 6.

231 Ibid., ch. 8.

232 Ibid., ch. 34.

loving attentiveness to God."[233] He employs the metaphor of the "secret ladder" to suggest that each person is trapped in the narrow confines of fears, petty judgments, and violence until he or she breaks free of the "prison" of intellect, memory, and the acquisitive will and travels down the ladder of silent contemplation "[w]ith no other guide than the one that burn[s] in [the] heart."[234] To focus on memory is to dredge up the feelings, whether positive or negative, associated with past events that necessarily distract one from the present moment wherein the mystery of God is always being revealed. Therefore, one must not store in the memory "the objects of hearing, sight, smell, taste, or touch but leave them immediately and forget them."[235] Far better, St John states, "to learn to silence the faculties so that God may speak."[236]

Christians who live and love their way into thinking, rather than the opposite, are constrained from negative appraisals of the intentions or conduct of others. Many of the Protestant mystics also reveal this insight. Like the example left by Christ in the Scriptures (Mt 18: 15–18), Menno Simons refused to judge the internal state of those who outwardly violated the ways of God. Christians are to "observe each other unto salvation" in all "becoming ways" such as teaching, warning, and consoling but in no way greater than in "unfeigned love until we increase in God and become united in faith."[237] Like the early Christian examples of communal discipline, Simons was careful to distinguish between an excommunication warranted for the purpose of encouraging inner renewal and one motivated by anger and denigration of the offender: "For we do not want to expel any, but rather to receive; not to amputate, but rather to heal; not to grieve, but rather to give comfort, not to condemn, but rather to save."[238] George Fox, frequently imprisoned for this faith, was often led by God to challenge judges directly who "oppress servants in their wages" or put people to death "for cattle and for money and small things."[239] He writes to his followers: "Above all things take heed of judging one another for in that ye may destroy one another, and leave one another behind … and eat out the good of another."[240]

Out of this stance of self-forgetfulness and unrestricted compassion comes joy and union, not judgment or memory of sin. Julian of Norwich states it was

---

233 St John of the Cross, "The Ascent of Mount Carmel," in *The Collected Works of St. John of the Cross*, eds Kieran Kavanaugh, OCD and Otilio Rodriguez, OCD (Washington, DC: ICS Publications, 1979), II, 12, 8.

234 Ibid., Stanza 3.

235 Ibid., III, 2, 14.

236 Ibid., III, 3, 4.

237 Menno Simons, "Admonition on Church Discipline," in *The Complete Writings of Menno Simons*, trans. Leonard Verduin (Scottdale, PA: Herald Press, 1956), p. 411.

238 Ibid., p. 413.

239 George Fox, "The Journal," in *Quaker Spirituality*, ed. Douglas V. Steere (New York: Paulist, 1984), pp. 67, 74.

240 Fox, "The Epistles," in *Quaker Spirituality*, p. 132.

revealed to her "in an instant" that even our moral failures and tragedies are made well in the loving gaze of God: "But I did not see sin, for I believe that it has no kind of substance, no share in being, nor can it be recognized except by the pain in causes. And it seems that this pain is something for a time, for it purges us and makes us know ourselves and ask for mercy; for the Passion of our Lord … comforts readily and sweetly with his words, and says: But all will be well, and every kind of thing will be well."[241] This revelation is the same as that given in the Gospel of John when Jesus comes to those who betrayed him, hidden in fear and shame, and embraces them and liberates them with a breath of peace and forgiveness (Jn 20: 22–23).

Summary

Throughout our survey of this momentous period, we have witnessed various and sometimes contradictory teachings among Christians. On one hand, law and justice began to derive their legitimacy primarily from sources extraneous to the gospel, such as the needs for order and security. The Roman social ideal of an "immutably organized" and stratified world was kindled anew.[242] A hierarchical society, patterned upon a hierarchical church, in turn patterned upon a hierarchical supernatural order, was a persistent theme in the literature of the day, nowhere more noticeably that in the work of John of Salisbury. His famous metaphor of the "body politic" aptly expresses one of the principal convictions of the era: "The prince is the head; the senate the heart; judges and governors the eyes, ears and tongue; officials and soldiers provide the hands; and those who serve the prince are the torso.[243] St Thomas was another noted exponent of this political theology: "[F]aith in Christ does not void the order of justice but strengthens it. Now the order of justice requires that subjects obey their superiors, else the stability of human affairs would cease. Hence faith in Christ does not excuse the faithful from the obligation of conforming to the policies of secular princes."[244]

Additionally, the consolidation of papal authority by means of law transformed not only the internal structure of the church but also provided the ideological and legal template for the emerging states of Europe. Canonists and theologians created a sharp distinction between the concepts of sin and crime, institutionalizing the public litigation of "criminal" offenses under the new inquisitorial judicial method. Law was released from its explicit connection to human relationships and became an independent moral entity with its own integrity. Crime was conceived not only as an offense against others, but also a transgression of law. In this new

---

[241] Julian of Norwich, *Showings*, Short Text, trans. Edmund Colledge, O.S.A. and James Walsh, S.J. (New York: Paulist, 1978), ch. XIII.

[242] LeBras, "Canon Law," p. 343.

[243] John of Salisbury, *Statesman's Book*, V, 2.

[244] Aquinas, *ST*, II-II, Q. 104, a. 6.

"legal culture," as Edward Peters suggests, those clergy with an eye to a position in the papal court were increasingly trained not in theology but in law, and "the content of papal decisions became more and more professionally juridical."[245]

Yet, on the other hand, as LeBras notes, just as its neo-Platonic theology accepted inequalities in wealth, influence, and opportunity in "submission to the chances of birth," there were still vibrant evangelical strains of a firm commitment to both the protection of the oppressed and the solidarity of the faithful, regardless of social status.[246] People balked at cooperating in judicial proceedings that would bring suffering or death upon their peers; and they openly celebrated the liminal moments that at God's bidding freed the condemned and exposed the pretensions of the powerful and the fatal limitations of human justice.

In retrospect, it was inevitable that the architectonic cosmic and social vision of Gregory VII and many medieval theologians would topple due to internal ecclesiastical tensions and contradictions, not to mention the Renaissance and the birth of humanism. Nominalists like Ockham, neo-Scholastics, among them Vitoria and Suarez, new political thinkers such as Marsilius of Padua and Wycliffe, and Protestant reformers, all refashioned the terrain on which discussions of law and judgment were conducted. A multi-faceted reaction to the dualist and legalist mentality of the institutional church yielded bold ideas concerning the nature of law, its binding force, and the integrity of conscience and personal autonomy.

Each of these developments weakened the organic framework of natural law and began the process of allowing the individual to determine the legitimacy of either ecclesiastical or political statutes. For Ockham and Suarez, fidelity to the church and to Christ was in no way mitigated by a principled reaction to the ontological authority imputed to law, whether positive or natural. They were joined in their opposition by other influential thinkers who were intent on ending papal designs upon temporal power and elevating instead a freestanding source of political authority in the people themselves.

Luther, Calvin and many of their theological confreres helped retrain the eyes of Christians to see law not as the manifestation of divine order but simply as a restraint on evildoers and a reminder that all share a common sinful orientation. The pedagogical function of law was also given due place but, in the end, the repressive and punitive function of law and the stake of Christians in maintaining it was rarely, if ever, questioned.

All of these varying influences intensified the internal drama over salvation and its relation to law and society. The freedom of the Christian from external sources of control was won at a high price. The classical medieval pattern of a place for every person and every person in his or her place gave way to the personal quest for salvation and to an all-powerful state that assumed, in many respects, the immediacy and influence once accorded to the imminent God. As Gauchet notes, at the end of Middle Ages the citizen and the believer were increasingly alone

245 Edward Peters, *Inquisition* (New York: The Free Press, 1988), p. 53.

246 LeBras, "Canon Law," p. 353.

and isolated, and it was Christian religion, more than any other cause, that bore responsibility for this alienation.[247] Taylor states that once faith began to be defined by this inward dynamic, the Middle Ages effectively came to an end.[248]

Classical medieval Catholicism maintained that the goal of every person is union with God. It made the assumption that law grounded in reason was necessary for the fulfillment of the quest for this union. For their part, reformers, beginning with the early Franciscans and including Jesuit neo-Scholastics and many of the Protestant divines, took a more Augustinian approach that law is grounded in the vagaries of the human will. Perhaps each would have benefited from another idea of Augustine, namely that desire is the force behind the will. The question for Christians is, in other words, not whether law and judgment are grounded in will or reason, but what should Christians desire. Certainly human rights are worth desiring, but should followers of Jesus seek rights without primary attention to the cross? Brian Tierney notes that as Christians began to desire more and more inner freedom from political and ecclesiastical control, the tension between the objective sense of right and the internal sense of power increased in scope and import. In such an atmosphere, the way was prepared for Hobbes and the Enlightenment to argue that the subjective interpretation was the only correct ethical choice.[249]

---

247 Gauchet, *Disenchantment*, p. 66.

248 Taylor, *Secular*, p. 227.

249 Ibid., pp. 50–51.

Chapter 5

Twilight of the Gods: Rights, Reason, and Disenchantment

Our task in this chapter is to investigate the movements that led to a structural and spiritual dualism in which law and punitive judgment, deriving their force and legitimacy from the interests of the state and the individual, were placed in an ethical category separate from the demands of the gospel. This definitive rupture in what has been termed the "sacred canopy" can be traced to the Enlightenment.[1] Much in Christian history preceded and prepared the ground for the belief that the external autonomy of civil society and its laws, and the internal autonomy of the individual and his or her conscience, can function without a conscious responsibility to the church and a necessary accountability to the message of Christ. Yet, despite the very human tendency of each generation of Christians to seek political and material security rather than the narrow way of evangelical perfection, the latter continued to haunt and inform even the most pragmatic answers to what Troeltsch termed "the social problem."[2]

In the Enlightenment, however, the very language of faith was transformed to dismiss to a large degree the relevance of the non-judgmental and non-violent teachings of Jesus in deference to practical, pragmatic concerns of the state and the lives of its citizens. Not only philosophical but also theological movements began to posit the centrality of power within the state, reason within the individual and associations of individuals, and a rationally grounded ethic over the radical demands of the gospel.

We will begin with an overview of speculative thought on law, judgment, and Christian ethics among several principal Enlightenment thinkers, then discuss the dismissal of a specifically Christian ethic in favor of the philosophy of Deism and the concept of civil religion. We will conclude with specific references to the way in which law and judgment impacted the practice of criminal justice.

---

1 Peter Berger, *The Sacred Canopy* (New York: Anchor Books, 1967). It is noteworthy that the secularization thesis still in vogue in the Sociology of Religion continues to trace itself to changes occurring in the late twentieth century, rather than the legal and philosophical developments in the Middle Ages and the Enlightenment.

2 Troeltsch, *Social Teaching*, vol. 1, pp. 30–34.

Humanism, Rationalism, and the Limits of Equality

All of its demerits in jettisoning law from a necessary accountability to the teachings of Jesus notwithstanding, the medieval synthesis of God, the human person, and civil society by means of law had the virtue of keeping a transcendent vision of justice as a corrective that, at the very least, allowed for eruptions of "communitas" into a legal structure that had been created for the purpose of eliciting obedience and insuring order. The thought of Victor Turner is suggested in this light. He argued that only in "liminal" periods of "anti-structure" that exist when the laws and the powers they serve no longer are capable of enforcing a strict disciplinary regimen, can the celebration of vibrant community take place—a community whose very vibrancy is predicated on the absence of judgment and the essential place it holds in the "hierarchical system of politico-legal-economic positions."[3] This "liminality" was clearly evident in those times already mentioned when each year convicted prisoners were released by communal consent and political decree in order to point to a divine mercy that mocks all feeble and inevitably violent human attempts to do justice.[4]

In his own study of legal transformation during this period, Manlio Bellomo reveals how, in Thomist fashion, medieval legal codes featured innumerable local ordinances (*ius proprium*) that drew upon the principles of the natural law (*ius commune*) to provide their moral legitimacy, yet each was seen to contain and divulge "only a tenuous glimmer of the Justice that was absolute, divine, hence eternal."[5] In the humanist philosophy of the period, however, legal scholars critical of both Roman and canon law argued that the relationship between the two approaches should be severed and a fully local common law given complete autonomy and authority.[6]

Harold Berman notes that humanist thinkers mounted a concerted attack on traditional legal sources at the philological, synthetic, and systematic levels.[7] The hallmark of this new approach was an application of a widely held belief

---

3 Victor Turner, *The Ritual Process* (Ithaca: Cornell University Press, 1969), pp. 94–97, 106–08.

4 "Judges deal pain and death. That is not all that they do. Perhaps that is not what they usually do. But they *do* deal death, and pain. From John Winthrop through Warren Burger they have sat atop a pyramid of violence." See Robert Cover, "Violence and the Word," *Yale Law Journal* 95 (1986), p. 1609.

5 Bellomo, *Common Legal Past*, p. xiii.

6 Ibid., pp. 204–05.

7 The philological critique centered on the meaning of terms utilized by Justinian, particularly in the *Digest*. The synthetic critique focused on omitting vast amounts of the *Digest* and organizing positive law according to general principles found in Justinian's *Institutes*. The systematic critique led to a new organization of legal principles drawn from a wide variety of sources whose meaning derived from reason and conscience. See Berman, *Law and Revolution II*, pp. 102–09.

of Protestant theology that salvation is an individual rather than communal quest. Law, like redemption, was understood as an internal process. It was not that God was fully absent from the writing, understanding, and enforcing of law, but "hidden" from the eyes of the unenlightened. Just as God's plan for social harmony in a Calvinist rendering was hidden in the souls of the elect whose duty it was to enact its principles, so the true interpretation and application of law was "implanted in the reason and conscience of the faithful jurist."[8]

One result of this new legal epistemology was an unprecedented emphasis placed upon reason as the source and monitor of truth in place of revelation, particularly the truth proclaimed in the gospel. It was due in large part to a widespread "disenchantment" with the churches themselves. The wars of religion did nothing to advance the trust once accorded to scriptural truth and, more to the point, those who proclaimed it. As Michael Oakeshott attests, if the political philosophers took "a sombre view of the human situation," dealing largely with a perceived "darkness" shrouding humans and their common affairs, religion and religious conflict were a principal cause of the problem.[9] Hobbes is but one of the leading thinkers of the age whose dedication to reason and to a scientific and expressly materialist depiction of the forces propelling the universe were fueled by bitter experience with theological bickering. He viewed the world solely in the mirror of rationality and consciously excluded "things infinite, things eternal, final causes, and things known only by grace or revelation."[10]

Rousseau and Montesquieu, while not as pessimistic about the human condition as Hobbes, were each as disaffected by the conduct of the church in France as was Hobbes with the churches in England. These writers exhibited the dualism common in the period in not eschewing the value of religious laws for the conduct of Christians, but strictly relegating those laws to a matter of personal salvation. In their schema, which became the dominant one of the era, God functions in a vastly different domain and it is pointless to try to fathom, let alone enact divine justice. Human religion, in the words of Rousseau, is "purely inward worship of Almighty God" and neither affects or is affected by matters of state and "all things of this world."[11] At one point, Montesquieu avows that there are "crimes against religion," but God has to avenge the rupture of His own decrees. Laws of the state, on the other hand, are of this world. They are not based upon biblical witness but solely upon human reason.[12]

---

[8] Ibid., p. 110.

[9] Michael Oakeshott, "Introduction," in Thomas Hobbes, *Leviathan* (Oxford: Basil Blackwell, 1960), pp. vii–xlvi.

[10] Ibid., p. xx.

[11] Jean Jacques Rousseau, *The Social Contract*, trans. Willmoore Kendall (Chicago: Henry Regnery, 1954), IV, viii.

[12] Baron de Montesquieu, *The Spirit of the Laws*, trans. Thomas Nugent (New York: Colonial Press, 1899), I, 3; XII, 4.

Spinoza, too, experienced bitter disappointment with religious bigotry and its use of power to eliminate religious opposition. His Jewish ancestors had moved to the Netherlands to escape persecution at the hands of the Spanish Inquisition but the religious tolerance proclaimed by the Reformed Church evaporated in the wake of the Arminian theological controversy.[13] Spinoza comments that the laws passed in this atmosphere were "more apt to provoke men than reform them" and that at the heart of theological conflict was not "great zeal for truth … but great ambition to rule."[14]

In such a world, the traditional Christian concept of theological contingency is bereft of its foundation. Dating back to thinkers like Augustine, contingency was rooted in a trust in a beneficent divine providence that provided solace in life's tragic moments at the same time as it fostered a deep humility as a counterweight to human attempts to control their own destinies. Its hallmark was a belief in the gratuitousness of life and of history. The turn to reason and natural rights, both accorded divine origin, transferred faith in providence to faith in oneself. Grotius remarks that "natural right is not susceptible of change, even by God," while Hobbes proclaims: "For after the Bible was translated into English, every man, nay every boy and wench that could read English, thought they spoke with God Almighty, and understood what he said … Every man became a judge of religion, and an interpreter of the Scriptures to himself."[15]

Hobbes is duly noted for, and his thought often unfairly reduced to, an anthropology pitting all against all—along with his rhetorical asides on the nastiness and brutishness of human existence. These flashy snapshots can serve to distract the reader not only from the complexity of Hobbes' thought but also from the fact that his dismissal of transcendent constraints on human reason and human interests was shared widely by his contemporaries and intellectual descendents.[16] The idea here is not the rejection of God by most of the leading Enlightenment thinkers, including, and even especially, Hobbes, but the belief that knowledge of God's existence and will for humankind are found not from faith, grace, and scripture alone, as the reformers insisted, but through the use of reason. As Michael Buckley notes, the foe against which these influential thinkers railed

---

[13] Benedict de Spinoza, *The Political Works*, ed. and trans. A.G. Wernham (Oxford: Clarendon, 1958), p. 3.

[14] Ibid., v.

[15] Grotius, *Law of War and Peace* , I, x; Hobbes is quoted in Spinoza, *The Political Works*, p. 1.

[16] Spinoza writes that "it is very rare for sovereigns to issue commands which are utterly foolish, for their main task … is to plan for the common good and direct everything by the dictate of reason … In addition, there is less danger of foolish decrees in a democracy: first because it is practically impossible for the majority … to agree on a piece of folly; and secondly because of the basis and aim of democracy … to restrain men as far as possible within the bounds set by reason." Spinoza, "Tractatus-Theologico Politicus," in *The Political Works*, XVI. See also, Montesquieu, *Laws*, I, III.

was not God but established religion. They were advocates of "natural religion," believing that evidence for the divine was obtainable independent of confessional allegiance or theological speculation. Such natural religion was believed capable of judging the validity of religious claims. Knowledge of God and God's truth were thus to be attained without appeal to the church and "even more critical ... without appeal to Christ."[17] Jurists in the seventeenth and eighteenth centuries would replicate their philosophical contemporaries, locating the ideal of human existence in a state of nature wherein the individual endowed with natural rights exercises true dominion.[18]

Descartes, who was so instrumental in erecting a fully mechanical understanding of the universe based on analytic geometry and a universal mathematics, was prompted as much by a desire to defend religion from the skepticism of writers like Montaigne as a love of philosophical speculation. His fear that atheism was "at the gates" prompted his spiritual director, Cardinal Berulle, to claim that Descartes' efforts to reveal that only certitude could stymie the critics of faith would lead to his eternal salvation.[19] Ironically, the casualty in all of this was faith itself. Descartes, true to his convictions, arrived at his famous proof for the existence of God by first, in effect, eliminating the possibility of certain knowledge anywhere save in human reason: "I have always been of the opinion that the two questions respecting God and the soul were the chief of those that ought to be determined by help of philosophy rather than theology."[20]

There is thus a strict division between the created subject and creation, including the subject's own body: "I here remark, in the first place, that there is a vast difference between the mind and body, in respect that body, from its nature, is always divisible, and mind is entirely indivisible."[21] More generally, his method of universal doubt, made famous in his reflection that all apparent manifestations of reality have no more credibility than the reality of objects experienced in one's dreams, led to the supposition that the certitude for which he sought could only be located in the intellect.[22]

That Descartes was to find the solution to intellectual discord in the certainty provided by the *cogito* (I think therefore I am) and, stemming from God's goodness, mathematics, greatly augmented the growing assurance not only among the educated elites but also among Christian theologians that reason and

---

17 Buckley, *Atheism*, p. 38.

18 Roscoe Pound, *An Introduction to the Philosophy of Law* (New Haven: Yale University Press, 1954), p. 17.

19 Buckley, *Atheism*, pp. 69, 72.

20 Rene Descartes, "Meditations on the First Philosophy," in *Discourse on Method and the Meditations*, trans. John Veitch (Buffalo: Prometheus, 1989), Dedication.

21 Ibid., "Meditations," VI.

22 Ibid., "Meditations," I.

its accompanying natural theology were sufficient to provide the truths for both ecclesiastical and civic life.[23]

Individual Freedom and the Power of the State

Not only were reason and science safer paths to a peaceful and truthful existence for thinkers like Hobbes, the only sure footing through the mire of human malevolence was categorically not the path of final causes and internal virtue so foundational to the "heathen philosophy" of Aristotle and Aquinas, but the security provided by absolute political power: "For the Lawes of Nature … of themselves, without the terrour of some Power, to cause them to be observed, are contrary to our naturall Passions, that carry into Partiality, Pride, Revenge, and the like."[24] Only by the conferral of "all their power and strength upon one Man, or upon one Assembly of men, that may reduce all their Wills … into one Will" can a social body live rightly and in peace.[25]

Rousseau, in like fashion, acknowledges that all power comes from God but quickly adds: "The same is true, however, of all sickness. Are we, then, forbidden to call in a doctor?"[26] The doctor to whom he refers is the political sovereign, the executor of the general will of the people, whose task it is to provide "the greatest of all goods, the good that ought to be the goal of every system of laws … liberty and equality."[27] This goal is a far different matter than the "freedom of the children of God" celebrated by St Paul (Rom 8: 21), a life lived in the grace and joy of the Holy Spirit in which an internal reservoir of faith detaches the Christian from the chains of materialism and social conformity. The goals of which Rousseau speaks are dependent upon the donation of the political authority: "nothing save the power of the state ever makes its individual members free."[28]

Kant's devout Lutheran faith provided for him a starting point not dissimilar from that of Hobbes. The former's primordial state of conflict echoes the ontological state of sin and darkness in which humans reside before election in Christ: "Whatever a man may have done in adopting a good disposition … he

---

[23] Descartes establishes the certainty of his own existence ("This alone is inseparable from me. I am—I exist"). He then proceeds to establish the goodness of God upon which truths of logic and mathematics can be established. "Meditations," II–V. See also Buckley, *Atheism*, pp. 81–85.

[24] Thomas Hobbes, *Leviathan*, ed. C.B. McPherson (London: Penguin, 1968), IV, XLVI; II, XVII.

[25] Ibid., II, XVII.

[26] Rousseau, *Social Contract*, I, iii.

[27] Ibid., II, xi.

[28] Ibid., II, xii.

nevertheless started from evil, and this debt he can by no possibility wipe out."[29] While all have the means of achieving salvation, and of living in an "ethical commonwealth" in which divine commands are expressed in "laws of virtue," Kant agrees with Hobbes that by nature humans require a "juridico-civil state" marked by "coercive laws," to offset the ravages of the war of all against all.[30]

Even Spinoza, who believed that everything in the universe was "in God" and who rejected Hobbes's bitter deductions concerning human nature wrote: "All men certainly seek their own advantage, but seldom as sound reason dictates; in most cases appetite is their only guide, and in their desires and judgments of what is beneficial they are carried away by their passions, which take no account of the future or anything else." He therefore concluded that "no society can exist without government and force, and hence laws to control and restrain the unruly appetites and impulses of men."[31]

The social contract theory of political origins intensifies the reliance on law that already had taken on an imposing metaphysical status in the Middle Ages. At the same time, it created the seeds of its own demise. For if law, backed by the force of the executive branch of government and its judicial arm, is the sole medium for the attainment of the unambiguous goods of "liberty and equality," then what is not unlawful falls within the domain of freedom. Locke writes that every human being is "naturally free" and nothing can "put him into subjection to any Earthly Power, but only his own consent."[32] The result is an infusion of lifeblood into the concept of "purely penal law." It is related in this case to what Hobbes calls "the silence of the law." In effect, Hobbes argues, if it is not illegal, the free person is "not hindered to doe what he has a will to." Accordingly, "where the Sovereign has prescribed no rule, there the Subject hath the liberty to do, or forebeare, according to his own discretion."[33]

In such a framework, free-thinking persons and their numerous Christian counterparts, now trusting in reason to weigh correctly the optimal moral course, found themselves in need of law and state power in a way for which the contract theorists failed to account. Political authority was charged not only to restrain those "unruly appetites and impulses" of their fellow citizens prohibited by law, it was also charged to protect their individual rights. Yet the self and its demands for autonomy, and a purely subjective determination of goods worth pursuing, more and more began to impose its will not only upon areas outside the explicit reach of the law, it also began to provide the framework wherein law itself was interpreted. Hobbes makes mention of this innate self-centeredness: "It is consequent also …

---

29 Immanuel Kant, *Religion within the Limits of Reason Alone*, trans. Theodore M. Greene and Hoyt B. Hudson (New York: Harper, 1960), II, I, C.

30 Ibid., III, I, I–II.

31 Spinoza, "Tractatus Theologico-Politicus," V.

32 John Locke, *Two Treatises of Government*, ed. Peter Laslett (Cambridge: Cambridge University Press, 1960), II, viii, 119.

33 Hobbes, *Leviathan*, II, XXI.

that there be no Propriety, no Dominion, no Mine and Thine distinct; but only that to be every mans that he can get; and for so long as he can keep it."[34] Montesquieu laments such a lack of political virtue and notes that in despotic societies and in those with high levels of class distinction "nobody aims at equality … they all aspire to superiority."[35] The dilemma in either case is that such a state, as Rousseau noted, is on the way to ruin.[36] Its only remedy is to legislate more and more law and, by such means, seek to control greater areas of the internal domain.[37]

In this expanding universe of legal sanctions, one in which Rousseau claimed that if one's moral opinion does not conform to the general will "that merely proves that [he or she] was mistaken," the practice of Christianity, even one compromised by an excessive legalism and individuality, is perceived as a threat to social harmony. What Rousseau referred to as the "Christianity of Gospels" does not have "any assignable point of contact with political society."[38] Indeed, he writes that Christ was "bent on establishing a spiritual kingdom on earth—an enterprise which forced a wedge between the political system and the theological system, and so undermined the unity of the state."[39] Hobbes is acknowledged by Rousseau to be the only Christian writer who "has clearly perceived both the disease and remedy" in the conviction that everything must "be subordinated to political unity." But, for all of his mistrust of the Christian churches, Rousseau contends that even Hobbes failed to see "that Christianity, given its domineering cast of mind, could not keep house with the system being advocated, and that the interest of the priest would in the long run prevail over the interest of the state."[40]

The Rational and Cultured Christian

Christians in the Enlightenment do not by and large appear to have sided with Rousseau's either/or dialectic concerning faith and citizenship. Rather, the great minds of the day sought to reconcile Christian faith with the vision of rationality, human agency, and political ethics shared by the writers mentioned in the previous section.

---

34 Ibid., I, 13

35 Montesquieu, *Laws*, V, 4.

36 Rousseau, *Social Contract*, III, xv.

37 Gauchet claims that "modernist individualist theories of the social contract appeared as soon as so-called absolute power was actually installed." See *Disenchantment*, p. 58.

38 Rousseau, *Social Contract*, IV, viii.

39 Ibid.

40 Ibid. Hobbes contended that Christianity (save the Catholic Church) would not pose a threat to the rule of the Leviathan due to Christ's teaching to render unto Caesar the things of Caesar. See *Leviathan*, III, xlii. For his trenchant comments on the papacy, see IV, xlvii.

Kant famously posited that transcendental concepts such as God, the world, and the human person are "mere ideas," lacking both "stability and objective reality" if viewed from the perspective of speculative reason. In his Second Critique, he retrieves the moral system explained in the *Groundwork of the Metaphysics of Morals*, maintaining that only in the use of practical reason—the path of methodical argument and logical deduction—can humans achieve moral freedom and come to know what is knowable about the deepest metaphysical issues.[41]

This moral freedom is exemplified in Kant's idea of the "good will": "It is impossible to conceive anything at all in the world, or indeed even beyond it, that could be considered good without limitation except a good will."[42] But the good will is fully dependent upon reason whose "true vocation" is "to produce a will that is good."[43]

Contrary to the contemplative belief that God is one with all things and can be known by a loving and purely non-cognitive attentiveness to reality, Kant continues to extend the dualist contention already seen in thinkers like Descartes that creation, while providing the possibility for faith, is in great part opaque and ambiguous without the concentration upon the self and its rational powers.[44] In this, Kant actually reinvigorates the formal separation between the internal forum of conscience and the external forum of statutory law in medieval Catholicism. In both cases the Christian reacts to law, not the gospel, as the independent variable, whether the inner moral law or the promulgated outer law.[45]

The result is a specific form of rationality, one that as we have seen is patterned upon pragmatic politics, inner autonomy, and either mathematical/scientific certitude or, in the case of Kant, analytical deduction. As Alasdair MacIntyre has pointed out, it is not that Christians are irrational; they simply have a different

---

41 "Now, the concept of freedom, insofar as its reality is proved by an apodictic law of practical reason, constitutes the *keystone* of the whole structure of a system of pure reason, even of speculative reason; and all other concepts (those of God and immortality), which as mere ideas remain without support in the latter, now attach themselves to this concept and with it and by means of it get stability and objective reality, that is their *possibility* is *proved* by this: that freedom is real, or this reveals itself through the moral law." Immanuel Kant, "Critique of Practical Reason," in *Practical Philosophy*, trans. Mary J. Gregor (Cambridge: Cambridge University Press, 1996), Preface (5:4).

42 Kant, "Groundwork of the Metaphysics of Morals," in *Practical Philosophy*, Section I (4:393).

43 Ibid., I (4:396).

44 "Thus I see before me order and purposiveness in nature, and need not proceed to speculation in order to assure myself of their *reality*; instead, it is only in order *to explain* them that I need *to presuppose a Deity* as their cause; but, since an inference from an effect to a determined cause, especially to a cause so precise and so completely determined as we have to think in God, is always uncertain and doubtful, such a presupposition cannot be brought further than the degree of being the most reasonable opinion for us as human beings." Kant, "Critique of Practical Reason," in *Practical Philosophy*, II, II, VIII (5:142).

45 Durham, "Criminal Law," pp. 224–25.

system of rationality than that forwarded by the Enlightenment, whose guiding metaphor is not the Bible but what he terms the "encyclopaedia."[46] Adam Gifford, whose yearly Gifford lectures on Christian theology arguably remain one of the highest professional honors an invited speaker can receive, was an associate of Thomas Spencer Baynes, the editor of the Ninth Edition of the *Encyclopaedia Britannica*. The latter's philosophy invoked "knowledge rather than opinion," and Gifford, in step with Baynes, bequeathed his fortune to expositions on religion "that treat their subject as a strictly natural science … I wish it to be considered just as astronomy or chemistry is."[47]

Kant (1724–1804) would have been an excellent candidate for the honor had he lived into the late nineteenth century. A great deal of his philosophical speculation was centered on the effort to place religion strictly within the bounds set by the human intellect. Like Descartes, the effort was an honest one—an attempt to lead the reader to faith by the path of reason. For Kant, there is a moral law and it is eternal and unimpeachable. Christ is the word of God, the paradigmatic ethical teacher, and "it is our universal duty to elevate ourselves to this ideal of moral perfection."[48] The question for Kant, no less than for us, is how do we fashion our lives to fit that perfect model? For him, the means to do so has been provided "irresistably" by "pure moral legislation, through which the will of God is primordially engraved in our hearts."[49] The one whom we seek, the Christ, is to be found and emulated "nowhere but in our own reason."[50]

One of the leading thinkers in the generation after Kant who diligently studied the former's thought was Friedrich Schleiermacher. He attempted to make Christianity once again suitable to those children of the Enlightenment, those "cultured despisers" who, as noted earlier, found in reason and nature all of the truth they believed was lacking in religions generally, and Christian faith particularly. His was an apologetic task that, in the words of Stanley Hauerwas, aimed at making Christian faith credible to the world rather than the world credible to Christian faith.[51] Schleiermacher speaks thus to his cultured interlocutor: "Let us deal honestly with one another. You do not like religion; we started from that assumption. But in conducting an honest battle against it … you do not want to have fought against a shadow." His aim is to reveal the level to which "the disposition of various cultivated peoples," the manifestation "of polite love and beneficial support of one another," are the true substance of the very thing they

[46] Alasdair MacIntyre, *Three Rival Versions of Moral Inquiry* (Notre Dame: Notre Dame University Press, 1990), p. 19.

[47] Ibid., pp. 9, 19.

[48] Kant, *Reason Alone*, II, I, A.

[49] Ibid., III, I, V.

[50] Ibid., II, I, B.

[51] Stanley Hauerwas and William Willimon, *Resident Aliens* (Nashville: Abingdon, 1989), pp. 30–48.

have scorned.[52] Thus he gently chides the reader: "If only you knew how to read between the lines! All holy writings are like the modest books there were in use some time ago in our modest fatherland, which treated important matters under a sketchy title." Christianity is in the end not faith at all but the feelings of "heartfelt compassion" or "the remorse over everything in us that is hostile to the genius of humanity."[53]

The nineteenth century saw a great outpouring of sentiments similar to those orchestrated by Schleiermacher in which Christians tied their faith to the values of an educated, polite, and affluent society. The universal religious feelings first enunciated by the moral sense theorists were translated into "purity crusades" and temperance movements. Christianity had become a religion of "pragmatists," and upon this faith, now based on middle class "morality and humanity," was "constructed the religious foundations of modern society."[54]

Several clear orientations concerning law and judgment emerge from this brief survey. Whether one concentrates on religion as fully contained within reason or one's feelings, the radical demands in the teachings of Jesus have been fully circumscribed within movements internal to the nature of every human being. From the perspective of those who view Christian faith as coincidental with benevolent or sympathetic feelings, law and judgment retain the independence they were accorded in medieval Catholicism and in emerging secular legal orders; and they lie largely outside the purview of Christian ethics. From the outlook of rationalists such as Kant, the teachings of Christ are a subset of purely intellectual forces aimed in the optimal sense at creating an ethical commonwealth in which "people make laws in accord with a sense of reciprocal rights." From a negative perspective, they constitute a repressive mechanism to restrain the malevolent who in "perversity of heart" follow "maxims of the will that are contrary to the law."[55] In both cases, law and judgment are set free of the strict constraints placed upon them in the gospel.

Deism and Civil Religion

It was noted that for Rousseau, as with his predecessor Montesquieu, one's faith and relationship with the divine were purely personal matters. God judges human

---

52 Friedrich Schleiermacher, *On Religion: Speeches to its Cultured Despisers*, trans. Richard Crouter (Cambridge: Cambridge University Press, 1988), Second Speech.

53 Ibid.

54 David Pivar, *Purity Crusade: Sexual Morality and Social Control* (Westport, CT: Greenwood Press, 1973), p. 158. See also Ann Douglas, *The Feminization of American Culture* (New York: Anchor Press, 1988); Mary P. Ryan, *Cradle of the Middle Class* (New York: Cambridge University Press, 1981); Svend Ranulf, *Moral Indignation and Middle Class Psychology* (New York: Schocken, 1964).

55 Kant, *Reason Alone*, III, I, III; I, III.

conduct in God's own way and in God's own time, but the rules governing the eternal realm cannot be enacted in civil society. The latter are not necessarily inimical to the ways of God as revealed in Scripture; they have an entirely different function, a point Rousseau noted that Hobbes understood clearly.[56] Another idea expressed by Hobbes that surely caught the eye of Rousseau was that the sovereign is the "supreme pastor to whom all pastors owe obedience" and that "[a] ll that is Necessary to Salvation, is contained in two Vertues, Faith in Christ, and Obedience to Laws."[57]

Rousseau was shrewd enough, however, to understand what Machiavelli had observed nearly three centuries before him, namely that religions in general, and one can assume Christianity in particular, are irreplaceable forces of social control, as long as they concur with prevailing political ideals. Machiavelli counsels all who would rule effectively "to uphold the foundation of the religion of their countries," to preserve "the purity of all religious observances and treat them with proper reverence," for in so doing "it is easy to keep their people religious, and consequently well-conducted and united."[58]

It matters little whether there is any truth to the claims of the specific faith. "Sagacious rulers" will emphasize "the belief in the miracles that are celebrated in religions, however false they may be."[59]

But religion cannot be tolerated as a divisive force. Machiavelli laments the corruption and "decadence" of the early sixteenth century Catholic Church and states "that the nearer people are to the Church of Rome, which is the head of our religion, the less religious are they."[60]

Rousseau forcefully avows both of the contentions raised by Machiavelli. He was convinced that "each citizen must have a religion requiring him to cherish his duties."[61] This conviction was an extension of his concept of the general will: "no society can possibly exist save as there is a point at which all the interests concerned are in harmony … I affirm then that sovereignty is purely and simply the exercise of the general will."[62]

We have already noted, however, that like most of the philosophers about whom we have spoken, he was deeply distrustful of established religion. What distinguishes his thought was a particular wariness of "public" Christianity. For him, it was a far greater threat than Machiavelli supposed. Whereas the latter lamented the corruption of the church of his day, Rousseau's suspicions of Christianity were far broader. For him, the entire faith, save for private devotion,

---

56 Rousseau, *Social Contract*, IV, viii.

57 Hobbes, *Leviathan*, III, xlii, xliii.

58 Niccolo Machiavelli, "The Discourses," in *The Prince and the Discourses*, trans. Luigi Ricci and E.R.P. Vincent (New York: The Modern Library, 1950), I, xii.

59 Ibid.

60 Ibid.

61 Rousseau, *Social Contract*, IV, viii.

62 Ibid., II, I.

was far too focused on a set of political goods contrary to those of benefit to the state: "Christian teaching does more to undermine than to promote the good health of the state." This "religion of the priest … drives a wedge between citizenship and piety."[63]

What Rousseau proposed was the novel and enduring concept of civil religion. As would Comte in the century following him, Rousseau understood that the wedding of law and public mores under the umbrella of divine authority was crucial to political unity. If people could transfer the awe, devotion, and obedience that faith in God often engenders to the state and to its sovereign, the factionalism and rebelliousness so detrimental to societies based upon the social contract, wherein "we, as a community take each member into ourselves as an indivisible part of the whole," could be avoided.[64]

He thus proposed that the nation become a "divine" body, an alternative church if you will, with the requisite "gods," "patrons," "dogmas," and "rites" that both comprise any religion and, more importantly, provide its ability to influence substantially the conduct of its adherents.[65] Here, private theological opinion is of little import as long as the citizen is inspired "to cherish his duties" and "regards as infidel … whatever lies outside the single nation."[66] The sovereign can then "fix the tenets of a purely civil creed" and "can banish from the state anyone who does not believe them."[67] Like Rousseau, Montesquieu can then state with a sense of religious fervor that virtue is not the set of disciplinary practices necessary to lead the good life or, for the Christian, to conform one's way of seeing and one's actions to those of Christ, but simply "love of the republic."[68]

Many social thinkers have noted the brilliance and endurance of Rousseau's schema. Robert Bellah is but one contemporary sociologist who has charted both the validity and influence of civil religion, particularly in the United States. He contends that, at its best, it enables American political practice to be chastised since the civil creed retains a modest conception of the God of Jesus; it has, however, normally been a tool of repression for the dissident, a catalyst for xenophobia, and a divine justification, as Rousseau suggested, to view outsiders not only as enemies but as infidels.[69]

Whatever its beneficial effects at achieving a unified national purpose, civil religion in all of its forms, but especially as conceived by Rousseau, relies on

---

63 Ibid., IV, viii.

64 Ibid., I, vi.

65 Ibid., IV, viii.

66 Ibid.

67 Ibid.

68 Montesquieu, *Laws*, V, 2.

69 Robert Bellah, "Civil Religion in America," in *Beyond Belief* (New York: Harper & Row, 1970), pp. 168–86. See also Carl L. Bankston, *Public Education, America's Civil Religion* (New York: Teachers College Press, 2009); Robert Wuthnow, *Producing the Sacred: An Essay on Public Religion* (Champagne: University of Illinois Press, 1994).

a particular conception of God—one not only categorically different than the God who appears in Jesus, but also a God far above the warp and woof of day-to-day human activities. This is a God whose principal characteristic is an ethic of division, an ethic wherein conduct unbecoming of national ideals is to be punished, both here and in the afterlife. Speaking of the American expression of this phenomenon, Bellah states: "The God of the civil religion is not only rather 'unitarian,' he is also on the austere side, much more related to order, law, and right than to salvation and love."[70]

All of this helps explain why Deism rose to prominence first in England and then throughout the continent at the end of the seventeenth century. A focus on reason, the confluence of the rights-bearing individual and the nation constituted to insure those rights, the initiation of market economies coupled with a distrust in organized religion, and a belief in truths revealed in nature, led to a belief in a distant God whose providential care was sewn into the matter of the universe rather than revealed through creeds and dogmas. It was, as Charles Taylor suggests, a new "social imaginary," one in which "the saving action of Christ" as well as "the life of devotion and prayer" were rarely invoked.[71] Michael Buckley notes that Catholic writers shared in the race to rationalize Christianity along with their Protestant counterparts. Ostensibly, as with Descartes, the aim was to offer skeptics of religion a foothold in reasonable faith on their otherwise unimpeded descent into atheism. Leading theologians invoked the argument from design to make a case for God as the "great architect," or portrayed the deity in a form of "Platonized Epicurianism." Like Taylor, Buckley notes, however, that "the theologian will look in vain" for a detailed Christology or an exploration of religious experience.[72]

In the Deist creed, revealed in concepts like Rousseau's general will, concern for the self meshes perfectly with concern for the political community, and the overarching value is one of social and moral order. A concept of similar import that emerged in conjunction with Deism was the "impartial spectator." Developed initially by what were termed the "moral sense theorists" in England at the turn of the eighteenth century, this notion highlighted the fact that humans are naturally motivated to work for the well-being of others. Any person, by removing him or herself from the heat of the moment and engaging in rational reflection, can discover these benevolent tendencies and is capable of acting upon them. The dualist foundation of the concept can be noted in the thoughts of one of its most well-known patrons, Adam Smith: "When I endeavour to examine my own

---

70 Bellah, "Civil Religion," p. 175.

71 The social imaginary is a confluence of cultural images, stories, and ideas that make "shared practices possible" and create "a widely shared sense of legitimacy." Taylor, *Secular*, pp. 171–72; 225.

72 Buckley, *Atheism*, p. 63. Taylor argues that a decisive error was made by the Council of Trent in attempting to reconcile the traditional natural law with the emerging concepts of natural law propounded by rights theorists. See *Secular*, p. 128.

conduct, when I endeavour to pass sentence on it … it is evident that, in all such cases, I divide myself, as it were, into two persons; and that I, the examiner and judge, represent a different character from that other I, the person whose conduct is examined into and judged of. The first is the spectator … The second is agent, the person whom I properly call myself."[73]

This general sense of sympathy with our fellows, as Mill would later note, produces in like degree a desire to punish.[74] Smith writes: "When we see one man oppressed or injured by another, the sympathy which we feel with the distress of the sufferer seems to serve only to animate our fellow-feeling with his resentment against the offender. We are rejoiced to see him attack his adversary in his turn, and are eager and ready to assist him … for defense, or even for vengeance within a certain degree."[75]

The lasting contribution of Smith to world history, of course, came not from his corpus of writings in moral philosophy, but from his contention that the moral sense theorists, principal among them his teacher, Francis Hutcheson, were wrong about divine providence. Specifically, Smith famously argued that God's providential guidance, functioning in history as an "invisible hand," can turn the selfish human endeavors of "two different orders of people who had not the least intention to serve the public" into widespread sources of "universal opulence." Smith is speaking of the "great proprieters" on one hand and "merchants and artificers" on the other who, "from a view to their own interest, and in pursuit of their own peddler principle of turning a penny wherever a penny was to be got," lacked both "knowledge" and "foresight of that great revolution which the folly of the one, and the industry of the other, was gradually bringing about."[76] Here the traditional sense of a providence that humbles all human attempts at self-enlargement yields to one that exalts personal avarice.

The impact of this new "social imaginary" was profound, not only for Christians of that era; it continues to have great explanatory relevance for widely held contemporary attitudes. The influence of the ethos of individual self-interest, of a narrow sense of national identity, and of a distant God whose message is not revealed in the life of the Incarnate Word but in natural reason and sentiments, marked the appearance of understandings of law and judgment fully severed from the teachings of Christ. Why leave all behind to follow Jesus, or "sell all you have

---

73 Adam Smith, "The Theory of Moral Sentiments," in D.D. Raphael (ed.) *British Moralists 1650–1800* vol. II (Oxford: Clarendon, 1969), III, I.

74 "The same powerful motives which command the observance of these primary moralities enjoin the punishment of those who violate them; and as the impulses of self-defense, of defense of others, and of vengeance are all called against such persons, retribution, or evil for evil, becomes closely connected with the sentiment of justice, and is universally included in the idea." John Stuart Mill, *Utilitarianism* (Indianapolis: Bobbs-Merrill, 1957), ch. 5.

75 Smith, "Moral Sentiments," II, I, ii.

76 Adam Smith, *The Wealth of Nations* (London: Penguin, 1970), I, i; III, iv.

and give it to the poor" so as to have "treasure in heaven" (Mk 10: 21), when one can prosper financially and still be in harmony with God's benevolent providence? Why "deny oneself, pick up the cross and follow" (Mk 8: 34) in order to learn the art of Christian discipleship, when one has all of the needed moral resources within one's natural sentiments guided by the use of impartial reason? Thus were many "enlightened" Christians freed from the sacrifices entailed by a costly discipleship, as well as the strict constraints Christian tradition often placed on both law and judgment. The result was a new approach to crime and punishment.

Humane and Profitable Punishment

It must be stated at the outset that however one interprets its relation to Christian ethics, the new ethos characterized by the separation of church and state, the rise of democratic movements, and the concentration on human dignity, initiated many noble and deservedly lasting social and intellectual changes. Humanist concerns for social levelling, the focus on the rights of the individual as inherent powers guaranteeing unbiased treatment from the sovereign power, and the emerging philosophy of utilitarianism, all contributed to a diminishment in the terrible suffering endured in prisons in Europe, America, and beyond.[77]

Penal reform was a major focus of the utilitarians, especially Beccaria and Bentham. In answer to the shocking abuses common in all places of detention, they developed a theory of punishment that accompanied the continued transformation of law into an independent source of spiritual and moral legitimacy. This new correctional paradigm reflected anthropological and moral beliefs of the day in which the human person was pictured as a blank slate, fully impressionable to social influences and able to be molded by the values of order and efficiency so dear to the emerging capitalist economies. The resultant approach to criminal justice

[77] Jeremy Bentham formulated the hedonic calculus to support his contention that humans always seek to maximize pleasure and minimize pain. This includes Christian ascetics in his opinion who, in their desire for pain, simply misapply utilitarian theory. See "An Introduction to the Principles of Morals and Legislation," in Raphael, *British Moralists*, IV, i–vii; II, ix. Leading penal reformers in Europe such as Cesare Beccaria, Bentham, and John Howard were also influential in the rise of the penitentiary movement in the United States. The issues raised there prompted the French government to dispatch Alexis de Tocqueville and Gustave de Beaumont to study American prisons and recommend changes for French penal justice. The study they produced helped spread the new experiments in criminal justice to prisons around the globe. See Cesare Beccaria, *On Crimes and Punishments*, trans. Henry Paolucci (Indianapolis: Bobbs-Merrill, 1963); Jeremy Bentham, "Panopticon: Or, The Inspection House," in *The Works of Jeremy Bentham* (Edinburgh: W. Tait, 1843); John Howard, *The State of the Prisons* (London: W. Eyres, 1777); Gustave de Beaumont and Alexis de Tocqueville, *On the Penitentiary System in the United States and its Application to France*, trans. Francis Lieber (Philadelphia: Carey, Lea, and Blanchard, 1833).

has endured to a significant degree in contemporary penal systems, particularly those in traditionally "Christian" societies.

Some of the best features of the Enlightenment appear in stark contrast to some of the worst features of the Christian churches. Both Protestants and Catholics, for the most part, had fully succumbed to the belief that the state and its laws are good in themselves, meant to insure the order that God had ordained for human society. A large volume of literature, much of it consisting of sermons delivered in judicial contexts, testifies to the role Christian ministers frequently played as voices justifying punishment and execution of enemies of the government. Randall McGowen notes that at "the scaffold a wicked example was put to good use. Evil became altered; the whole ritual became a sermon." Additionally, he writes that "the narrative revealed by the ceremony was not exhausted by the suffering. For instance, the death helped to remind viewers that chaos and destruction would follow the dissolution of hierarchy and order."[78]

The church built on the life and teachings of Christ had, in many respects, now so fully embraced the hegemony of law and punitive judgment that it not only practiced them in its domain, it had become their herald in the political arena as well.

New Theories of Punishment

As noted, prison reform was a very important issue for many of the leading intellectuals of the Enlightenment. Innovations in epistemology, especially with Descartes, joined with new legal, social, and anthropological theories to refashion misanthropic approaches to punishment and infuse them with egalitarianism and a rising sense of humanism.

The first, and in many ways the most notable, of the reformers was Cesare Beccaria who, in 1764, recast the language and practice of criminal justice with his groundbreaking monograph, *On Crimes and Punishments*. What made the treatise so attractive was Beccaria's ability to translate the major ideas of his intellectual predecessors into an issue that had been smoldering in the public conscience.

Beccaria assumed a Hobbesian anthropology wherein "each individual … will always endeavor to take away from the mass, not only his own portion, but to encroach on that of others."[79] Rather than conclude, however, that selfish humans deserve a penalty commensurate with their unconquerable selfishness, he reasoned from a moral theory grounded, like that of Hutcheson and Smith in "the indelible

---

[78] Randall McGowen, "The Body and Punishment in Eighteenth Century England," *The Journal of Modern History* 59 (1987), pp. 665–66. Francesco Compagnoni provides an overview of Catholic attitudes to torture and capital punishment and reveals that, save for isolated voices of abolition, both were affirmed by the hierarchy from the mid-fourth century at least until the middle of the twentieth century. See "Capital Punishment," pp. 39–53.

[79] Beccaria, *Crimes*, ch. I.

sentiments in the heart of man," that the social contract ought to permit the "smallest portions possible" of punishment: "What *right*, I ask, have men to cut the throats of their fellow-creatures? Certainly not that on which the sovereignty and laws are founded."[80] In this he affirms the "general will" of Rousseau and lauds "the great" Montesquieu for the insight that punishments not based upon "absolute necessity" are signs of tyranny.[81]

The theory that emerges is based on the certainty furnished by "mathematical exactness" rather than the tradition of established religion which has been "commonly abused": "The motives which religion opposes to the fear of impending evil, and the love of life, are too weak, as they are too distant, to make any impression on the senses."[82] It is in utility that Beccaria finds the ideal philosophical and analytical vehicle to bear a new model of criminal justice based upon deterrence. Since "pleasure and pain are the only springs of action in beings endowed with sensibility," if one can tailor the amount of punishment to that degree that will make the "strongest and most lasting impressions on the minds of others, with the least of amount of torment to the body of the criminal," one will have honored both the need of society for order and the right of the offender to the maximum degree of pleasure and happiness possible.[83]

The deep humanity of the theory and its immense and inestimable benefit to the hapless and abused prisoners must be acknowledged with gratitude and admiration. Not only did Beccaria rail eloquently and forcefully against the death penalty, he also vilified the use of torture: "Can the groans of a tortured wretch recall the time past, or reverse the crimes he has committed?"[84]

Beccaria's notions of criminal justice were immediately successful and he became a popular personage in the salons of Europe. His work was also read eagerly around the globe, nowhere more fervently than in the United States.[85] The idea of basing punitive theory upon deterrence rather than simple retribution was also widely emulated. The Napoleonic criminal code which served as a model for numerous legal systems in other jurisdictions was based principally on the concept of deterrence.[86] But of the many who were profoundly moved by Beccaria's treatise, perhaps no one was more naturally disposed to do so than Jeremy Bentham. Since Bentham believed that utility governed all human action, he concurred with Beccaria that it was a not a matter of speculation but calculation that would point

---

80 Ibid., ch. II, XXVIII.

81 Ibid.

82 Ibid., ch. XVIII.

83 Ibid., ch. XII.

84 Ibid.

85 Editions of the book were published in Charlestown in 1777 and Philadelphia in 1778. The work was also printed as a serial in 1786 in both the *New Haven Gazette* and *Connecticut Magazine*. See Louis P. Masur, *Rites of Execution* (New York: Oxford University Press, 1989), p. 52.

86 Berman, *Law and Revolution II*, p. 12.

to the optimal treatment for human malevolence. He also duplicated Beccaria's schema that the level of chastisement necessary to deter both the actual offender and future offenders can be dramatically lessened as long as the response to infractions is swift, certain, and its rationale clearly communicated.[87]

Bentham was careful to defend the commitment to equality before the law and especially to minimize punishment only to the degree necessary to insure legal compliance. In keeping with the precise nature of his mind and his fondness for mathematical exactness, he suggested that a disproportion in punishment, especially if corporal punishment is to be inflicted, could best be avoided if a spanking machine was utilized: "A machine might be made, which should put in motion certain elastic rods of cane or whalebone, the number and size of which might be determined by the law: the body of the delinquent might be subjected to the strokes of these rods, and the force and rapidity with which they should be applied, might be prescribed by the Judge: thus everything which is arbitrary might be removed."[88]

The humanitarian impulse at the heart of these reforms, whatever we may think of them from the comfort of our vantage point, both motivated and reflected a growing sense throughout Europe that would emerge fully in nineteenth-century romanticism. The public, especially the cultured and educated classes, were growing more and more weary and horrified over torture, the public abuse of prisoners, and the festive and sadistic atmosphere surrounding capital punishment. One historian notes that the public evinced a growing sorrow over the death and suffering of others for no other reason than that they "were increasingly perceived as fellow human beings."[89] It was part of a movement with roots in the Renaissance and the "inner worldly asceticism" of the Reformation which permeated "public administration, the world of lawyers, and the liberal professions," a set of ceremonial attitudes, "borrowed from traditional aristocratic ideals in decline but never rejected." Among them, there was a renewed sense of "self-control, detachment, courtesy, authority, paternalism, [and] dignity of gesture and demeanor."[90]

Many European states abolished torture in the second half of the eighteenth century.[91] Thereafter, as Pieter Spierenburg observes, attention was turned to banning the exposure of the corpses of the executed, especially children: "The

---

[87] Jeremy Bentham, *The Rationale of Punishment* (Honolulu: University Press of the Pacific, 2004), I, VI, vii–viii; Beccaria, *Crimes*, ch. XLVII.

[88] Bentham, "Principles," XIV, viii; *Punishment*, II, I.

[89] Pieter Spierenburg, *The Spectacle of Suffering* (Cambridge: Cambridge University Press, 1984), p. 185. McGowen makes a similar argument tied to new conceptions of the body. See "Body and Punishment."

[90] Bellomo, *Common Legal Past*, pp. 8–9; Douglas, *Feminization*. Concerning "inner worldly asceticism," see Weber, *Protestant Ethic*, pp. 155–83.

[91] Edward Peters attributes the abolition movement to the new conception of natural law that featured "the natural dignity of humans." He cites Beccaria, Bentham,

display of the dead bodies of capitally punished delinquents was discontinued in Western Europe around 1800 … There can be no doubt that increased public sensitivity moved the authorities to act. Abandonment of the custom was usually motivated by calling it a relic of the 'barbarity of former times.'"[92]

Finally, movements originated at that time that would, by the mid-nineteenth century, culminate in a widespread abandonment of the practice of public executions. Among the outspoken advocates for the abolition of capital punishment in England were legal scholars such as William Blackstone, William Eden, and Samuel Romilly. Their commitment to bloodless punishment was driven in large part by the ideas dear to the Enlightenment, especially "the new evolution of the individual."[93] In the United States, the movement was driven in part by the feeling that if an "antichristian" brutality marked the monarchical regime from which Americans had broken away, a true republic, in the words of Benjamin Rush, would be "the best repositor[y] of the Gospel" and show greater moderation in the treatment of its captives.[94]

That the ideas we have discussed still have a place in European jurisprudence and penal practice is validated in James Whitman's recent study of the differences between the current practice of punishment in the United States and Europe. He notes that some European countries that trace their criminal statutes to the Enlightenment, and specifically to the Napoleonic codes of the early nineteenth century, are committed to the belief that both the judicial and punitive stages of law enforcement must be governed by a "levelling-up" principle. Unlike the politics of punishment in America that seeks equality by means of "levelling-down," the practice in these jurisdictions is that equality under the law means that offenders should be treated with the same deference shown to those of the upper classes.[95]

There are rich ironies in this brief account of the movement for a humane penal regimen, comprised mainly of proponents of Deism and natural religion. For the most part, Christians of that time, both Catholic and Protestant, had been fully initiated into the belief that civil law and its mechanisms of judgment and corporal punishment were necessary and morally acceptable complements to Christian ethics. Or, perhaps better put, Christians were now largely imbued with a dualist worldview, one that placed the creed and dogmas of faith in one dimension of life called "religion," and placed ethics, especially social ethics, fully within the domain of reason and law. Church and state were allies and law was their common language. Louis Masur notes this in relation to the ritual of execution in the early American republic where extant "gallows literature" reveals that criminals were in virtually all cases depicted as "naturally vicious" agents who "embraced iniquity

---

and John Howard as particularly influential in orchestrating this philosophy. See, *Torture* (Philadelphia: University of Pennsylvania Press, 1985), pp. 87, 99.

92 Spierenburg, *Spectacle*, p. 190.

93 McGowen, "Body and Punishment," pp. 667–69.

94 Quoted in Masur, *Rites of Execution*, pp. 61, 66.

95 Whitman, *Harsh Justice*, pp. 117–19.

despite the best efforts of pious parents and benevolent rulers; prisoners described themselves as 'naturally inclined to vice.' It was up to the individual whether or not to 'indulge in vicious passions' ... and the responsibility of society to punish those who did."[96]

Figures such as Beccaria and Bentham as well as most of their reform-minded colleagues found themselves in opposition to the "Christian ethics" they had witnessed and in which they had been raised. They are to be commended for a legacy of sensitivity to human suffering. They were, however, just as dedicated to law and judgment as their Christian counterparts, not as a means of inflicting bodily pain, but as means of social control.

The Economy of Discipline

In his well-known study of the origins of the "punitive panoply" of modern Western societies, Foucault contends that the penitentiary, which came into prominence in the late eighteenth century, was its dominant metaphor; it was "the penalty of civilized societies."[97] For, as Foucault asks, "[h]ow could the prison not be the penalty *par excellence* in a society in which liberty is a good that belongs to all?"[98] Punishment always reflects the values of society and, as we have noted in this chapter, the Enlightenment commitment to equality required the establishment of legal and criminal codes that not only "defined the power to punish as a general function of society," but were also "exercised in the same manner over all ... and in which each individual was equally represented."[99]

Of course, a new politics of punishment reflects not only a different set of ethical norms, it also requires a new understanding of human nature and, to a significant degree, as Marxist scholars have insisted, reflects the economic system in the given jurisdiction.[100]

The new anthropological view was given its characteristic trait in the rejection by philosophers such as Hobbes and Locke of any innate moral ontology. We saw that Hobbes began his quest for the ideal political arrangement by insisting that the human person is "governed every one by his own law" as well as by "a mechanistic-materialist politics" that springs "from a mechanistic and materialist universe."[101] He thus rejected the teleological focus of "heathen" philosophers

---

[96] Masur, *Rites of Execution*, p. 37.

[97] Michel Foucault, *Discipline and Punish*, trans. Alan Sheridan (New York: Vintage, 1979), pp. 231–32.

[98] Ibid., p. 232.

[99] Ibid., p. 231.

[100] Several works explore the relationship between economy and punishment. See, e.g., Dario Melossi and Massimo Pavarini, *Prison and the Factory*, trans. Glynis Cousin (New York: Macmillan, 1981); Georg Rusche and Otto Kirchheimer, *Punishment and Social Structure* (New York: Russell & Russell, 1968).

[101] Hobbes, *Leviathan*, IV, xlvi; Oakeshott, "Introduction," *Leviathan*, xviii–xix.

such as Aristotle and Aquinas, who believed that the human person was naturally impelled to the good, to virtue, to life in society, and to contemplation.[102]

Locke bore a similar antagonism to the classical natural law philosophers and to the "falseness of the supposition" that there are "certain innate principles ... stamped upon the mind of man; which the soul receives in its very first being, and brings into the world with it."[103] Rather, Locke argued that all knowledge is produced by sensory experience and the mental operations triggered by the senses such as "thinking, doubting, believing, reasoning, knowing, [and] willing."[104] The mind is, in his famous formulation of the *tabula rasa*, "white paper, void of all characters, without any ideas."[105]

This new interest in a social engineering model of epistemology was to be transferred to the treatment of social delinquents. As Michael Ignatieff remarks in his study of the first English penitentiaries: "If all ideas, including moral ones, were derived from external sensation, it followed that people could be socialized by taking control over their sources of sensation."[106] At the same time, he notes that the materialism of figures such as Hobbes was "the idealist force" behind the penitentiaries: "In the symbolic system that materialist assumptions made possible, managing the self and managing other men became analogous to the management of machines."[107]

These innovations emerged during the time of the industrial revolution in England. It had antecedents in the formation of what were termed workhouses, or "bridewells," in England in the late sixteenth century: "In England, the bridewells were established for the confinement and deterrence of 'masterless' men thrown into the highways by the dissolution of Catholic monastic charity, the breakup of feudal retinues ... and the steady pressure of population growth on a small and overstocked free labor market."[108] The logic was to intervene in the lives of vagrants, petty criminals, and the morally corrupt by forcing upon them habits of industry and social propriety.[109]

The early "bridewells," however, were exemplars of neither order nor industriousness; and the logic that governed their operation was driven more by

---

102 Hobbes, *Leviathan*, IV, xlvi; Aquinas, *ST*, I, XII, viii, ad. 4; Aristotle, *Ethics*, II, X.

103 John Locke, "An Essay Concerning Human Understanding," in *Great Books of the Western World* 35, ed. Robert Maynard Hutchins (Chicago: Encyclopedia Britannica, 1952), I, I. I ff.

104 Ibid., II, I, ii–iv.

105 Ibid., II, I, ii.

106 Michael Ignatieff, *A Just Measure of Pain* (New York: Pantheon, 1978), p. 67.

107 Ibid., p. 68.

108 Ibid., pp. 11–12.

109 Randall McGowen, "The Well-Ordered Prison," in Norval Morris and David Rothman (eds) *The Oxford History of the Prison* (New York: Oxford University Press, 1995) pp. 83–84; J. Thorsten Sellin, *Slavery and the Penal System* (New York: Elsevier, 1976), pp. 71–74.

pragmatic economic concerns and a utilitarian commitment to deterrence than an impulse to reform or to ennoble what one charter called "rogues, vagabonds, idle, loitering, and lewd persons" by means of labor.[110] For the most part, the work was conceived as a punishment for their dissolute behavior. The Dutch philosopher, Dirck Coornhert, wrote in 1567 of the function of these workhouses that had quickly spread to Holland. His argument was that those who were not trustworthy enough for enforced public work, yet not as reprehensible as those destined for galley slavery, were to be confined and given work not as a means of reform but for purely economic motives.[111]

Not all advocates of the workhouse were so narrowly focused, and the Calvinist-inspired theology of thinkers such as Coornhert was to be augmented by the philosophical principles of writers such as Hobbes and Locke, as well as the moral commitments of Beccaria and Bentham. In other words, an economically proficient and effective system of punishment, faithful to Enlightenment principles, could only be achieved to the degree that it was rational. It was in this area that Bentham's ideas were most effective. As we noted earlier with the spanking machine, he argued that the most pragmatic and morally defensible conception of administering pain was one that was impersonal; and the punishment would be humane precisely to the degree that it *was* impersonal. Punishment thus joined itself to the scientific orientation and the hedonic calculus. In the words of Ignatieff, it was "an objective use of pain by the state for the regulation of the egoistic calculus of individuals."[112] And, in deference to the sensibilities of the cultural elites and growing middle class, it was banned from places of commerce and public enjoyment. Repression, in the words of Spierenburg, had become a private affair.[113]

Although Bentham's design for a penitentiary, the Panopticon, was never adopted in England, it was adopted elsewhere and exhibited both his moral vision and mechanistic technique.[114] Whatever the goals of the keepers: "punishing the incorrigible … reforming the vicious, confining the suspicious, employing the idle … instructing the unwilling … or training the rising race in the path of education," Bentham insisted that the solution lay in "a simple idea in Architecture!"[115] In his design, the cells were arranged in circular layers with a guard tower in the center with viewing portals that enabled the officers to see into each cell without being seen themselves: "the more constantly the persons to be inspected are under the

---

110 Quoted in Sellin, *Slavery*, p. 73.

111 Thorsten Sellin, *Pioneering in Penology* (Philadelphia, University of Pennsylvania Press, 1944), pp. 23–24.

112 Ignatieff, *Just Measure*, p. 76.

113 Spierenburg, *Spectacle*, p. 193.

114 It did influence the construction of a number of penitentiaries throughout the world, including the United States. See James Jacobs, *Stateville: The Penitentiary in Mass Society* (Chicago: University of Chicago Press, 1977).

115 Bentham, "Panopticon," Preface, Letter I.

eyes of the persons who should inspect them, the more perfectly will the purpose of the establishment have been attained. Ideal perfection … would require that each person actually be in that predicament, during every instant of time."[116]

Despite the rather modest degree of institutional emulation, the ideas behind the Panopticon were larger than those of its creator. Foucault argues that the social vision of the experiment, what Bentham termed "a new mode of obtaining power over the mind," presages perfectly the growth and contemporary flowering of the national security state, obsessed with observation and control: "The contract may have been regarded as the ideal foundation of law and political power; panopticism constituted the technique, universally widespread, of coercion. It continued to work in depth on the juridical structures of society, in order to make the effective mechanisms of power function in opposition to the formal framework that it had acquired. The 'Enlightenment,' which discovered the liberties, also invented the disciplines."[117]

This new vision of social organization and crime control to which Christians lent their support as theologians, philosophers, jurists, politicians, and citizens was given evidence by de Tocqueville in his visit to American penitentiaries in the 1830s. He described in detail the debate between the rational, painful, and economically driven penal organization named after its prototype at the facility in Auburn, New York, and the monastic-inspired penitentiary founded by the Quakers in Philadelphia. The author noted that the latter "produces more honest men, and that of New York more obedient citizens."[118] De Tocqueville encouraged France to adopt Pennsylvania's monastic model, but his native country, like the United States and virtually every other nation, chose the opposite. France opened the prison at Mettray shortly after de Tocqueville's report. In its military discipline, its impersonal social arrangement (inmates referred to by a number), its corporal discipline, and its work regimen, the facility, in Foucault's words, exemplified "the model in which are concentrated all the coercive technologies of behavior."[119]

Whatever his differences with the thinkers we have discussed in this chapter, Hegel is a perfect example of a leading intellectual—and, at least in his early writings, a Christian one—who exemplified the degree to which political power took on a sacred resonance. For him, and most of his contemporaries, the state and its laws had become an unquestioned good, an instance of the divine, and

---

[116] Ibid., Letter I.

[117] Bentham, "Panopticon," Preface; Foucault, *Discipline and Punish*, p. 222. David Garland is one contemporary criminologist who has written on the phenomenon of continual social observation and supervision that continues the idea behind the Panopticon. He calls the trend, "criminologies of everyday life." See, *Culture of Control*, pp. 182–83.

[118] Beaumont and Tocqueville, *Penitentiary System*, p. 60.

[119] Foucault, *Discipline and Punish*, p. 293.

an incarnation of that "higher entity which even lays claim to this very life and property and demands its sacrifice."[120]

Hegel rejected the social contract precisely because he believed that the state exists "on lines that are fixed and absolute."[121] Yet he strikes the same chord as Rousseau and many others in his contention that the ruling power must function "with mechanical necessity," must compel "the activity of every individual to accord with the general will," and that all citizens "must therefore venerate the state as a secular deity."[122] In that light, he exemplified the attitude so prevalent now in the retributive thrust of many contemporary societies, impatient with the relevance of "the subjective aspect of crime," and dismissive of the importance of "trivial psychological ideas of stimuli, impulses too strong for reason, and psychological factors coercing and working on our ideas."[123] Rather, Hegel insisted that crime is wrong because the "right" is established in the laws and customs of a particular people; therefore, "punishment is inherently and actually just."[124] It is "something in itself truly infinite and absolute."[125]

The figures we have surveyed in this section and throughout this chapter are only a sample of the mind of the age. While different in many ways, and Hegel is certainly different than many of the thinkers we have surveyed, I have tried to show that there were crucial similarities among them in the areas of law, judgment, and punishment. The movements set in motion by the Enlightenment were driven both explicitly and implicitly by a transformed Christian consciousness that had so elevated divine transcendence, and minimized divine immanence, that the power of humans both as individuals and in civil concert was enhanced to a degree once reserved to God alone. Gauchet stresses this point continually: "The more God is thought of and venerated as the Wholly Other, the less his creatures' existence is perceived and treated by them as being controlled by something other." What really changed, in the last analysis, was the legal narrative. All systems of law, as has been noted, are narrative based; they reflect the foundational story of a society—its myth, with all of the attendant cosmic underpinnings, whether real or implied. Christians had for centuries been editing the story of the life of the "lawless" Christ with a growing legalism, a weakening of a broad sense of kinship with the image of God in everything and everyone, and a commensurate desire to control and punish the conduct of others in deference to their own narrowly defined conception of the good. In the absence of the example of Christ, in the absence of a God to be loved and worshipped as immanent in all of creation, a new

---

120 G.W.F. Hegel, *Philosophy of Right*, trans. T.M. Knox (London: Oxford University Press, 1967), p. 71.

121 Ibid., p. 285.

122 Ibid.; G.W.F. Hegel, *Natural Law*, trans. T.M. Knox (Philadelphia: University of Pennsylvania Press, 1975), p. 85.

123 Hegel, *Philosophy of Right*, p. 70.

124 Ibid.

125 Hegel, *Natural Law*, p. 92.

narrative had taken hold of the Christian imagination: law had became the sacred "other" that holds us together.[126]

[126] Gauchet, *Disenchantment*, p. 38.

Chapter 6
Law and Judgment in Modern Society

We have traced up to this point the movements in Christian history that fractured the unitive and contemplative ethic of Jesus. In the life of Christ, one finds an attitude of total presence to creation and to the other; one in which a compassionate stance precedes and effectively dismisses a reliance on law or the need of the ego to compare, to analyze, to fear, or to judge. It has been shown that a slow process of pragmatic and organizational compromise so diminished the message of Jesus that, by the dawn of the modern era, a dualism between sacred and secular, person and society, and God and the world had effectively transformed the structure of Christian consciousness. Harold Berman writes that "it was not the rise of Protestant Christianity in the sixteenth and seventeenth centuries but rather the decline of Protestant [as well as Roman Catholic] Christianity ... that led to the substitution of the new *–isms*, new overriding faiths in the nation, the individual, the private accumulation of wealth and the supremacy of rational calculation."[1]

In Catholic circles, after the Council of Trent (1545–1563) moral theology became a field of study in and of itself, detached from philosophical theology and scripture. The Christian ethic was presented in the format of abstract manuals written to assist confessors in determining levels of culpability and the appropriate penance for specific sins.[2] For two centuries, the new discipline was absorbed in debates on the issue of probablism. The latter was an elaborate system of moral analysis meant to determine the responsibility and level of culpability of the individual Catholic to ecclesiastical and secular law in particular situations.[3] This new approach to ethics reduced virtually the entire Christian life to a series of rules, often with strict penances attached for their violation and, equally often, terminal consequences for the soul of the negligent. As one author states, the excessive focus on probablism and the determination of guilt "led to the sterility of the whole moral theological endeavor and to a rather general disregard of the unique character of Christian morality."[4] Ironically, for a church that had condemned modernism in the mid-nineteenth century, the manual tradition was

---

[1] Berman, *Law and Revolution II*, p. 24.

[2] Bernard Haring, *The Law of Christ*, trans. Edwin G. Kaiser (2 vols, Westminster, MD: New Press, 1961), vol. 1, pp. 18–20. Charles Curran writes: "Trent understood the sacrament of penance primarily in juridical terms, with the priest acting as a judge to determine whether absolution is to be given or denied." See *Catholic Moral Theology in the United States* (Washington: Georgetown University Press, 2008), p. 2.

[3] Mahoney, *Moral Theology*, pp. 135–43.

[4] Haring, *Law*, p. 21.

deeply infused with the subject–object duality that dominated the Enlightenment, and the independent variable in its meticulous deliberations was not the Gospel, but law.

On the Protestant side, historicism came to the fore in the nineteenth century among the Reformation's liberal descendents. It was highly polemical (as were Catholic writings), carried the weight of inner-worldly asceticism, a rejection of monastic and contemplative spirituality, and, perhaps to a degree even greater than Catholicism, an embrace of the Enlightenment duality between faith and reason.[5] The fundamentalist reaction to liberalism at the end of the nineteenth century did little to change the basic conclusions of liberals: that salvation was largely an individual affair, won by obedience to law; and, certainly in America, that the institutions of government and economy were ordained and blessed by God and deserved the full allegiance of the Christian faithful: "Insofar as the kingdom was conceived in social terms the faith in its coming was transformed into a belief in progress. The judgment was really past. It had occurred in a democratic revolution. The life now lived in the land of promise was regarded as the promised life, and no greater bliss seemed possible than was afforded by the extension of American institutions to all the world."[6]

With this as background, the task of this chapter is to reveal the particular ways that law and punitive judgment developed now that they were so often conceived by Christians to have rational and moral legitimacy. The thesis in brief is that the ethical principles of lawmakers, jurists, and political leaders became in large part the ethical principles of most Christians.

We will trace three main areas of legal development in the proceeding pages: legal positivism, legal realism, and narrative accounts of the law. The chapter will conclude with a section describing the specific ways these movements have impacted the practice of criminal justice.

Legal Positivism

The new interpretation of natural law found most prominently in Enlightenment writers such as Hobbes, Locke, and Rousseau, the strict acceptance of social order seen in figures such as Hegel, and utilitarian theories concerning what law is and what it ought to be, yielded in the late nineteenth century to a positivist,

---

[5] Troeltsch writes of Ascetic Protestantism: "Through its ecclesiastical ideal, which merges into the ideal of the Free Churches, the democratic constitution of its individual congregations, as well as of its general ecclesiastical structure, its autonomous individualism … and its systematic and positive industry, it has become one of the basic causes of the immense changes in modern society." See *Social Teaching*, II, p. 818.

[6] H. Richard Niebuhr, *The Kingdom of God in America* (New York: Harper, 1959), p. 183. On the development of fundamentalism, see George M. Marsden, *Fundamentalism and American Culture* (New York: Oxford University Press, 1980).

sociological approach that was "governed by laws as completely beyond the power of conscious human control as the movements of the planets."[7] Positivism was centered on "abstract universals of theoretic jurisprudence" in an effort to establish "fundamental accepted rules specifying the essential lawmaking procedures."[8] It is the quintessential liberal theory of law in which action and agent are formally separated and in which it is believed that the attentiveness by judges to legal rules can safely isolate what they do from who they are.[9] Positivism sought to treat law "as a manifested fact of social authority or power, to be studied for what it is and does, not for what it is trying to do or become."[10]

The reasons for this shift in juridical philosophy were, upon reflection, somewhat predictable. In a disenchanted world absent of divine immanence and with the rise of the autonomous individual whose rights and interests had taken on an unprecedented priority, fact and value, what is and what ought to be were increasingly perceived as distinct. David Hume is the most famous of the empiricists who argued in this vein but he echoed a sentiment with growing resonance among the Christian faithful that reason functions on a plane different from that of truth or falsehood: "actions do not derive their merit from a conformity to reason, nor their blame from a contrariety to it; and … as reason can never immediately prevent or produce any action by contradicting or approving of it, it cannot be the source of moral good and evil."[11]

A positivist approach to law can also be traced to the fact that the conception of natural law at the heart of the social contract theories is a negative concept rather

---

[7] Pound, *Introduction*, pp. 22–23; *Interpretations of Legal History* (Cambridge, MA: Harvard University Press, 1923), pp. 71–74. Ronald Dworkin traces legal positivism back to utilitarianism, especially the philosophy of Bentham. See *Taking Rights Seriously* (Cambridge, MA: Harvard University Press, 1977), p. vii.

[8] Oliver Wendell Holmes, "The Path of the Law," *Harvard Law Review* 10 (1897), p. 458; H.L.A. Hart, "Positivism and the Separation of Law and Morals," *Harvard Law Review* 71 (1958), p. 603. Alan Watson states that law is "largely autonomous and not shaped by social needs" but emerges from the "culture of the lawyers and especially of the lawmakers," those who "have control of the accepted mechanisms of legal change." It is "in large measure … dictated by the tradition relating to the law that prevails among the legal elite." See *The Evolution of Law* (Baltimore: Johns Hopkins University Press, 1987), pp. 93, 118.

[9] Oliver Wendell Holmes alludes to this formal dualist approach in discussing how ancient sources of legal authority have given way to judicial attentiveness to legislation and communal expediency: "And as the law is administered by able and experienced men, who know too much to sacrifice good sense to a syllogism, it will be found that, when ancient rules maintain themselves … new reasons more fitted to the time have been found for them, and that they gradually receive a new content, and at last a new form, from the grounds from which they have been transplanted." *The Common Law* (Boston: Little Brown, 1881), p. 36.

[10] Fuller, *Morality of Law*, p. 145.

[11] David Hume, "A Treatise of Human Nature," in D.D. Raphael (ed.), *British Moralists 1650–1800* (2 vols, Oxford: Clarendon Press, 1969), vol 2, III, I, I.

than the positive one that appeared in medieval theory. Persons live in society not as an extension of the ancient belief that humans are social, seek to promote the common good, and *a fortiori* are obliged to sacrifice for that greater good, but in order to maximize liberty and allow only the most minimal constraints of that liberty as the security of their persons and property will allow.[12]

Similarly, we have noted how the translation of utilitarian ethics into law, especially with the writings of Beccaria and Bentham, was characterized by a mechanistic and scientific approach, a "calculus," that sought to place the least amount of pain or hindrance upon the human person in order to insure his or her compliance with statutes enacted by authoritative decree.

In all of these approaches, law is "made" rather than "found." It is, above all else, a set of rules for orderly governance. In the words of one of the leading voices of the movement, John Austin, laws are "general commands of a sovereign authority enforced by threat of sanction."[13] Ronald Dworkin states that for legal positivists, law is "a set of special rules used by the community directly or indirectly for the purpose of determining which behavior will be punished or coerced by the public power."[14] The authority of law is self-referential; a law is a law whether or not "we happen to dislike it, or though it vary from the text, by which we regulate out approbation and disapprobation."[15]

Law is "not the manifestation of a supernatural authority," or a reflection of communal values of decency and fair play but, according to another of its principal spokespersons, Hans Kelsen, "a specific social technique," "not a problem of morals."[16] Moreover, Kelsen insisted that for these reasons, neither was law concerned with a value-laden and "political" term like justice: "The tendency to identify law and justice is the tendency to justify a given social order. It is a political not a scientific tendency."[17]

This is not to say that law for the positivists is consciously inimical to cherished moral norms. Hart speaks of "justice in the administration of law ... something which prevents us from treating it as if morally it is utterly neutral, without any necessary contact with moral principles."[18] Oliver Wendell Holmes, America's foremost defender of the theory, spoke of "the secret root" of a judge's communal concern "from which the law draws all the juices of life" and of "the remoter and more general aspects of the law" that can connect "with the universe and catch

---

[12] Pound, *Introduction*, p. 25.

[13] Quoted in Frank S. Alexander, "Beyond Positivism: A Theological Perspective" in Witte and Alexander, *The Weightier Matters of the Law* (Atlanta: Scholars Press, 1988), p. 253.

[14] Dworkin, *Rights*, p. 17.

[15] Quoted in Hart, "Positivism," p. 596.

[16] Hans Kelsen, *General Theory of Law and the State*, trans. Anders Wedberg (New York: Russell & Russell, 1961), pp. xiv–xv, 5 [orig. pub. 1945].

[17] Ibid., p. 5.

[18] Hart, "Positivism," p. 624.

an echo of the infinite."[19] Yet Hart, in the same passage just quoted, dismisses any talk of justice in the law save for its procedural aspects, and Holmes was best known for assertions such as the following: "I should be glad if we could get rid of the whole moral phraseology which I think has tended to distort the law."[20] In its formal administration, then, morality was formally distinct from law, and if their union should take place, it was more a matter of coincidence than design.[21]

The fact that positivists, among many others, claim that law is fundamentally a "scientific" exercise in power and social control is probably shocking to no one. The interests of those who promulgate and enforce legal statutes ultimately taint even the natural law, which prides itself on incarnating the eternal truth into human social life. Jeffrey Stout states that a "transcendent thing-in-itself, even if we suppose it exists, wouldn't help until we described it in our terms—at which point we would no longer be appealing to a thing-in-itself but rather to ... beliefs, habits of description, and patterns of reasoning that belong to a cultural inheritance."[22] Similarly, Hauerwas stresses that the default value of law, including natural law, is still power. Constraint, threat, and punishment are necessary cognates of the legal process; and these stand in stark contrast to the message of Christ that truth never needs violence to reinforce the validity of its claims.[23] Oddly enough, in the end, the process of enforcement, if not explicit legal content, links positivists and legal traditionalists in a classic positivist formulation: however reprehensible it may seem, law is still law and must be obeyed.[24]

The links to purely penal law are quite striking. Recall that for Suarez, law, save those instances of it directly reflecting biblical teaching, was an exercise in the will of the sovereign for order and control, rather than an act whereby reason implements universal ethical principles. The political subject was bound in conscience to submit to the penalty if he or she should violate it, but the law itself was "amoral" and could be ignored if one's conscience was convinced that disobedience was licit. Holmes remarks that, like the yearly exercise in creative accounting employed by American taxpayers claiming exemptions and deductions from the Internal Revenue Service, citizens recognize law not as a moral consensus but as a "business" and always consider "how far they will run the risk of coming

---

19 Holmes, *Common Law*, p. 35; "Path of the Law," p. 478.

20 Quoted in Bayne, *Conscience*, p. 21.

21 Hart states: "It is in no sense a necessary truth that laws reproduce or satisfy certain demands of morality, though in fact they have often done so." Quoted in Alexander, "Beyond Positivism," p. 253.

22 Stout, *Ethics*, p. 23.

23 Stanley Hauerwas, *The Peaceable Kingdom* (Notre Dame: University of Notre Dame Press, 1983), pp. 15, 61.

24 Hart states that even if an individual could demonstrate that a legal requirement was morally wrong, "the demonstration of this would not show the rule not to be (or to be) law." See "Positivism," p. 626.

against what is so much stronger than themselves."[25] Lawrence Friedman argues that law is an "instrument" wielded "by people in power … to push or pull toward some definite goal."[26] Kelsen states that law, like every political ideology, "has its root in volition, not in cognition; in the emotional, not in the rational element of our consciousness; it arises from certain interests, or, rather, from interests other than the interest of truth."[27]

For the positivist, the "hard cases" that fall outside the province of existing legislation require decisions that in turn produce more legislation. The opinion of the judge in such a case "is written in language that seems to assume that one or the other party had a pre-existing right to win the suit, but that idea is only a fiction. In reality, he has created new legal rights, and then applied them retrospectively to the case at hand."[28] Recall that there are now, only in the federal courts, hundreds of thousands of laws in the United States for which a guilty party can be subject to criminal penalties.[29]

What is revelatory in this reference to *realpolitik*, voluntarism, and the natural affinity they have to legal positivism is not that people need better legal theories to embrace or react against, but that Christians in great numbers concur with so many of their basic assumptions. Law, for many Christians, is necessary to keep us from sliding into hell, yet, strangely enough, the game theory of law referred to in the reference to underhanded ways to avoid taxation, centers the moral conundrum not on the conformity of the action, say, to the life of Christ, but on "getting caught," and the personal loss that will ensue for the one who is so unfortunate. Here, Christian moral obligation, to the degree it is affirmed, is largely perceived as personal and distinct from one's economic and social conduct—the divide between fact and value. The conviction that the violence and self-interest of the world can only be transformed with the absolute truth of the cross has often ceded priority to a belief in the sacredness of law that has in turn reshaped the meaning and efficaciousness of the cross itself.

By beginning with the question of what the law is, legal positivism avoids the deeper and more important questions, certainly for Christians, of why law is needed in the first place and what purpose it serves.[30] A group of scholars, critical of the positivist shift, took up these questions and their insights are helpful for Christians seeking to refashion their understanding of law.

---

25 Holmes, "Path of the Law," p. 457.

26 Lawrence M. Friedman, *A History of American Law*, second edition (New York: Simon & Schuster, 1985), p. 29.

27 Kelsen, *General Theory*, p. xvi.

28 Dworkin, *Rights*, p. 81.

29 DeLong, "The New 'Criminal' Classes," in Healy, *Go Directly to Jail*, p. 9.

30 Alexander, "Beyond Positivism," p. 255.

Legal Realism

One of the founders of the school of legal realism in the twentieth century, Karl Llewellyn, insisted that the study of law should focus not on the creation of effective rules and procedures but on how it functions in practice. He also contended that ancient thinkers such as Aristotle, philosophers such as Machiavelli and Montesquieu, and more contemporary figures such as Max Weber, Louis Brandeis, and Felix Frankfurter all subscribed to the realist doctrine.[31]

Like the theological realist Reinhold Niebuhr, who insisted that reason is always to some degree "the servant of interest," and that despite the benign nature of the stated intentions of the ruling class, it always "arrogates an inordinate portion of social privilege to itself," Llewellyn understood the judicial process "as the imposition of the will of 'interested' parties."[32] He wrote that in an official or formal sense interest is independent of law, but, in pragmatic terms, the protection of interest "is the purpose of substantive legal rights, of legal rules, [and] of precepts of substantive law ... The rules and rights are not ends, but means. But they are means which in another aspect ... themselves become ends."[33]

Jerome Frank, a fellow realist and contemporary of Llewellyn, was less tactful in his estimation of the legal process. In fact, he believed that his colleague was, if anything, too optimistic in his contention that behind the "paper rules" there actually existed "real rules" that by rigorous analysis could be summoned to bring greater justice to legal proceedings.[34] Frank spoke of the "magical verbal devices" issued by judicial thinkers to conceal the fact "that one's rights to life, liberty or property are subject to ... crooked lawyers, crooked witnesses, mistaken witnesses, absence or death of witnesses, loss of documents, competence of lawyers, mistaken judges, biased judges, inattentive judges, stupid judges, crooked judges, inattentive juries [and] biased juries."[35]

A recent study on the perception of law by many in the public, as opposed to that of legal professionals, reveals some of the substance of the criticisms legal realists make of the courtroom experience. The book features the story of a poor victimized woman (Millie) who assumed, as was the case in her world, that a person like the judge would remember her and the letter she wrote describing her plight. She believed that relationships carried webs of meaning larger than rules. Her sad and fruitless experience prompted the following comment from the authors: "The rules, taxonomies, and operating procedures of the court flattened and froze time

---

31 Llewellyn, *Jurisprudence*, pp. v, 4–5.

32 Reinhold Niebuhr, *Moral Man and Immoral Society* (New York: Charles Scribner's Sons, 1932), pp. xiv–xv, 6–7; Llewellyn, *Jurisprudence*, p. 36.

33 Ibid., p. 14.

34 Frank called Llewellyn a "rule skeptic" and classified himself as a "fact skeptic." See Jerome Frank, *Courts on Trial* (Princeton: Princeton University Press, 1950), pp. 73–74; Llewellyn, *Jurisprudence*, p. 23.

35 Frank, *Courts on Trial*, p. 62.

into these separate occasions. The spatialized modes of knowledge abstracted the actors from continuing interactions and arranged them in static interpersonal roles, moments, and unconnected performances … The human interaction that Millie believed was to be embodied in the paper was instead preempted by it."[36]

Perhaps no one was more "realistic" and starkly pessimistic about the true function of law than Max Weber. The rule of law was, for him, the triumph of the most impregnable system of power in human history. Unlike patriarchal and charismatic forms of governance whose strength lies either in a time-honored display of authoritarian rule, or in the captivating personality of the prophet, the strength of the rule of law lies not in its outward show of force (although force is always in the shadows) but in its rationality.[37] Law gives the ruled the illusion that they have freely forged the chains that control aspects of their behavior and hides the architects of power safely behind the labyrinth of the economic and political bureaucracy.[38]

Thus, for Weber, a fully developed system of law is far more than rules or principles to govern human interaction but "the most rational known means of exercising authority over human beings."[39] By means of the impersonal and hierarchical nature of bureaucratic administration, and the technical expertise required for the legal professional (as indeed any advanced bureaucratic official), legal systems exercise "domination through knowledge."[40]

Just as Dworkin suggests that positivists use the expanding rules in modern legal systems retroactively to then justify the creation of those very rules, legal realists tend to assert that expanding statutory classifications disturb rather than clarify justice. To classify, in Llewellyn's mind, is "to build emphases, to create

---

36 Ewick and Sibley, *Common Place of Law*, p. 8. Similarly, Julia Davis, criticizing the impersonal metrics of establishing guilt and sentencing the culpable states: "The numbers imposed by the law are imposed by an act of will … It is order that is chosen, not discovered, and it is enforced by acts of power, not by the force of nature." Quoted in Katja Franko Aas, *Sentencing in the Age of Information* (London: Glasshouse Press, 2005), p. 25.

37 Weber, *Economy and Society*, p. 215.

38 Here is Weber's famous quote concerning the iron cage that best expresses his contention of the determinative power of the modern bureaucratic and legal state: "The Puritan wanted to work in a calling; we are forced to do so. For when asceticism was carried out of monastic cells into everyday life, and began to dominate worldly morality, it did its part in building the tremendous cosmos of the modern economic order. This order is now bound to the technical and economic conditions of machine production which to-day determine the lives of all the individuals who are born into this mechanism, not only those directly concerned with economic acquisition, with irresistible force. Perhaps it will do so until the last ton of fossilized coal is burnt. In Baxter's view the care for external goods should only lie on the shoulder of the 'saint like a light cloak, which can be thrown aside at any moment.' But fate decreed that the cloak should become an iron cage." See *Protestant Ethic*, p. 181.

39 Weber, *Economy and Society*, p. 223.

40 Ibid., p. 225.

stresses, which obscure some of the data under observation and give fictitious value to others."[41]

In this, the proponents of legal realism reproduce the skepticism of Oliver Wendell Holmes but turn it back upon him. Thinkers like Frank and Llewellyn were well aware of the sacred caste that law has assumed in the Christian West. But whereas the positivists were themselves the heirs of a Christian "moral" tradition, however seriously flawed for its own legalism, and proceeded to elevate juridical decrees to an independent and self-validating status by harvesting the moral fruit of that tradition, the realists consciously reconnected rules and principles. For behind the critique of the way a narrow ideology based on power and self-interest insinuates itself into the legislative process, they, save for Weber, sought to reestablish a legitimacy to law based on something other than law itself.

Llewellyn, writing of natural law, suggested it affords "a concrete guide to the making of proper positive law, and a concrete guide for the correction of positive law which has gotten itself badly and aberrantly made."[42] Frank was no less intent on unmasking the errors in the judicial process even as he pointed to something beyond it as a corrective for its abuses. Reviving the Thomist insistence that natural law is not positive law at all as much as the conditions necessary for the creation of anything worthy of the name, Frank states that it is useless to be content "with improving the legal rules." He desires the rejoining of what "is" and what "ought to be," for to separate "ethics from the judicial process is to pervert the latter."[43]

The legal realists aid in the task of exposing the sinister features of legalism in general and the moral agnosticism of legal positivism in particular. Their pessimistic appraisals remind us that law, as Weber and Frank contend, has taken on a phantom moral aura in which it is displayed as "fairly reliable, definite, and uniform," the perfect illusion for use by "legal magicians."[44] At their most sanguine, however, their appreciative references to medieval natural law ought to remind Christians not of how good law used to be before it consciously parted company with the ethic of Jesus, but of the way their own tradition erred in seeking to make morality dependent on law rather than the life and teachings of Christ.

Narrative Theories of Law

In recent years, an approach to law with fertile connections to some of the principal emphases of this book has arisen. Some legal scholars have allied themselves with the realist critique of the sterile, analytical format we have come to know in which an impregnable line is fashioned between law and lawbreaker. At the same time, they provide a context to explain illegality in a way that resists the impulse to judge

---

41 Dworkin, *Rights*, p. 81; Llewellyn, *Jurisprudence*, p. 27.

42 Llewellyn, *Jurisprudence*, p. 113.

43 Frank, *Courts on Trial*, pp. 362–72, esp. 371.

44 Ibid., p. 66.

if it is not accompanied by understanding and compassion. Legal positivism, in the words of some of these critics, has fashioned a system more and more impervious to moral challenge precisely because its very tenets are based not on stated moral commitments but on the will of lawmakers.[45]

For Robert Cover, communal standards of conduct that are embodied in legal provisions proceed from a community's tradition, its "epic" story of origin, and the "scriptures" or hallowed texts that proclaim its world-defining meaning.[46] Law in this framework is not self-validating but must continually derive its sustenance and applicability from a reflection upon the foundational narrative and the ways in which that narrative extends its trajectories in the imagination.[47]

Additionally, he recognizes that this relation between tradition, imagination, and ethical standards of conduct is in many ways unique to each community. People, as character ethicists remind us, perceive the world and come to understand its varied representations through the adjective that precedes the word, "ethics."[48] Some of the communities to which they render allegiance are "small and private, others immense and public," but it is these commitments that determine "what law means and what law shall be."[49]

Some of the philosophers who advocate punishment as communication echo in significant ways the sentiments just shared. Nils Christie argues that crime should be the starting point "for a real dialogue, and not an equally clumsy answer in the form of a spoonful of pain."[50] R.A. Duff states that punishment as an expression of social disapproval, however meticulously crafted in legal practice and parlance, is an empty exercise if the one punished does not understand why he or she has to suffer.[51] He suggests, in line with ancient Christian practice, that the punitive experience cannot be meaningful unless it is persuasive, unless the offender comes to see within the context of his or her own narrative that there is value in the penance imposed, so much so that they will come to accept it and will it for themselves.[52]

The legalism that evaluates all conduct solely in terms of conformity to its statutes fails not only to appreciate the inherent relation between narrative and character; it also judges as malevolent those who fail to adhere to its behavioral standards and justifies the insensitivity and violence that so often underlie the

---

45 Alexander, "Beyond Positivism," p. 278.

46 Cover, "Nomos," pp. 4–5.

47 Ibid., p. 5.

48 Hauerwas, *Peaceable Kingdom*, p. 1.

49 Cover, "Nomos," p. 7.

50 Quoted in John Braithwaite and Philip Petit, *Not Just Deserts* (Oxford: Clarendon Press, 1990), p. 1.

51 R.A. Duff, "Penal Communications: Recent Work in the Philosophy of Punishment," in Michael Tonry (ed.) *Crime and Justice* 20 (Chicago: University of Chicago Press, 1996), p. 33.

52 Ibid., p. 53. See also Braithwaite and Petit, *Just Deserts*, p. viii.

imposition of a punitive sentence. Even the benign intentions of judges, where they can still function with some discretionary power, are shadowed by the violence that is inherent in legal judgment: "For as the judge interprets, using the concept of punishment, she also acts—through others—to restrain, hurt, render helpless, even kill the prisoner ... Similarly, whether or not the judge and prisoner share the same philosophy of punishment, they arrive at the particular act of punishment having dominated and having been dominated with violence, respectively."[53] This implicit and explicit connection between law and indifference, if not hostility, to the culpable is noted by Grant Gilmore: "In Hell there will be nothing but law, and due process will be meticulously observed."[54]

Members of what is termed the New Haven School have been sharply critical of legal positivism generally and the Chicago School in particular; the latter made famous by free-market enthusiasts such as Milton Friedman and Richard Posner, whose strictly utilitarian approach to law and especially its relation to *laissez faire* economic principles accepts without reservation the current distribution of wealth and promotes government restraint upon any intervention into the economy save to insure efficient transactions.[55] This latter philosophy, owing much to positivist assumptions, is countered with the claim that "market failure is a pervasive phenomenon," that the current distribution of wealth is a cause of serious moral concern, and that law and public policy cannot be subservient to market transactions.[56]

Similarly, N.E. Simmonds reflects on the fact that while most citizens are content with the understanding that law is mainly local custom, a deeper reservoir of meaning must be plumbed to make morally coherent and satisfying the imposition of suffering and death on those who disobey the law.[57] In this, he and other contemporary legal theorists hint at the fact that the partition of facts and values, reflecting the dualism that has so marred the integrity of Christian ethics, must give way to at least a serious conversation concerning the nature of law itself and the many ways that it not only masks prejudice and violence but also fractures a Christian approach based upon the ontological unity of all in Christ.

The realism, the punitive restraint, the call for a renewed conversation about the relation between law and sources of revealed wisdom that characterize the thought of many of the theorists referred to in this section are, despite their importance in

---

53 Cover, "Violence," p. 1609.

54 Grant Gilmore, *The Ages of American Law* (New Haven: Yale University Press, 1977), p. 111.

55 George E. Garvey, "A Catholic Social Teaching Critique of Law and Economics," in Michael McConnell, Robert F. Cochran, Jr. and Angela C. Carmela, *Christian Perspectives on Legal Thought* (New Haven: Yale University Press, 2001), p. 229.

56 Ibid.

57 N.E. Simmonds, *Law as a Moral Idea* (Oxford: Oxford University Press, 2007), p. 14.

aiding Christians to rethink the purpose and validity of law and judgment, still the opinion of a minority both in the legal community and in the population at large.

In America and other nations of the world, the social turmoil that began in the 1960s, accompanied by a withering of the reliance by many on formerly cherished institutions, among them the church, has resulted in a legal explosion driven by fear of and hostility to social misfits on one hand, and a reliance on the courts to intervene on behalf of personal interests on the other. Milton Friedman noted that the weakening of social cohesion in the later decades of the twentieth century produced on the part of the public at large an expectation of retributive justice and a "general expectation of recompense" for wrongs endured.[58] Warren Burger, writing in 1982 as Chief Justice of the United States Supreme Court, observed and lamented this vast expansion of law into the void created by the decline of allegiance to family, church, and neighborhood: "Remedies for personal wrongs that once were considered the responsibility of institutions other than the courts are now boldly asserted as legal entitlements."[59]

There is still a deep divide among Christians between those who affirm law as an exercise of power, control, and punishment, and those who call those characteristics, as well as the role of law itself, into question.[60] In one sense, then, legal positivism is still the coin of the juridical realm, but for the Christian those deeper and unanswered questions often linger in the background. Christians are a people whose "epic" story, and the lives of many of its most cherished prophets and saints, among them Christ himself, are written in a grammar suffused with illegality, imprisonment, torture, and death—all justified by established legal procedure. For Christians, therefore, the sources of wisdom reveal that those who fail to abide by the law are at least as morally praiseworthy as those who render judgments and enforce violent penalties when the codified norms are not obeyed.

There is as yet no indication that a consensus concerning the meaning of law can be reached, and certainly not one based upon what Berman calls "reasoned compassion."[61] In either case, that is not the intent of this brief summary of contemporary legal theory. What I have hoped to show is that a substantial number of the finest legal minds have realized that something very serious takes place both morally and spiritually in the specialized mechanics of the criminal court. In their opinion, law is neither neutral nor objective, and it is inseparable from the exercise of power and the infliction of pain. Christians must at least reconsider this reality, one that Dworkin understands very well: "Day in and day out we send people to jail, or take money away from them, or make them do things they do not want to do, under coercion of force, and we justify all of this by speaking of such persons as having broken the law … Even in clear cases … we are not able

---

58 Kermit L. Hall, *The Magic Mirror: Law in American History* (New York: Oxford University Press, 1989), p. 308.

59 Ibid.

60 Cover, "Nomos," p. 18.

61 Berman, *Law and Revolution II*, pp. 129–30.

to give a satisfactory account of what that means, or why that entitles the state to punish or coerce."[62]

This ambiguity needs to be addressed by Christians because what is at stake is not simply a proper understanding of law and judgment or the "correct" interpretation of the Christian ethic, but the lives of countless men and women being crushed beneath the weight of a legal and criminal justice system implicitly, if not explicitly, sanctioned by their consent.

Criminal Justice

We have already spoken at some length in the Introduction on contemporary criminal justice practice. The intent in this short synopsis is to orchestrate the widespread confusion about meaning that shadows much of what transpires in the prisons and jails both in America and abroad. This confusion is particularly pertinent to our study as the early Christian practices of penance and prayer, combined with a vivid image of Christ and many of the saints as prisoners, led to the inauguration of confinement as a penitential journey, not an act of punitive judgment, and the inauguration of a methodology of transformation and reintegration whose structural shell strangely persists amidst the aimlessness and despair of the contemporary prison.[63]

Studies reveal that while many citizens continue to hope that incarceration will improve the character and conduct of offenders, the vast majority believe (despite statistical evidence to the contrary) that the criminal threat to society is increasing, and desire that lawbreakers be incapacitated and punished in the hopes of deterring future criminal acts.[64]

Meanwhile, many of those whose task it is to chart the course of and implement criminal justice policy reveal a lack of confidence in the validity, let alone the morality, of the entire edifice of penal confinement. It is rife with economic

---

62 Dworkin, *Rights*, p. 15.

63 See the discussion in Chapter 3 as well as some of my own work on the Christian roots of the modern penal system. Skotnicki, *Criminal Justice and the Catholic Church*; "Foundations"; "God's Prisoners."

64 On the plurality of ends that the public desires from its criminal justice system, see "Changing Public Attitudes Toward the Criminal Justice System" (Open Society Institute, 2002) available at http://www.soros.org. In 2009, 74 percent of Americans believed that there was more crime in the U.S. than in the previous year. See *Sourcebook of Criminal Justice Statistics Online*, http://www.albany.edu/sourcebook/pdf/t2332009. Meanwhile, the FBI reports: "Preliminary figures indicate that, as a whole, law enforcement agencies throughout the Nation reported a decrease of 5.5 percent in the number of violent crimes brought to their attention for 2009 when compared with figures reported for 2008." See http://www.fbi.gov/ucr/prelimsem2009/index.html. Franklin Zimring states that fear of violent crime more than the prevalence of violent crime has motivated the enormous expansion of the penal system. See *Crime is not the Problem* (New York: Oxford University Press, 1997), p. xi.

adventurism, widespread violence and human degradation, class and racial disparities, and a growing sense of pessimism that recalcitrant human behavior can be satisfactorily corralled given the assumptions concerning law, human nature, and punishment currently in vogue.

As has been noted in the preceding pages, one of the reasons that a positivist approach has achieved such a pronounced legitimacy among legal professionals and scholars is its claim that law need not involve itself in questions of "value." Recalling Hans Kelsen, many are convinced that if law is promulgated it has validity; if it is obeyed, it has efficacy; and if it is disobeyed, it warrants punishment.[65]

In step with the thin moral, not to mention Christian, foundations of the current structure, David Garland comments that repeated evidence "of unrestrained state authority, of arbitrary power and the violation of civil liberties no longer figure so prominently in public concern."[66] In similar fashion, Jonathan Simon discusses how public attitudes favoring personal responsibility and will in criminal cases over social and structural impediments have enabled political authorities to imprison vast numbers of economically distressed citizens rather than be forced to address the need for "fundamental changes in the status quo of wealth and power."[67]

It was noted in the Introduction that the architects of criminal justice policy, reflecting the unequal distribution of wealth and social leverage so prevalent in contemporary society, have turned the penal system into a "kind of reservation, a quarantine zone in which purportedly dangerous individuals are segregated in the name of public safety." This has been carried out with exquisite efficiency in the U.S., where over two million people are housed in a system "resembling nothing so much as the Soviet Gulag," most of whom "are drawn from classes and racial groups that have become politically and economically problematic."[68]

Perhaps even more poignantly, like Foucault before him, Garland suggests that the efficient, bureaucratic, and bloodless technique of legal and punitive institutions exists as a negative image of a public seething with rage and hungering for violent retribution against those perceived as threatening: "Considered in formal terms, today's death penalty is a mirror image of a public torture lynching—an inverse image, a disavowal, calculated to resist any such accusation. But substantively, many of the same social forces that previously prompted lynchings nowadays

---

65 Kelsen, *General Theory*, pp. 29–30.

66 Garland, *Culture of Control*, p. 12.

67 Jonathan Simon, *Governing Through Crime: How the War on Crime Transformed American Democracy and Created a Culture of Fear* (New York: Oxford University Press, 2007), pp. 25–26.

68 Garland, *Culture of Control*, p. 178.

prompt capital punishment ... much the same public structures that permitted lynchings then, enable capital punishment now."[69]

Garland is but one of many contemporary scholars who have held up the mirror of violence and racism before society and its justice system. The sheer number of impassioned exposés exploring inequality and mistreatment in the field of criminal justice suggests that many accounts are written in the hope that the public and its officials will see the reflection of their own narrowness, fear, and violence in the way the convicted are treated.[70] Numerous scholars and advocates also offer hopes of different strategies for the supervision of communities; for intervention in the lives of those prone to arrest; for diversion programs into vocational, educational, and recovery programs instead of incarceration; for similar opportunities and safeguards extended to the hundreds of thousands leaving custody each year; and for the implementation of restorative as opposed to adversarial justice.[71]

One of the reasons for the continued resonance of the legal and punitive philosophy now in place lies in the baffling multiplicity of theoretical templates that have been proposed to direct the recurring questions of why we punish, whom we punish, and how much punishment they deserve.

Michael Tonry has for years edited the annual volume describing research in the discipline of criminal justice and provides vivid evidence of this organizational disharmony that stymies attempts to address successfully a host of troubling tensions. He notes that utilitarian theory (indeterminate sentences, parole) held sway for much of the twentieth century, followed by the ascent of retributive theory (objectivity in sentencing) in the 1970s. This punitive turn was quickly augmented in the last decades of the century with emphases on deterrence (mandatory minimum sentences, truth in sentencing laws), and incapacitation (three strikes laws, sex offender registry). Tonry states that what we now have is nothing more than a "muddle" of approaches in which scattered attempts at rehabilitation, community-based corrections, and restorative justice have been joined to all of

---

[69] David Garland, "The Peculiar Forms of American Capital Punishment," *Social Research* 74 (2007), p. 457. See also, Foucault, *Discipline and Punish*, pp. 10–12.

[70] Noted Australian criminologist and restorative justice advocate John Braithwaite and his colleague write: "A society which feels morally comfortable about sending thousands of terrified young men and women to institutions in which they are bashed, raped, and brutalized, stripped of human dignity, denied freedom and speech and movement, has a doubtful commitment to freedom." Braithwaite and Petit, *Just Deserts*, p. 6.

[71] On community policing and intervention, see Todd Clear and Harry Dammer, *The Offender in the Community* (Belmont, CA: Wadsworth, 2000). On diversion programs, see Philip Fennell (ed.), *Criminal Justice in Europe: A Comparative Study* (Oxford: Clarendon, 1995); Franklin E. Zimring, *American Juvenile Justice* (New York: Oxford University Press, 2005). On released offenders, see Joan Petersilia, *When Prisoners Come Home* (New York: Oxford University Press, 2003). On Restorative Justice, see Braithwaite, *Crime, Shame and Reintegration*; *Restorative Justice and Responsive Regulation* (Oxford: Oxford University Press, 2002); Jane Dickson-Gilmore and Carol LaPrairie, *Will the Circle be Unbroken?* (Toronto: University of Toronto Press, 2005).

the above.[72] It is not hard to see that in such a cacophony of competing voices what is left in place when the last speaker has finished is the approach to law and judgment currently in operation. Cover refers to the above as "jurispathology" in which judges confronting "the luxuriant growth of a hundred legal traditions … assert that this *one* is law and destroy or try to destroy the rest."[73]

From a somewhat different perspective, some suggest that the practical result of the fact/value distinction in democratic societies is that the status quo comes to be acknowledged as reflecting the precise way things ought to be. De Tocqueville spoke glowingly of the democratic and egalitarian influences in the American public, and at the same time of the projection of their aristocratic and authoritarian shadow upon the legal system, particularly the class bias evident in the treatment of the suspected delinquent. He states that even in a civil case, the poor person cannot meet the bail assigned to keep him from detention "and if he is obliged to wait for justice in prison, he is speedily reduced to distress. A wealthy person, on the contrary always escapes imprisonment in civil cases; nay, more, if he has committed a crime … Nothing can be more aristocratic than this system of legislation."[74] Brague writes that in compensation for the prevalent separation of law and morality, modern societies exert "a pressure on themselves that tends to identify what is with what should be. That gentle pressure may turn out in fact to be more tyrannical than ever."[75]

However one views the merits or demerits of the various theoretical strategies just mentioned, each to varying degrees begs the deeper concerns posed in this book. Those concerns, as seen in the observation about the punitive orientation of the public at large, involve the perception among average citizens, many Christians among them, that law and judgment by their very natures are meant to divide rather than unite, and to punish rather than forgive. Christians have by and large forgotten that it is a formidable moral decision to judge, let alone condemn another: "[W]e have lost the old conviction that judging and punishing are morally fearsome acts. We have a far weaker sense than our ancestors that we should doubt our own moral authority when judging other human beings."[76]

---

[72] Michael Tonry, "Purposes and Functions of Sentencing," in Michael Tonry (ed.), *Crime and Justice: A Review of Research* 34 (Chicago: University of Chicago Press, 2006), pp. 1–2.

[73] Cover, "Nomos," p. 53.

[74] Alexis de Tocqueville, *Democracy in America* (New York: Alfred A. Knopf, 1945), I, II.

[75] Brague, *Law*, p. 239.

[76] Whitman, *Origins*, pp. 211–12.

Chapter 7
How Should Christians Think About Law and Judgment?

As religious traditions are passed down from one generation to the next, inevitable changes occur both in those who hear the narrative as it is interpreted to them and in the narrative itself. The story of Christ is very much a case in point. Each generation of Christians learns and then retells the story of Jesus and what his teachings reveal about how they should live. What is critical to the process, according to Gadamer, is a realization of the inevitable "prejudices" that accompany the hearing and interpreting of the message. Prejudice in this sense is not a pejorative term but an exercise in the sociology of knowledge.[1]

Where a problem *does* occur is in the contention that one can communicate *without* prejudice. In other words, the difficulty is not that perception is shaped by language and culture, nor that we see the world through the lens of self or group interest; it is the belief, made all the more plausible since the Age of Reason, that it is possible to observe history, and in the present case the gospel, with an objectivity shorn of distortion, by no other means than the proper use of reason itself.[2] Gadamer states that this "false power" granted to reflection, especially in the dichotomy it creates between authority and the thinking subject, is based upon a "fallacious idealism" and is "a mistake fraught with ominous consequences."[3]

Eric Wolf shares much of this concern in his analysis of intellectual currents in the Christian West that have done so much to create "people without history." Beginning with the empirical assumption that simple observation reveals the interconnectedness of life in all of its forms, he wonders aloud about the "education" garnered from a strict taxonomy of knowledge into academic

---

[1] Hans-Georg Gadamer, *Philosophical Hermeneutics*, trans. David E. Linge (Berkeley: University of California Press, 1976), pp. 8–9. See also, Clifford Geertz, "Ideology as a Cultural System," in *The Interpretation of Cultures* (New York: Basic Books, 1973), pp. 194–233.

[2] "In this objectivism the understander is seen—even in the so-called sciences of understanding like history—not in relationship to the hermeneutical situation and the constant operativeness of history in his own consciousness, but in such a way as to imply that his own understanding does not enter into the event." Gadamer, *Hermeneutics*, p. 28.

[3] Ibid., p. 33.

disciplines and the overarching dualism of the Western mind that has transformed "dynamic interconnected phenomena into static, disconnected things."[4]

The preceding chapters of this book have sought to account for the ways in which Christians, in effect, have become people without history. The descendents of those who ardently believed with St Paul that Christ is "the end of the law" (Rom 10: 4) have come in large numbers to make compliance with law, either ecclesiastical or civil, the measure of moral and spiritual worth, and, in equally great numbers, to make it the hand bearing the weapon of justifiable retribution upon those who have violated its provisions.

It has been maintained that the desire for order and control that made legal infractions offenses in their own right, independent of obligations of love for God and neighbor, was a principal factor in this change—initially in the church, and soon thereafter in the state. In the process, the immanence of God in creation, the oneness of all in Christ (Col 1: 16), largely gave way to a divided world and a divided soul in which belief governed the metaphysical realm, while power—the external power of the state and the internal power of the rights-bearing citizen—governed life in the world. Ours became a world of law: law in service to the security and economic interest of society, and law in service to the interests of the individual. As a result, Christ, now no longer perceived as a threat to legalism and to all dualist formulations that would divide the innocent and guilty, became the defender of the political regime, of private gain, of retributive punishment for lawbreakers, and, for many Christians, a lawgiver as formidable as Hammurabi, Solon, Justinian, or, for that matter, Moses.

This final chapter will first discuss several contemporary Christian approaches to the questions that have been raised in this book concerning law, judgment, and punishment. It will conclude with an attempt to summarize two interrelated contentions that, in this author's opinion, are essential to Christian ethics: a non-judgmental, indiscriminately compassionate, and legally minimalist stance that accompanies and indeed derives from a contemplative spirituality.

Law and Judgment in Contemporary Christian Ethics

One of the ways to frame the questions for Christians concerning the legitimacy of law, judgment, and punishment is epistemological: what constitutes knowledge? It has been suggested here that Christian history has provided a continuum, one side of which mirrors the knowledge derived from an unconditional acceptance, the other from a reasoned and objective distance.

The methods used to fashion an ethic for Christians often fall into the latter camp. Some proponents of natural law, despite their substantial disagreement with the modern understanding of both the human person and the state, share

---

[4] Eric R. Wolf, *Europe and the People Without History* (Berkeley: University of California Press, 1982), pp. 4–5, 7.

with the mindset established during the Enlightenment a belief not only that law and judgment are morally necessary and conceptually defensible in themselves, but also that a reasonable jurist can render an interpretation of human behavior, acceptable in Christian terms, "at a distance" from the one being judged. John Finnis, for example, a leading voice among contemporary natural law theorists, understandably rejects a positivist approach that would render law "a vast rubbish heap of miscellaneous facts described in a multitude of incommensurable terminologies."[5] On the other hand, Finnis proceeds from the Thomist insistence that law, if properly promulgated, must be obligatory since it shares in the perfection of divine reasoning. As such, he "presumptively" equates a moral obligation "if not a compelling demand of justice" to legal enactments representing "a disciplined acquisition of accurate knowledge about human affairs."[6] Such "knowledge" comes to "the reflective and critical theorist in his effort to convert his own … practical prejudices into reasonably true judgments about what is good and practically reasonable."[7]

The difference between the above approach and the objective formulae for judicial sentencing currently in vogue in many nations is more one of technique than basic moral premises. Both believe that punishment is a rational process governed by rules. The format for the current distribution of punitive sentences varies mainly in its computer-driven procedural guidelines "for achieving mathematical certainty, consistency, and clarity of thought."[8]

Other thinkers similarly favor a rational defense of punishment based upon a view of justice whose very substance would be tarnished if mitigated by too much compassion. Albert Alschuler, for example, stresses the supererogatory nature of mercy: it surpasses by definition the demands of justice that a balance be maintained between what we give and what we get. While acts of mercy are laudatory, and could conceivably be instituted as law in cases where the victims of crime petition the court to lessen or even dismiss punishment in certain instances, in objective terms they violate the "giving-receiving ratio."[9] The failure to punish persons who willingly reject the social responsibility implied in lawful conduct is "improper" and "makes selfish action more likely."[10]

The idea of punishment restoring a divinely ordained balance upset by sinful behavior is, of course, very old. It was invoked by thinkers such as Anselm and Aquinas, among others, and is still in evidence in natural law thinkers such as

5 John Finnis, *Natural Law and Natural Rights* (Oxford: Clarendon Press, 1980), pp. 16–17.

6 Ibid., pp. 14–15, 16–17.

7 Ibid., pp. 16–17.

8 Aas, *Sentencing*, p. 71.

9 Albert W. Alschuler, "A Plea for Mercy," in Rothchild et al., *Doing Justice to Mercy*, pp. 94–95.

10 Ibid., p. 94. This is reminiscent of St Anselm who stated that were God not to punish, divine justice itself would be called into question. *Why God*, I, 12.

Finnis, Fuchs, and Porter, who argue, in Christian terms, for the legitimate use of coercive action by the state.[11]

John Stackhouse and Oliver O'Donovan are among those who offer what might be termed a realist account of law, judgment, and punishment, affirming the tension between the "now and not yet" quality of the reign of God.

Stackhouse, invoking the thought of C.S. Lewis, Reinhold Niebuhr, and Dietrich Bonhoeffer, and allying himself with the "Christ and Culture in Paradox" model of H. Richard Niebuhr, believes that Christian ethics has too much to offer the world to remain as aloof as "sectarians" like Hauerwas and John Howard Yoder recommend. On the other hand, graced by the presence of Christ and the Holy Spirit, the church is motivated by a vision of the Reign of God too universal to embrace the easy accommodation, current among many evangelicals, between Christian moral commitments and nationalist politics.[12] The paradox, as presented by Stackhouse, affirms a dualism between the world and God, who at times resembles the impartial spectator of Adam Smith: "Amid this swirl, Christianity affirms faith in God as the one who sits in the heavens and who enjoys the perfect vantage point from which to tell us what we need to know."[13] At the same time, a similar dualism is affirmed within the individual who, with the proper resources of the tradition, can think his or her way into a proper Christian response: "The Christian, then, thinks as carefully as she can, according to the standards of her culture—in trust that, under the providence of God, such thinking will be adequate to fulfilling her vocation."[14]

In terms of law and punitive judgment, Stackhouse, echoing the position of Paul Ramsey and, ultimately, Martin Luther, contends that Christians should support the legitimate use of coercion for legal infractions, in accord with a belief that such force is legitimated by God, but also minimize violence in accord with the compassion of Christ: "[S]ociety needs to be protected by violence—legal, authorized, monitored, and minimal violence, but violence nonetheless … Whether it's called coercion or legitimate and proportionate violence, somebody

---

[11] Anselm states: "Hence it is absolutely wrong and even impossible for man to receive from God what God intended to give him, if he does not render back to God all that he took from him; so that as God has lost it through him, so He was to regain it through him." *Why God*, I, 23. Finnis claims that punishment "seeks to restore the distributively just balance of advantages between crime and law-abiding, so that, over the span of time which extends from before the crime until after the punishment, no one should actually have been disadvantaged … by choosing to remain within the confines of the law." See *Natural Law*, p. 263. See also Josef Fuchs, *Natural Law* (New York: Sheed & Ward, 1965) Pt. II, ch. 5; Jean Porter, *The Recovery of Virtue* (Louisville: Westminster/John Knox, 1990), pp. 31–32, 128–31; *Natural and Divine Law* (Grand Rapids: Eerdmans, 1999), p. 286.

[12] John G. Stackhouse, *Making the Best of It* (New York: Oxford University Press, 2008), p. 6.

[13] Ibid., p. 168.

[14] Ibid., p. 172.

has to exercise it in the divinely instituted capacity of government. Why would God's people not play a part in such a system?"[15]

In somewhat similar but more nuanced terms, O'Donovan contends that a principal function of secular governments, the true sign of their authority, is the judgment entailed in rendering acts of moral discrimination.[16] This duty traces itself directly to the command of God that Israel institute judges to resolve conflictual communal issues and the teaching of St Paul that civil authority is empowered "to reward the just and punish the evil" (Rom 13: 4).[17]

Despite these assurances of the moral and religious legitimacy of judgment, O'Donovan states that in Christ a set of "new terms" for the understanding of politics and political authority are presented that are based in salvation history."[18] Against this infinite horizon, he claims that to assume "the role of the judge is to leave the position of evangelical strength and to enter the sphere of human weakness and political shame."[19]

Reminiscent of Christian realists like Reinhold Niebuhr, O'Donovan honors the tension between an immanent Christian responsibility for justice in the world ("The self-judging Christian is, of course, good for society and its organs of judgment") and the transcendent self-sacrificial love of Christ, acknowledging that one must judge but do so with a concomitant sense of humility and care: "Our judgment is never more truthful in its correspondence to God's judgment than when it acknowledges its own severely limited capacity for truth."[20] Furthermore, in the light of God's final judgment, and the realization that its formulations are merely "interim," society, like the individual Christian, is free "not to judge."[21]

In the choice between the teachings of Christ and those of the Mosaic code and the contested verse of St Paul in Romans 13, O'Donovan reveals the notion that Christians can, in their public persona, sanction state intervention into the lives of the unlawful and the punishment of those who are guilty but, on a private level, suspend judgment or not "perpetuate the act of judgment": "So although private vengeance has to be condemned, the desire for vengeance must be allowed its proper point of entry into the public realm, where it both commands and legitimates political authority."[22] In another passage, he writes: "Wrong and

[15] Ibid., p. 282. Luther, "Secular Authority," in *Martin Luther: Selections from His Writings*, VI; Paul Ramsey, *The Just War* (New York: Scribner, 1968).

[16] O'Donovan, *Judgment*, p. 7.

[17] Ibid., pp. 3–4.

[18] Ibid., p. 5.

[19] Ibid., p. 86.

[20] Ibid., pp. 312, 22. Reinhold Niebuhr, *An Interpretation of Christian Ethics* (San Francisco: Harper & Row, 1963), chapters 5, 6.

[21] O'Donovan, *Judgment*, p. 238.

[22] Ibid., p. 25.

nothing else, is the necessary condition, but also the sufficient condition, for governmental intervention."[23]

In a striking observation, O'Donovan writes that the desire for punitive judgment that inevitably arises has been answered in the life of Christ and, therefore, given Christian freedom, we must "judge for ourselves" in light of his revelation.[24] Ideally, he, like Stackhouse, hopes that judgment will be governed by attentive communication, free of abuse and manipulation, and a sense of "ours" rather than "mine," but the "ours" seems to be undermined continually by the premises established not only concerning the biblical warrant to punish but also in the legitimacy given to the legal and punitive determination of "right" and "wrong."[25]

Some of the concerns shared by O'Donovan concerning the creation of a communicative "we" in the context of judgment can be found among Christian thinkers in the area of restorative justice. As noted in the last chapter, restorative justice seeks to transform the adversarial method of the judicial adjudication of wrongs by focusing on vitally important notions, especially for the Christian, of penance, restitution, and reconciliation.[26] Its leading voice in the United States, Howard Zehr, summarizes its governing emphases in stating that crime is, above all, an act of harm done to others and to human relationships (thus not primarily a legal violation); it summons a set of obligations on the part of offenders to seek to remedy the wrong that has been done; and it proposes that through respectful dialogue the "stakeholders" in the offense can arrive at a mutually agreeable settlement of the infraction and, ideally, a reconciliation of offender and victim.[27]

In their admirable desire to address some of the glaring errors in contemporary criminal justice, not the least of which being its punitive emphasis—based in large part on a perceived polarity between those on each side of legal compliance—restorative advocates tend to reproduce that polarity in the acceptance of law as

---

23 Ibid., p. 62. Jeffrie Murphy holds a similar view that punishment is fitting from a Christian perspective so long as "vindictive passion" has been quelled. See "Christian Love and Criminal Punishment," in Witte and Alexander, *Christianity and the Law*, p. 229.

24 O'Donovan, *Judgment*, p. 238.

25 Ibid., pp. 243–49. The author states: "The art of penal development is the multiplication of a carefully differentiated range of intermediate assaults. Yet its horizon is the ultimate possibility of death itself" (p. 123).

26 See the discussion on the origins of penance in Chapter 3. John Braithwaite, perhaps the most respected advocate of the approach, notes that with the inauguration of private confession in the sixth century, the church institutionalized the practice of restorative justice. See *Restorative Justice*, p. 5. Christopher Marshall argues, much in line with the argument made in Chapter 3, that for punishment to have value, it must not be imposed but experienced in the offender's own recognition of the moral and spiritual harm done by the abuse of others. See *Beyond Retribution* (Grand Rapids, MI: Eerdmans, 2001), pp. 131–40.

27 Howard Zehr, *The Little Book of Restorative Justice* (Intercourse, PA: Good Books, 2002), p. 12–13.

an independent variable in the quest for a just resolution to criminal offenses. The nature of law itself for the Christian often escapes critical scrutiny.

In fairness, this oversight may be due to the desire to reform the system on behalf of the endless men and women who languish in jails and prisons, whose stories are virtually unheard, whose probable desire for reconciliation is systematically denied, and whose punishment lasts long after their release from custody. These laudable concerns, however, typically trade in the currency of what ethicists such as John Howard Yoder and Stanley Hauerwas call apologetics or "Constantinianism." The latter features the attempt by Christians to find a language for the gospel acceptable to the ears of the powerful and of their fellow citizens: "Apologetics is based on the political assumption that Christians somehow have a stake in transforming our ecclesial claims into intellectual assumptions that will enable us to be faithful to Christ while still participating in the political structures of a world that does not yet know Christ."[28]

My own concerns are not that there is something wrong with the desire to make things better for those enmeshed in the nets of the justice system, and less with the goals of restorative justice to achieve reconciliation between victims and their assailants. They lie with the fact that the attempts of Christians to reform the practices associated with criminal offenders involve the acceptance of punishment for legal infractions as morally necessary; and an inevitable result of this concession is the loss of those essential Christian commitments of unconditional love and forgiveness that will never be comprehensible from a state of mind in which law functions on a plane independent of the gospel.

Thus, Zehr can claim that restorative justice "is not primarily about forgiveness or reconciliation" as much as instituting a model "to rethink the needs which crimes create."[29] Christopher Marshall, basing his treatise on biblical teaching, places greater emphasis than Zehr upon forgiveness and reconciliation, but still contends, using scriptural exegesis, that "society is duty-bound to react against evil, to repudiate it in principle by social censure and condemnation and to seek its annulment or negation lest it spread like a disease."[30] Marshall also states: "Legal justice—the promulgation of laws and the prosecution and punishment of lawbreaking—operates largely at an impersonal level, as part of the social contract that binds society together." Despite the need for a more personalist approach to the resolution of criminal conflicts, he maintains that there is "much to be said for the legal system operating on an impersonal basis, not the least being its capacity to defend the innocent, control revenge, and prevent excessive punishment through carefully regulated judicial procedures."[31]

---

28 Stanley Hauerwas and William Willimon, *Resident Aliens*, p. 22. In similar fashion, Constantinianism "leads Christians to judge their ethical positions on the basis of how much Christian ethics Caesar can be induced to swallow without choking." Ibid., p. 72.

29 Zehr, *Restorative Justice*, pp. 8, 13.

30 Marshall, *Beyond Retribution*, p. 136.

31 Ibid., p. 271.

James Samuel Logan, although motivated by a commitment to "ontological intimacy," consistent with how I believe Christians are to see God's creation, recommends that the needs of the state and its legal system, not the teachings of Christ, be employed in dealing with "society's most violent and unrepentant felons." He states: "restorative justice is not a panacea. It is not necessarily a replacement for the legal system, nor is it necessarily an alternative to prison ... [It] takes justice seriously as it inches society in the direction of ontological intimacy."[32]

My own approach shares some of the concerns of the writers mentioned above, especially in the earnest and praiseworthy attempts to humanize criminal justice at the judicial level and bring about a communicative exchange, particularly between offenders and victims. The motivation, however, is not dictated by law, still less by agreement with the infliction of pain, but by the fact that the inclusive and unconditional love of Christ translates into defense of those being mistreated and love for those who mistreat them. For Christians, the neighbor is the next person in their field of vision. Responsibility to and love for him or her is not a law but a direct consequence of the fact that when I am seeing rightly, I am seeing the face of God in the wounded and those who wound them.[33]

The Christian ethic begins with repentance (Mk 1: 15). It cannot be forced upon the sinner. The teachings of Christ, and often those of St Paul, speak of the process in serious cases of disruptive behavior in which the church attempts, through temporary exclusion, to create the conditions for the offender to come to embrace contrition and restitution prior to reintegration (Mt 18: 15–18; II Cor 5: 16–19; 7: 8–10). These wise counsels formed the basis of the sacrament of penance and certain features of the monastic ethos, especially its penal philosophy.

It is thus coherent for Christians to affirm the need for solitude and seclusion in cases of violent behavior, ideally in an environment similar to that inaugurated in the early monasteries where offenders can come to see, not in a sorrow inflicted upon them by others, but in "a sorrow that comes from God," the love already in and around them from which they have become alienated (II Cor 7: 9). In practical terms, it would thus not be incongruous to agree that offenders may need to come to their own senses (Lk 15: 17) in the environment of contemporary correctional facilities. This, however, should not sanction the belief among Christians that the state, the collective "we," must punish lawbreakers.

---

32 James Samuel Logan, *Good Punishment?: Christian Moral Practice and U.S. Imprisonment* (Grand Rapids: Eerdmans, 2008), pp. 239, 233.

33 There are clear echoes here of the thought of Paul Ramsey and his deontological assertion that Christians are bound by duty to attend to the needs of the neighbor in the same way that the Good Samaritan cared for the beaten stranger. The difference with Ramsey is significant however: love is not a duty but a natural movement of the heart once one has overcome the ego's distortion of primal unity in service of order, boundaries, and security. See *Basic Christian Ethics*, pp. 92–103.

Christians may lack the resources, time, and commitment to put the ideas of the tradition into effect for bringing the alienated and destructive into harmony with God and creation.[34] In other words, this reluctant instrumental role conceded to law and punitive judgment does not seek to defend, in Christian terms, the right of the state to exercise legally sanctioned coercion or violence, though that is in fact what states and their judicial arm do. It is also, sadly, what Christians often do—those who have fallen under the sway of the dualism and disenchantment that have shaped Christian thought, especially in the last five centuries. Charles Taylor rightly notes that both Catholics and Protestants since that time could in effect do no other—given the constraints imposed by social forces and the limitations of theological reflection—than stress the primacy of the judicial-penal metaphor rather than that of grace and redemption.[35]

The Christian ethic should see retributive measures only as internal and self-imposed, never as a legitimate punitive expression upon those who have broken the law. This nuanced interpretation of punishment may seem like a semantic point but the "semantics" of the gospel are at risk, as is our way of seeing the world through Christian eyes, should we manifest a belief that law justifies the exclusion of others from our unconditional love and forgiveness.

The Last Judgment

Hobbes stated that on a life path crowded on one side with those invoking "great liberty" and, on the other, "much authority," "tis hard to passe … unwounded."[36] As has been shown throughout this volume, Christians have always found it difficult to honor and imitate "the freedom of the children of God" (Rom 8: 21) while pressed by the need to protect themselves and their possessions. They have found it even more difficult since the inauguration of the "modern age" wherein the very language we speak and in which the gospel is heard is driven by an exaltation of the ego and the defense of self-interest; and right alongside the need for security stands the edifice of law and the violent power that is its only sure support.

We have spoken much of the divided mode of apprehension that has made it possible for Christians on one hand to profess their faith in Christ and proclaim him as the Lord of their lives, and at the same time unashamedly judge others as worthy of punishment and even death. And in those cases where Christians sincerely lament or even protest the specific ways the enforcement of laws and the prosecution for their violation are conducted, the reforms for which they often aim

---

[34] That said, there are movements in many countries to establish faith-based prisons wherein Christian principles form the basis of the correctional regimen. See Jorge Crespo Toral, *Towards Freedom* (Washington, DC: Prison Fellowship International, 2000).

[35] Taylor, *Secular*, p. 652.

[36] Hobbes, *Leviathan*, Epistle Dedicatory.

take law, judgment, and punishment for granted—only the way they are applied needs emendation.

Duncan Forrester provides some explanation for this tendency in his notion that in the absence of a clear sense of what justice is or demands Christians find that the easiest course is to rely on the status quo, "and recognize precedent and public opinion as having some kind of moral authority."[37] Similarly, Hauerwas laments the fact that in civic conversation the term "justice" has no Christian variant. It is a word both believers and non-believers use uncritically and hence the entire concept is a "bad idea" for Christians, precisely because in the contemporary world, secular society sets the agenda for justice in a language saturated with apprehension, condemnation, and violence.[38]

There are two remedies for this muted evangelical language that can set the tone for a truly Christian voice, a voice that speaks of freedom unbounded by fear or hatred of the threatening, the enemy, or the criminal. The first is a function of memory, of tradition, of remembering in whose name we Christians "live and move and have our being" (Acts 17: 28). The second is a function of practice, of praying in the way I believe Jesus prayed: silently, attentively, openly, and lovingly before God fully manifest and yet fully hidden in every aspect of reality.[39]

Remembering Jesus

It was noted at the beginning of the chapter that Western men and women have been termed "people without history." The only "tradition" many of us know is the liberal political philosophy based upon "inalienable rights," the role of the state in providing and protecting them, and the independent moral authority of reason to situate those rights in an allegedly truthful way in the midst of life's shifting contours. Where history comes into play in this view, as Charles Pinches suggests, is commonly in the evoking of memory, whether in the family or in the nation—a memory that is often saturated in sentiments that can easily turn dangerous. He maintains that it is precisely for these reasons that Christians must rely on Scripture to re-narrate events, to place memory in a different context, particularly in those occurrences involving threats to individual pride or national

---

[37] Duncan Forrester, *Christian Justice and Public Policy* (Cambridge: Cambridge University Press, 1997), pp. 37–38.

[38] Hauerwas, "The Politics of Justice," in *After Christendom*, pp. 45–68.

[39] Heidegger reveals a contemplative orientation often in his writings. He states that "appearance, as the appearance 'of something,' does *not* mean showing itself; it means rather the announcing-itself by something which does not show itself." He then speaks of the need of silence, of "hearkening" to the depth of meaning being communicated in the world around us. See *Being and Time*, trans. John Macquarrie and Edward Robinson (New York: Harper & Row, 1962), pp. 52, 206–08.

hegemony. For such incidents regularly serve as pretexts for a guiltless thirst for revenge and violence.[40]

In the New Testament, memory cannot be separated from the faith that God is present in all of creation, gracing every creature and every moment, nor from the hope that God is not only redeeming humanity but that the cross, born lovingly amidst the daily dose of rejection, indifference, and ill-will, is the path of redemption for Christians and for all the world (Col 1: 16–20). The ability to align ourselves with the unfailingly generous mystery of love and meaning surrounding us contrasts with the preoccupation with nostalgia on one hand and an angry retribution on the other among many of our contemporaries, professed Christians among them, who lack the ability to connect memories of the past, whatever the sorrow or shame associated with them, to a vibrant source of peaceful and joyful hope.[41]

We need to remember that in Christ the way humans relate to God has changed decisively. It is no longer a relationship predicated upon law with the consequent and endless series of rewards and punishments before the vicissitudes of human moral compliance. St Paul, save for discrete passages, did not conceive of the Christian life in terms of law: "his ethics are grounded on the Spirit and on love of the neighbor."[42] Christ calls the disciples his "friends" (Jn 15: 15). He has not come to reprimand or to punish but to forgive his persecutors and betrayers, revealing his sacred wounds and, as with the apostle Thomas, inviting us to touch them (Jn 20: 27). *He* is the answer to human malevolence. His truth cannot be encoded in a series of statutes since it is the perfect union of the divine and the human, as shown in the rationally perplexing parable of the workers in the vineyard (Mt 20: 1–16).[43] Thus, not even the church can presume to reflect fully the enormity of divine favor and the unconditional regard God has for creation. As Pope Gelasius stated centuries ago, only Christ can simultaneously be "priest and king." The ancient emperors, some medieval pontiffs, and early leaders of the Reformation presumed this godlike design only to their dismay and, in the case of the latter two, the crippling of Christian witness.[44]

Law is and always will be a central focus of political institutions. Human beings require a *nomos*, a normative cosmos, revealing the need to "create a world of right and wrong, of lawful and unlawful, of valid and void."[45] This legal universe with its required modes of conduct is fully contingent upon the narrative a community adopts as its own truthful guide. Robert Cover, echoing Llewellyn, argues from his learned perspective that those who stand

---

40 Charles R. Pinches, *A Gathering of Memories* (Grand Rapids, MI: Brazos, 2006), p. 11.

41 Ibid., p. 154.

42 Sanders, *Paul*, pp. 103–04.

43 Taylor, *Secular*, pp. 706–07.

44 Gauchet, *Disenchantment*, p. 139.

45 Cover, "Nomos," p. 4.

in judgment must recognize this ineradicable tendency and how it shapes the way members of distinct communities within the wider national community perceive the world around them. Wise judges, therefore, must first reveal a careful and compassionate appreciation for the way ethical commitments shape legal compliance and "invite new worlds" into their field of vision rather than circumscribing them within their own.[46]

More to the point of our study, Cover notes that St Paul exemplifies the way the Christian narrative reshapes the story of the Jewish people and their fidelity to law by means of "a revolutionary allegorical extension" in the Epistle to the Galatians.[47] There, Paul compares the Jews to Hagar and Ishmael, "the firstcomers whose claim is based on law," with the Christians whom he compares to Sarah and Isaac "who lack any legal entitlement but who hold the divine promise of destiny." The upshot of this Pauline allegory is that the "whole edifice of law ... is torn down" before the mystery of Christian destiny.[48]

We have noted throughout the book that the ongoing problem for Christians has been how much of the narrative of a sacred bond that unites all of creation in Christ are they willing to surrender in order to accommodate the moral stance of those who protect their security and their rights. The fact that many Christians fail to see the image of God in criminal offenders, and judge human worth by legal or social standards other than those provided by Christ, does little to weaken the contention that an uncritical understanding of law cannot coexist with the gospel without the substantial weakening of the latter.

We need to remember that Christian ethics betrays its own moral and linguistic inheritance in even entertaining the question of whether we should inflict punishment. In the latter choice, as Miroslav Volf contends, human malevolence accomplishes a double triumph: "The first victory happens when an evil deed is perpetrated; the second victory, when evil is returned."[49] Rather, the engaging question, to which both the New Testament and Christian tradition provide ample direction, is how the alienated and abandoned can be restored to fellowship and communion. Rahner attests that the answer is taking each human being, especially those deemed criminal, "absolutely seriously": "And if we did look at [the criminal]

---

46 Ibid., p. 68. Llewellyn studied Native American judicial procedure and insisted that the sense of "we-ness" was profoundly superior to "arms-length attitudes" that characterize the "lawyer-style adversary procedure." He states that "we should scorn, even fear" such an approach, especially toward any community whose welcome is in question. See *Jurisprudence*, pp. 447–48.

47 Cover, "Nomos," p. 24.

48 Ibid.

49 Volf contends that biblical teaching emphasizes "exemplary memory" over "literal memory." Miroslav Volf, *The End of Memory: Remembering Rightly in a Violent World* (Grand Rapids: Eerdmans, 2006), pp. 9, 87–88.

like this, in reverent humility, then we would see Christ in him: the incarnate word of the Father, who is everywhere, honored and adored."[50]

We need also to remember how our oneness in Christ is the oneness of deeply flawed human beings, alienated from our true selves, constantly erecting barriers, protecting our fragile egos, judging, competing, and asserting a false preeminence over people more like us than we dare to admit: "So, then, we meet ourselves when we meet the prisoners in prison. They present our own image to us, that image which we must face continually, day after day, if we hope to find the grace of God for ourselves."[51] It is a diminishment of the truth of the eternal reach of the cross and its message of redemptive suffering to close ranks in the face of those who threaten us and threaten our worldview, even though that is what our unredeemed nature and our embattled self-images constantly try to do.[52] The more we know ourselves the less we can look down on anyone, a notion to which St Paul was a witness: "humbly look on others as superior to yourself" (Phil 2: 3). This is not a pious affectation but the "dark" truth to which the saints constantly attest. In the words of the medieval Franciscan mystic, Francisco de Osuna: "we learn more by falling than by ascending."[53]

St John of the Cross insisted that we can only come to know who God is through increasing clarity about who God is not. The "dark night" is the journey of faith that learns to cling to nothing—neither our accomplishments, nor our desires, nor our perceived worthiness, and certainly not our anger. Only in the loss of who we think we are can we come to know who we truly are. It is reminiscent of Christ's teaching: if you love your life you must lose it (Lk 9: 24).[54]

Furthermore, we must remember that we are called by Christ to love everyone and judge no one. After the fact, yes, as has been mentioned, something must be done with and for someone whose carelessness and lack of regard for others, not to mention him or herself, has assumed dominance in a heart made only for care. That said, proper judgment is not an expression of reason—the beleaguered "impartial spectator" trying fruitlessly to come to the truth in a polarized vacuum—but of grace. The first movement of the Spirit is to recognize the divine presence in others and to reverence and care for them. The God in us seeks union with God around us. In the human heart this movement is a grace that John Milbank, referencing Augustine, views not as a private possession that is earned, in the sense that one develops virtues, but something higher, a participation by a will enamored of God beyond the self "toward a sharing and ontological distribution … of the inexhaustible common good."[55]

---

50 Rahner, "The Prison Pastorate," in *Justice Reflections* 6 (2004), p. 7.

51 Ibid., p. 13.

52 Taylor, *Secular*, p. 655.

53 Osuna, *Spiritual Alphabet*, XIII, 1.

54 John of the Cross, "The Ascent of Mount Carmel," I–II; "The Dark Night," I–II, in *The Collected Works of St. John of the Cross*.

55 John Milbank, *Being Reconciled* (London: Routledge, 2003), p. 12.

The act of judgment is often an accusation, a finding of fault in the other, a standing above and apart. Our judgmental tendencies should be sobered by our earlier discussion of the etymology of the word "Satan." The noun for the ancient Hebrews meant both adversary and legal accuser.[56] Similarly, the Greek word for the devil, *diabolos*, stems from the verb *diaballo* meaning "to divide or set at variance; it then developed to the making of accusations; and then to slander, misrepresentation and deception."[57] In short, the devil in us is the ever-righteous judge of others.

We must remember, finally, that judgment, law, and the desire to inflict pain simply are not the way of Jesus. His authority was not an external force, nor was it a set of demands with the required punishment for failure to meet them. His was the way of the sower (Mk 4: 1–20), the sower of the imagination: telling stories, giving examples, none more compelling than the example of his own life. One can locate specific passages in the New Testament that speak of the Christian ethic in terms of legal compliance and righteous judgment, but to provide them primary significance would radically distort the message of Jesus, taking away his whole method of teaching and his way of reacting to human weakness.[58] Like the contemplative he was, Christ knew that change must come from within, from a purification of heart and vision. He provides the true example of a life grounded in openness and receptivity to God in all of creation. It is this contemplative stance that Christians need to adopt in order to begin to see and act the way that he did.

Putting on the Contemplative Mind of Christ

When John the Baptist stated concerning Christ, "He must increase; I must decrease" (Jn 3: 30), he summarized much not only of what Christian mystics have said over the centuries but also what seems to have been the spirituality of Christ himself in regard to God the Creator. An attitude of complete abandonment of self-will in favor of the divine will is revealed in events such as the Transfiguration (Mk 9: 2–8) and the agony in the garden at Gethsemane (Mk 8: 32–36). Many of the sayings of Christ center on the renunciation of the ego (Mt 16: 24–25), coupled with the belief that true life is not so much sought after as discovered already operative in the heart and in the world. Becoming detached from the enclosed love of family, ethnic group, nation, or religion invites that great love, in the words of Thomas Merton, "whose center is everywhere and whose circumference is nowhere."[59] The cost of obtaining the "buried treasure" (Mt 13: 44) or the "pearl of great price" (Mt 13: 45–46) that are God's way of being is no more than a trust that a richer, deeper, more love-filled life lies on the other side of the analytical self

---

[56] Day, *Adversary*, p. 15.

[57] Court, *Dictionary of the Bible*, s.v. Satan.

[58] See Biddle, *Missing the Mark*, p. 95; Zahl, *Grace*, p. 55.

[59] Thomas Merton, *Seeds of Contemplation* (New York: Dell, 1953), p. 52.

and, in the words of the early mystic St John Climacus, in offering to God "nothing but a speechless soul and a voiceless mind."[60]

Scripture suggests that the prayer of Christ was normally this immersion in contemplative silence. He spent long hours alone (Mk 1: 35; 6: 46–47; Mt 14: 23–24) and it is revealing that the only time he seems to have prayed verbally with the disciples was after such a period of quiet, in response to their query that he teach them to pray (Lk 11: 1–2).[61] The contemplative stance is necessary to all that Jesus did, forming a vision, a way of seeing that led him to puncture barriers that not only his religious persecutors found appalling—touching lepers (Mt 8: 1–4) and the dead (Mk 5: 40–41), befriending tax collectors and prostitutes (Mk 2: 16–17; Lk 7: 36–50), healing on the Sabbath (Mk 3: 1–6)—but also that his disciples found shocking: speaking with women in private (Jn 4: 27), playing with children (Mt 19: 13–15), and healing the vociferous Bartimeus (Mk 10: 46–48). This stance of universal regard, the fruit of a heart emptied of self and filled with God, led Jesus across political, religious, and ethnic fault lines that the fearful, "tribal" mind of his contemporaries had erected against outsiders, e.g. the Roman occupiers (Mk 8: 5–13), Samaritans (Lk 9: 51–56), the Syro-Phonecian woman (Mk 7: 24–30), or the tortured self-mutilator in the region of the Gadarenes (Mk 5: 1–20).[62]

The contemplative mind is also a "lawless" mind. As we have noted, law can do no other than reflect the ethical standards or ideals of a specific people or organization. This does not condemn law as something bad; still less does it denigrate those who sincerely adhere to its precepts. It does reveal, however, that without some type of conversion of one's heart and moral perspective to a broader, kinder, and more inclusive way of seeing, love will select between the worthy and unworthy and, all too often, between the law-abiders and the law-breakers.[63] We know that Christ did not transgress legal provisions in order to prove a point, or deliberately to infuriate his foes, but because his outlook was guided by a love that could do no other than heal when the sick and the troubled reached out to him. Thus Thomas Merton states that, like Christ, the contemplative will always be an "outlaw" in a world that so carefully judges who is and is not worthy of love, forgiveness, and care.[64]

In this light, it is most appropriate that the beautiful story of the appearance of the resurrected Christ to the frightened and concealed disciples reveals him simply breathing upon them pardon, reconciliation, peace, and the presence of the Holy Spirit (Jn 20: 19–23). In one whose every breath is so attentive and loving, there

60 St John Climacus, *The Ladder of Divine Ascent*, Step 5, 7.

61 Rohr, *The Naked Now*, p. 72.

62 David Berreby calls the either/or dualist mindset "tribal" thinking. See *Us and Them* (New York and Boston: Little Brown, 2005), pp. 16–17.

63 This is the argument of Henri Bergson who maintains that this wide and limitless love is best exemplified in the Christian mystics. See *Two Sources*, pp. 227ff.

64 Merton, "Rain," p. 14.

can be no polarity, no exclusiveness, and there are no boundaries; nor can there be judgment, even upon betrayers and doubters.

The contemplative is anything but an escapist. The world is not the problem; it is sacred through and through. The problem is self-absorption at the expense of the immanent divine presence everywhere. Thus Osuna writes, as did Pseudo Dionysius before him, that the divided mind, the dualist mind is the birthplace of the terrible things that we do. For here lies the very disquiet of the judgmental and accusatory "adversary": "whatever your actions your mind must accompany them and not wander in different directions, the body being in one place and the heart in another." A distracted mind is reminiscent of "Satan who intruded himself among the sons of God. When God, knowing his restlessness and turbulence and that he was never still nor recollected in his thoughts asked him: 'Whence comest thou?' Satan answered shamelessly: 'I have gone round about the earth, and walked through it.'" Osuna then addresses many of us with a similar rootless anxiety: "You [also] would be obliged to reply with Satan that you had been round the whole world with your wandering thoughts, for you had rejected no vain imaginations."[65]

To live in the moment is also to love the moment and the unfathomable God always present in that moment. John of the Cross defines prayer as nothing more than "to abide in … quietude with a loving attentiveness to God."[66] Osuna writes: "It cannot injure you to see and love God in everything you behold, looking on it as a gift from his hand."[67] One early medieval mystic wrote that we all live under a "cloud of unknowing," the path to be followed cannot become clear through any form of rational analysis, still less by dwelling upon the past. The only course, indeed the wisest of all, is to let go of all save a constant emitting of love from the heart.[68]

These contemplatives merely restate what Christ continually taught: that love alone fulfills all of the law (Mt 22: 36–40), and the words of St Paul that the whole law can be summarized in love of neighbor (Gal 5: 14). It is a love that cannot be created but is already possessed for the love of God is within us (Jn 14: 22).

Christians must learn to trust that this overwhelming love will love through us if only we can forget ourselves long enough each day to discover ourselves in the grasp of something infinitely tender and wise. We must place our hope in that

---

65 Osuna, *Spiritual Alphabet*, I, 2. Pseudo Dionysius states: "my advice to you as you look for a sight of the mysterious things, is to leave behind you everything perceived and understood, everything perceptible and understandable, all that is not and all that is, and, with your understanding lead aside, to strive upward as much as you can toward union with him who is beyond all being and knowledge." "The Mystical Theology," in *Pseudo Dionysius: The Complete Works*, ch. 1.

66 John of the Cross, "Ascent of Mount Carmel," in *The Collected Works of St. John of the Cross*, Kieran Kavanaugh, O.C.D. and Otilio Rodriguez, O.C.D. (eds) (Washington, DC: ICS Publications, 1979). II, XII, 8.

67 Osuna, *Spiritual Alphabet*, XVI, 4.

68 *The Cloud of Unknowing*, ch. 6.

abundant grace, no longer needing to judge or punish anyone. Richard Rohr states that this divine indwelling is not earned, "only recognized and realized … and fallen in love with." In a simple presence to creation, a breathing of Christ's own breath of peace and pardon, "you will be both overwhelmed and underwhelmed at the boundless mystery of your own humanity. You will know you are standing under the same waterfall of mercy as everybody else and receiving an undeserved radical grace." It is what Christ taught us to do but what we have so often forgotten in our attempts to control, to condemn, and to punish. "Without that underlying experience of God as both abyss and ground, it is almost impossible to live in the now; in the fullness of who I am … and almost impossible to experience the Presence that, paradoxically, always fills the abyss and shakes the ground."[69]

---

[69] Rohr, *Naked Now*, p. 22.

Bibliography

A Collection of the Laws and Canons of the Church of England, ed. and trans. John Johnson (Oxford: John Henry Parker, 1850).

Aas, Katja Franko, *Sentencing in the Age of Information* (London: Glasshouse Press, 2005).

Abelard, Peter, *Peter Abelard's Ethics*, trans. D.E. Luscombe (Oxford: Clarendon Press, 1971).

Acts of the Christian Martyrs, trans. Herbert Musurillo (Oxford: Clarendon, 1972).

Adams, Marilyn McCord, "The Structure of Ockham's Moral Theory," *Franciscan Studies* 46 (1986), pp. 1–35.

Alexander, Frank S., "Beyond Positivism: A Theological Perspective," in John Witte, Jr. and Frank S. Alexander (eds), *The Weightier Matters of the Law* (Atlanta: Scholars Press, 1988), pp. 251–84.

Alfonso X, *Las Siete Partidas*, ed. Robert I. Burns, trans. Samuel Parsons Scott (5 vols, Philadelphia: University of Pennsylvania Press, 2001).

Alschuler, Albert W., "A Plea for Mercy," in Jonathan Rothchild, Matthew Myer Boulton, and Kevin Jung (eds), *Doing Justice to Mercy* (Charlottesville: University of Virginia Press, 2007), pp. 92–100.

Ambrose, Saint, "Cain and Abel," in *The Fathers of the Church*, vol. 42, trans. John J. Savage (New York: Fathers of the Church, 1961).

________ "Letter 7," in O'Donovan, Oliver and Joan Lockwood O'Donovan (eds), *From Irenaeus to Grotius: A Sourcebook in Christian Political Thought* (Grand Rapids, MI: Wm B. Eerdmans, 1999).

________ "Sermon against Auxentius," in O'Donovan, Oliver and Joan Lockwood O'Donovan (eds), *From Irenaeus to Grotius: A Sourcebook in Christian Political Thought* (Grand Rapids, MI: Wm B. Eerdmans, 1999).

Anselm of Canterbury, Saint, *Why God Became Man*, trans. Joseph Colleran (Albany: Magi Books, 1969).

Aquinas, Saint Thomas, *On the Governance of Rulers*, trans. Gerald B. Phelan (London: Sheed & Ward, 1938).

________ *Summa Theologica*, trans. Fathers of the English Dominican Province (New York: Benziger, 1947).

________ *Truth*, trans. James V. McGlynn, S.J. (2 vols, Chicago: Henry Regnery, 1953).

________ *On the Truth of the Catholic Faith (Summa Contra Gentiles)*, trans. Vernon J. Burke (Garden City, NY: Image Books, 1956).

________ "Commentary on the Sentences," in O'Donovan, Oliver and Joan Lockwood O'Donovan (eds), *From Irenaeus to Grotius: A Sourcebook in Christian Political Thought* (Grand Rapids, MI: Wm B. Eerdmans, 1999).

Aristotle, *Ethics*, trans. J.A.K. Thompson (Harmondsworth, UK: Penguin, 1955).

________ *Metaphysics*, trans. John Warrington (London: Dent, 1956).

Augustine, Saint, *The Lord's Sermon on the Mount*, trans. John J. Jepson (Westminster, MD: Newman, 1948).

________ *The Problem of Free Choice* (*De Libero Arbitrio*), trans. Dom Mark Pontifex (Westminster, MD: Newman Press, 1955).

________ *City of God*, trans. Henry Bettenson (Harmondsworth, UK: Penguin, 1972).

________ "Letter from Augustine to Macedonius, Provincial Governor of Africa," in O'Donovan, Oliver and Joan Lockwood O'Donovan (eds), *From Irenaeus to Grotius: A Sourcebook in Christian Political Thought* (Grand Rapids, MI: Wm B. Eerdmans, 1999).

________ "Expositions of Psalms," in *The Works of St. Augustine*, ed. John E. Rotelle, trans. Maria Boulding, O.S.B. (Hyde Park, NY: New City Press, 2004).

________ "Letters," in *The Works of St. Augustine*, ed. Boniface Ramsey, trans. Roland Teske, S.J. (Hyde Park, NY: New City Press, 2004).

Bankston, Carl L., *Public Education, America's Civil Religion* (New York: Teachers College Press, 2009).

Barth, Gerhard, "Matthew's Understanding of the Law," in Gunther Bornkamm, Gerhard Barth and Heinz Joachim Held (eds), *Tradition and Interpretation in Matthew*, trans. Percy Scott (London: SCM, 1982), pp. 58–164.

Bartlett, Robert, *Trial by Fire and Water* (Oxford: Clarendon, 1986).

Basil, Saint, "The Long Rules," in *St. Basil: Ascetical Works*, trans. Sister M. Monica Wagner (New York: Fathers of the Church, 1950).

________ *Letters*, trans. Sister Agnes Clare Way, O.P. (Washington, DC: Catholic University of America Press, 1951).

Bauman, Richard A., *Crime and Punishment in Ancient Rome* (London and New York: Routledge, 1996).

Bayne, David Cowan, *Conscience, Obligation, and the Law* (Chicago: Loyola University Press, 1966).

Beaumont, Gustave de and Alexis de Tocqueville, *On the Penitentiary System in the United States and its Application to France*, trans. Francis Lieber (Philadelphia: Carey, Lea, and Blanchard, 1833).

Beccaria, Cesare, *On Crimes and Punishments*, trans. Henry Paolucci (Indianapolis: Bobbs-Merrill, 1963).

Bellah, Robert, "Civil Religion in America," in *Beyond Belief* (New York: Harper & Row, 1970), pp. 168–86.

Bellomo, Manlio, *The Common Legal Past of Europe*, trans. Lydia G. Cochrane (Washington, DC: Catholic University of America Press, 1995).

Benedict, Saint, *Benedict's Rule*, trans. Terrence G. Kardong (Collegeville, MN: Liturgical Press, 1996).

Bentham, Jeremy, "Panopticon: Or, The Inspection House," in *The Works of Jeremy Bentham* (Edinburgh: W. Tait, 1843).

________ "An Introduction to the Principles of Morals and Legislation," in D.D. Raphael (ed.), *British Moralists 1650–1800*, vol. II (Oxford: Clarendon, 1969).

________ *The Rationale of Punishment* (Honolulu: University Press of the Pacific, 2004).

Berger, Peter, *The Sacred Canopy* (New York: Anchor Books, 1967).

Bergson, Henri, *The Two Sources of Morality and Religion*, trans. R. Ashley Audra and Cloudesley Brereton (New York: Doubleday, 1935).

Berkovits, Eliezer, *Essential Essays on Judaism*, ed. David Hazony (Jerusalem, Shalem Press, 2002).

Berman, Harold, *Law and Revolution* (Cambridge, MA: Harvard University Press, 1983).

________ *Law and Revolution II* (Cambridge, MA: Harvard University Press, 2003).

________ "An Ecumenical Jurisprudence," in John Witte, Jr. and Frank S. Alexander (eds), *The Teachings of Modern Christianity on Law, Politics, and Human Nature* (2 vols, New York: Columbia University Press, 2006), vol. 1, pp. 752–64.

Bernard of Clairvaux, "On Consideration," in O'Donovan, Oliver and Joan Lockwood O'Donovan (eds), *From Irenaeus to Grotius: A Sourcebook in Christian Political Thought* (Grand Rapids, MI: Wm B. Eerdmans, 1999).

Bernstein, Alan, *The Formation of Hell* (Ithaca: Cornell University Press, 1993).

Berreby, David, *Us and Them* (New York and Boston: Little Brown, 2005).

Biddle, Mark E., *Missing the Mark: Sin and Its Consequences in Biblical Theology* (Nashville: Abingdon, 2005).

Bingham, Joseph, *Antiquities of the Christian Church* (London: William Straker, 1844).

Blackstone, William, *Commentaries on the Laws of England (1765–1769)* (4 vols, Oxford: Clarendon Press).

Boethius, *The Consolation of Philosophy*, trans. W.V. Cooper (New York: The Modern Library, 1943).

Bogira, Steve, *Courtroom 302* (New York: Alfred A. Knopf, 2005).

Bonaventure, Saint, "Defense of the Mendicants," in *The Works of Bonaventure*, trans. José de Vinck (4 vols, Paterson, NJ: St. Anthony Guild, 1966).

________ "The Life of St. Francis," in *Bonaventure*, trans. Ewert Cousins (Mahwah, NJ: Paulist, 1978).

Bornkamm, Gunther, *The New Testament: A Guide to its Writings*, trans. Reginald H. Fuller and Ilse Fuller (Philadelphia: Fortress, 1973).

________ "End Expectation and Church in Matthew," in Gunther Bornkamm, Gerhard Barth and Heinz Joachim Held (eds), *Tradition and Interpretation in Matthew*, trans. Percy Scott (London: SCM, 1982), pp. 15–51.

Bowsky, William M., *A Medieval Italian Commune: Siena Under the Nine* (Berkeley: University of California Press, 1981).

Brague, Remi, *The Law of God*, trans. Lydia G. Cochrane (Chicago: University of Chicago Press, 2008).

Braithwaite, John, *Crime, Shame, and Reintegration* (Cambridge: Cambridge University Press, 1989).

________ *Restorative Justice and Responsive Regulation* (Oxford: Oxford University Press, 2002).

Braithwaite, John and Philip Petit, *Not Just Deserts* (Oxford: Clarendon Press, 1990).

Branden, Robert Charles, *Satanic Conflict and the Plot of Matthew* (New York: Peter Lang, 2006).

Brown, Peter, "Religious Coercion in the Later Roman Empire," *History* 48 (1963), pp. 283–305.

________ *Augustine of Hippo* (New York: Dorset Press, 1986).

Brugger, E. Christian, *Capital Punishment and Roman Catholic Tradition* (Notre Dame: University of Notre Dame Press, 2003).

Buber, Martin, *I and Thou*, trans. Walter Kaufman (New York: Charles Scribner's Sons, 1970).

Buckley, Michael, S.J., *At the Origins of Modern Atheism* (New Haven: Yale University Press, 1987).

Bultmann, Rudolf, *Theology of the New Testament*, trans. Kendrick Grobel (2 vols, New York: Charles Scribner's Sons, 1951).

Cadorette, Curt, "Legion and the Believing Community: Discipleship in an Imperial Age," in Michael Budde and Robert Brimlow (eds), *The Church as Counterculture* (Albany: State University of New York Press, 2000), pp. 153–69.

Calvin, John, *Calvin: On God and Political Duty*, ed. John T. McNeill (Indianapolis: Bobbs-Merrill, 1950).

________ *Calvin's Institutes*, ed. Hugh T. Kerr (Louisville: Westminster/John Knox, 1989).

Cameron, Averil, *Christianity and the Rhetoric of Empire* (Berkeley: University of California Press, 1991).

Chodorow, Stanley, *Christian Political Theory and Church Politics in the Mid-Twelfth Century* (Berkeley: University of California Press, 1972).

Clark, David W., "Voluntarism and Rationalism in the Ethics of Ockham," *Franciscan Studies* 31 (1971), pp. 72–87.

Clasen, Claus-Peter, *Anabaptism: A Social History, 1525–1618* (Ithaca and London: Cornell University Press, 1972).

Clear, Todd and Harry Dammer, *The Offender in the Community* (Belmont, CA: Wadsworth, 2000).

Clement of Alexandria, "The Instructor," in *The Ante-Nicene Fathers*, vol. 2, eds Rev. Alexander Roberts and James Donaldson (New York: Charles Scribner's Sons, 1925).

________ "The Stromata," in *The Ante-Nicene Fathers*, vol. 2, eds Rev. Alexander Roberts and James Donaldson (New York: Charles Scribner's Sons, 1925).

Clement of Rome, Saint, "The Letter to the Corinthians," in *The Apostolic Fathers*, vol. 1, trans. Francis X. Glimm (New York: Christian Heritage, 1947).
Climacus, Saint John, *The Ladder of Divine Ascent*, trans. Archimandrite Lazarus Moore (London: Faber and Faber, 1959).
Compagnoni, Francesco, "Capital Punishment and Torture in the Tradition of the Catholic Church," in Franz Bockle and Jacques Pohier (eds), *The Death Penalty and Torture* (New York: Seabury, 1979), pp. 39–53.
Court, John M., *Dictionary of the Bible* (London: Penguin, 2007).
Cover, Robert, "Nomos and Narrative," *Harvard Law Review* 97 (1983), pp. 4–68.
________ "Violence and the Word," *Yale Law Journal* 95 (1986), pp. 1601–29.
Cox, Harvey, *When Jesus Came to Harvard* (Boston: Mariner Books, 2004).
Curran, Charles, *Directions in Fundamental Moral Theology* (Notre Dame: University of Notre Dame Press, 1985).
________ *Catholic Moral Theology in the United States* (Washington: Georgetown University Press, 2008).
Cusac, Anne Marie, *Cruel and Unusual: The Culture of Punishment in America* (New Haven: Yale University Press, 2009).
Cyprian, Saint, *The Lapsed*, trans. Maurice Bevenot, S.J. (Westminster, MD: Newman Press, 1957).
________ *The Letters of Cyprian of Carthage*, trans. G.W. Clark (2 vols, New York: Newman Press, 1984).
D'Arcy, M.C., S.J., *St. Thomas Aquinas* (Westminster, MD: Newman, 1955).
Davies, W.D., *Invitation to the New Testament* (Garden City, NY: Doubleday, 1966).
Dawson, Christopher, *The Making of Europe* (New York: Meridian, 1958).
Day, Peggy L., *An Adversary in Heaven: Satan in the Hebrew Bible* (Atlanta: Scholars Press, 1988).
De Vaux, Roland, O.P., *Ancient Israel: Its Life and Institutions*, trans. John McHugh (New York: McGraw Hill, 1961).
Dean, Trevor, *Crime in Medieval Europe* (Harlow, UK: Longman, 2001).
DeLong, James V., "The New 'Criminal' Classes: Legal Sanctions and Business Managers," in Gene Healy (ed.), *Go Directly to Jail* (Washington, DC: The Cato Institute, 2004), pp. 9–44.
Delumeau, Jean, *Sin and Fear*, trans. Eric Nicholson (New York: St. Martin's, 1983).
Denziger, Henry, *The Sources of Catholic Dogma*, trans. Roy J. DeFerari (St. Louis: B. Herder, 1957).
Descartes, Rene, *Discourse on Method and the Meditations*, trans. John Veitch (Buffalo: Prometheus, 1989).
Dickson-Gilmore, Jane and Carol LaPrairie, *Will the Circle be Unbroken?* (Toronto: University of Toronto Press, 2005).
Didache, trans. Robert A. Kraft (New York and Toronto: Thomas Nelson & Sons, 1965).
Dodd, C.H., *Gospel and Law* (New York: Columbia University Press, 1951).

Douglas, Ann, *The Feminization of American Culture* (New York: Anchor Press, 1988).

Drapkin, Israel, *Crime and Punishment in the Ancient World* (Lexington, MA: Lexington Books, 1989).

Duff, R.A., "Penal Communications: Recent Work in the Philosophy of Punishment," in Michael Tonry (ed.), *Crime and Justice* 20 (Chicago: University of Chicago Press, 1996), pp. 1–97.

Dunbabin, Jean, *Captivity and Imprisonment in Medieval Europe, 1000–1300* (Houndmills, UK: Palgrave Macmillan, 2002).

Durham, W. Cole, "Religion and Criminal Law: Types and Contexts of Interaction," in John Witte, Jr. and Frank S. Alexander (eds), *The Weightier Matters of the Law* (Atlanta: Scholars Press, 1988), pp. 193–227.

Dworkin, Ronald, *Taking Rights Seriously* (Cambridge, MA: Harvard University Press, 1977).

Edgerton, Samuel, *Pictures and Punishment* (Ithaca: Cornell University Press, 1985).

Elias, Norbert, *The Civilizing Process*, trans. Edmund Jephcott (2 vols, New York: Urizon, 1978).

Erasmus, "The Complaint of Peace," in O'Donovan, Oliver and Joan Lockwood O'Donovan (eds), *From Irenaeus to Grotius: A Sourcebook in Christian Political Thought* (Grand Rapids, MI: Wm B. Eerdmans, 1999).

Erikson, Kai, *Wayward Puritans* (New York: Wiley, 1966).

Ewick, Patricia and Susan S. Sibley, *The Common Place of Law* (Chicago: University of Chicago Press, 1998).

Falk, Ze'ev, *Hebrew Law in Biblical Times* (Jerusalem: Wahrmann Books, 1964).

Favazza, Joseph, *The Order of Penitents* (Collegeville, MN: Liturgical Press, 1988).

Feeley, Malcolm and Jonathan Simon, "The New Penology: Notes on the Emerging Strategy of Corrections and its Implications," *Criminology* 30 (1992), pp. 449–74.

Fenn, Richard, *The Persistence of Purgatory* (Cambridge: Cambridge University Press, 1995).

Fennell, Philip (ed.), *Criminal Justice in Europe: A Comparative Study* (Oxford: Clarendon, 1995).

Figgis, John Neville, *The Divine Right of Kings* (New York: Harper, 1965).

Fingarette, Herbert, "The Meaning of Law in the Book of Job," in Stanley Hauerwas and Alasdair McIntyre (eds), *Revisions* (South Bend, IN: Notre Dame University Press, 1983), pp. 249–86.

Finnis, John, *Natural Law and Natural Rights* (Oxford: Clarendon Press, 1980).

Forrester, Duncan, *Christian Justice and Public Policy* (Cambridge: Cambridge University Press, 1997).

Foucault, Michel, *Discipline and Punish*, trans. Alan Sheridan (New York: Vintage, 1979).

Fox, George, "The Epistles," in *Quaker Spirituality*, ed. Douglas V. Steere (New York: Paulist, 1984), pp. 129–36.

________ "The Journal," in *Quaker Spirituality*, ed. Douglas V. Steere (New York: Paulist, 1984), pp. 59–125.

Frank, Jerome, *Courts on Trial* (Princeton: Princeton University Press, 1950).

Frend, W.H.C., *The Rise of Christianity* (Philadelphia: Fortress, 1984).

Fretheim, Terence E., *God and World in the Old Testament* (Nashville: Abingdon, 2005).

Friedman, Lawrence M., *A History of American Law*, 2nd edition (New York: Simon & Schuster, 1985).

Fuchs, Josef, *Natural Law* (New York: Sheed & Ward, 1965).

Fuller, Lon, *The Morality of Law* (New Haven: Yale University Press, 1964).

Gadamer, Hans-Georg, *Philosophical Hermeneutics*, trans. David E. Linge (Berkeley: University of California Press, 1976).

Garland, David, *The Culture of Control* (Chicago: University of Chicago Press, 2001).

________ "The Peculiar Forms of American Capital Punishment," *Social Research* 74 (2007), pp. 435–64.

Garnsey, Peter, *Social Status and Legal Privilege in the Roman Empire* (Oxford: Clarendon, 1970).

Garvey, George E., "A Catholic Social Teaching Critique of Law and Economics," in Michael McConnell, Robert F. Cochran, Jr. and Angela C. Carmela, *Christian Perspectives on Legal Thought* (New Haven: Yale University Press, 2001), pp. 224–40.

Gauchet, Marcel, *The Disenchantment of the World*, trans. Oscar Burge (Princeton, NJ: Princeton University Press, 1997).

Geertz, Clifford, "Ideology as a Cultural System," in *The Interpretation of Cultures* (New York: Basic Books, 1973), pp. 194–233.

Geltner, G., *The Medieval Prison* (Princeton: Princeton University Press, 2008).

Gerson, Jean, "On Church Power and the Origin of Law and Right," in O'Donovan, Oliver and Joan Lockwood O'Donovan (eds), *From Irenaeus to Grotius: A Sourcebook in Christian Political Thought* (Grand Rapids, MI: Wm B. Eerdmans, 1999).

Gilmore, Grant, *The Ages of American Law* (New Haven: Yale University Press, 1977).

Ginzberg, Louis, *Legends of the Bible* (New York: Simon and Schuster, 1956).

Girard, Rene, *Violence and the Sacred*, trans. Patrick Gregory (Baltimore: Johns Hopkins University Press, 1977).

Given, James B., *Inquisition and Medieval Society* (Ithaca: Cornell University Press, 1997).

Goebel, Julius, Jr., *Felony and Misdemeanor* (Philadelphia: University of Pennsylvania Press, 1976).

Goffman, Erving, *Stigma* (Englewood Cliffs, NJ: Prentice Hall, 1963).

Gratian, "Decretum Gratiani," in *Corpus Iuris Canonici* (Lyon, 1616).

Gregory the Great, "Epistles," in *A Select Library of Nicene and Post-Nicene Fathers of the Christian Church*, Philip Schaff and Henry Wade (eds), trans. Rev. James Barmby (Grand Rapids, MI: William B. Eerdmans, 1956).

Griffith, Lee, *The Fall of the Prison* (Grand Rapids: Eerdmans, 1993).

Grotius, Hugo, *The Law of War and Peace*, trans. Francis W. Kelsey (Indianapolis: Bobbs-Merrill, 1925).

Hall, Kermit L., *The Magic Mirror: Law in American History* (New York: Oxford University Press, 1989).

Hamilton, Bernice, *Political Thought in Sixteenth Century Spain* (Oxford: Clarendon Press, 1963).

Haring, Bernard, *The Law of Christ*, trans. Edwin G. Kaiser (2 vols, Westminster, MD: New Press, 1961).

Harries, Jill and Ian Wood (eds), *The Theodosian Code* (Ithaca: Cornell University Press, 1993).

Hart, H.L.A., "Positivism and the Separation of Law and Morals," *Harvard Law Review* 71 (1958), pp. 593–629.

Hauerwas, Stanley, *A Community of Character* (Notre Dame: University of Notre Dame Press, 1981).

________ *The Peaceable Kingdom* (Notre Dame: University of Notre Dame Press, 1983).

________ *After Christendom* (Nashville: Abingdon, 1991).

________ *Dispatches from the Front* (Durham, NC: Duke University Press, 1994).

________ "The Nonviolent Terrorist," in Michael L. Budde and Robert W. Brimlow (eds), *The Church as Counterculture* (Albany: State University of New York Press, 2000), pp. 89–104.

________ *Performing the Faith* (Grand Rapids, MI: Brazos, 2004).

Hauerwas, Stanley and William Willimon, *Resident Aliens* (Nashville: Abingdon, 1989).

Head, Thomas, "Saints, Heretics, and the Fire: Finding Meaning through the Ordeal," in Sharon Farmer and Barbara H. Rosenwein (eds) *Monks and Nuns, Saints and Outcasts* (Ithaca: Cornell University Press, 2000), pp. 200–34.

Healy, Gene (ed.), *Go Directly to Jail* (Washington, DC: The Cato Institute, 2004).

Hegel, G.W.F., *Philosophy of Right*, trans. T.M. Knox (London: Oxford University Press, 1967).

________ *Natural Law*, trans. T.M. Knox (Philadelphia: University of Pennsylvania Press, 1975).

Heidegger, Martin, *Being and Time*, trans. John Macquarrie and Edward Robinson (New York: Harper & Row, 1962).

Helmholz, R.H., "The Early History of the Grand Jury and the Canon Law," *University of Chicago Law Review* 50 (1983), pp. 613–27.

________ "Western Canon Law," in John Witte, Jr. and Frank S. Alexander (eds), *Christianity and the Law: An Introduction* (Cambridge: Cambridge University Press, 2008), pp. 71–87.

Heschel, Abraham, *Between God and Man* (New York: Harper & Brothers, 1959).

________ *The Prophets* (New York: Harper & Row, 1962).
Hobbes, Thomas, *Leviathan*, ed. C.B. McPherson (London: Penguin, 1968).
Holmes, Oliver Wendell, *The Common Law* (Boston: Little Brown, 1881).
________ "The Path of the Law," *Harvard Law Review* 10 (1897), pp. 457–78.
Holstenius, Lucas, *Codex Regularum Monasticarum et Canonicarum* (Graz: Akademische Druck-U. Verlagsanstalt, 1957).
Hooker, Richard, *The Laws of Ecclesiastical Polity* (London: J.M. Dent, 1954).
Howard, John, *The State of the Prisons* (London: W. Eyres, 1777).
Huizinga, J, *The Waning of the Middle Ages* (New York: Doubleday, 1954).
Hume, David, "A Treatise of Human Nature," in D.D. Raphael (ed.), *British Moralists 1650–1800* (2 vols, Oxford: Clarendon Press, 1969).
Ignatieff, Michael, *A Just Measure of Pain* (New York: Pantheon, 1978).
Ignatius of Antioch, Saint, "To the Ephesians," in *The Apostolic Fathers*, vol. 1, trans. Gerald G. Walsh, S.J. (New York: Christian Heritage, 1947).
Illich, Ivan and David Cayley, *The Rivers North of the Future* (Toronto: Anansi, 2005).
Irenaeus of Lyons, "Against Heresies," in O'Donovan, Oliver and Joan Lockwood O'Donovan (eds), *From Irenaeus to Grotius: A Sourcebook in Christian Political Thought* (Grand Rapids, MI: Wm B. Eerdmans, 1999).
Irwin, John, *The Jail: Managing the Underclass in American Society* (Berkeley: University of California Press, 1985).
________ *The Warehouse Prison* (Los Angeles: Roxbury, 2005).
Ives, George, *A History of Penal Methods* (Montclair, NJ: Patterson Smith, 1970).
Ivo of Chartres, "Decretum," in J.P. Migne, *Patrologiae Cursus Completus*, vol. 161 (Paris: 1845).
Jacobs, James, *Stateville: The Penitentiary in Mass Society* (Chicago: University of Chicago Press, 1977).
John of Paris, "On Royal and Papal Power," in O'Donovan, Oliver and Joan Lockwood O'Donovan (eds), *From Irenaeus to Grotius: A Sourcebook in Christian Political Thought* (Grand Rapids, MI: Wm B. Eerdmans, 1999).
John of Salisbury, *The Statesman's Book of John of Salisbury* (*Policraticus*), trans. John Dickinson (New York: Russell & Russell, 1963).
John of the Cross, Saint, *The Collected Works of St. John of the Cross*, Kieran Kavanaugh, O.C.D. and Otilio Rodriguez, O.C.D. (eds) (Washington, DC: ICS Publications, 1979).
Johnson, Luke Timothy, *Reading Romans* (New York: Crossroad, 1997).
Johnson, Paul, *A History of the Jews* (New York: Harper & Row, 1987).
________ "Law in Early Christianity," in John Witte, Jr. and Frank S. Alexander (eds), *Christianity and Law: An Introduction* (Cambridge: Cambridge University Press, 2008), pp. 53–69.
Johnston, Norman, *Forms of Constraint* (Urbana, IL: University of Illinois Press, 2000).
Julian of Norwich, *Showings*, Short Text, trans. Edmund Colledge, O.S.A. and James Walsh, S.J. (New York: Paulist, 1978).

Jung, Kevin, "Fallibility and Fragility," in Jonathan Rothchild, Matthew Myer Boulton and Kevin Jung (eds), *Doing Justice to Mercy* (Charlottesville: University of Virginia Press, 2007), pp. 206–21.

Justin Martyr, "Dialogue with Trypho," in *Writings of St. Justin Martyr*, ed. Thomas B. Falls (New York: Christian Heritage, 1948).

Kamen, Henry, *The Spanish Inquisition: A Historical Revision* (New Haven: Yale University Press, 1997).

Kant, Immanuel, *Religion within the Limits of Reason Alone*, trans. Theodore M. Greene and Hoyt B. Hudson (New York: Harper, 1960).

________ *Practical Philosophy*, trans. Mary J. Gregor (Cambridge: Cambridge University Press, 1996).

Kantorowicz, Ernst, *The King's Two Bodies* (Princeton, NJ: Princeton University Press, 1957).

Kasemann, Ernst, *Commentary on Romans*, trans. Geoffrey W. Bromily (Grand Rapids, MI: William B. Eerdmans, 1980).

Keane, Philip, *Christian Ethics and the Imagination* (Ramsey, NJ: Paulist, 1984).

Kelsen, Hans, *General Theory of Law and the State*, trans. Anders Wedberg (New York: Russell & Russell, 1961).

King, Martin Luther, "Letter from the Birmingham Jail," in *Why We Can't Wait* (New York: Harper & Row, 1964), pp. 76–95.

Koester, Craig R., *The Word of Life: A Theology of John's Gospel* (Grand Rapids, MI: William B. Eerdmans, 2008).

Krauss, Karl, *Im Kerker* (Freiburg and Leipzig, 1895).

Kristof, Nicholas D., "Priority Test: Health Care or Prisons?" *New York Times*, August 18, 2009.

Kushner, Harold S., *When Bad Things Happen to Good People* (New York: Avon, 1981).

Lactantius, *The Divine Institutes*, trans. Sister Mary Francis McDonald, O.P. (Washington: Catholic University of America Press, 1964).

Leap, Terry L., *Dishonest Dollars* (Ithaca and London: Cornell University Press, 2007).

LeBras, Gabriel, "Canon Law," in C.G. Crump and E.F. Jacobs (eds), *The Legacy of the Middle Ages* (Oxford: Clarendon Press, 1926), pp. 321–61.

LeGoff, Jacques, *The Birth of Purgatory*, trans. Arthur Goldhammer (Chicago: University of Chicago Press, 1981).

Levinson, Bernard, *Legal Revision and Religious Renewal in Ancient Israel* (New York and Cambridge: Cambridge University Press, 2008).

Llewellyn, Karl, *Jurisprudence: Realism in Theory and Practice* (Chicago: University of Chicago Press, 1962).

Locke, John, "An Essay Concerning Human Understanding," in *Great Books of the Western World* 35, ed. Robert Maynard Hutchins (Chicago: Encyclopedia Britannica, 1952).

________ *Two Treatises of Government*, ed. Peter Laslett (Cambridge: Cambridge University Press, 1960).

Logan, James Samuel, *Good Punishment?: Christian Moral Practice and U.S. Imprisonment* (Grand Rapids: Eerdmans, 2008).
Louis, Saint, *The Etablissements de Saint Louis*, ed. and trans. F.R.P. Akehurst (Philadelphia: University of Pennsylvania Press, 1996).
Luna, Eric, "Overextending the Criminal Law," in Gene Healy (ed.), *Go Directly to Jail* (Washington, DC: The Cato Institute, 2004), pp. 1–7.
Luther, Martin, "Explanation of the Psalms," in *Luther's Works*, vol. 13, trans. Daniel E. Poellot (St. Louis: Concordia, 1956).
________ "Lectures on Genesis," in *Luther's Works*, vol. 1, trans. George V. Schick (St. Louis: Concordia, 1956).
________ "Lectures on Romans," in *Luther's Works*, vol. 25, trans. Walter G. Tillmanns (St. Louis: Concordia, 1956).
________ "Lectures on the Sermon on the Mount," in *Luther's Works*, vol. 21, trans. Jaroslav Pelikan (St. Louis: Concordia, 1956).
________ *Martin Luther: Selections from His Writings*, ed. John Dillenberger (New York: Anchor, 1961).
Luzzato, R. Moshe Chayim, *The Knowing Heart*, trans. Shraga Silverstein (Jerusalem and New York: Feldheim, 1982).
Machiavelli, Niccolo, "The Discourses," in *The Prince and the Discourses*, trans. Luigi Ricci and E.R.P. Vincent (New York: The Modern Library, 1950).
MacIntyre, Alasdair, *Whose Justice? Which Rationality?* (Notre Dame, IN: University of Notre Dame Press, 1988).
________ *Three Rival Versions of Moral Inquiry* (Notre Dame: Notre Dame University Press, 1990).
Mahoney, John, *The Making of Moral Theology* (Oxford: Clarendon, 1987).
Maitland, F.W., *The Constitutional History of England* (Cambridge: Cambridge University Press, 1968).
Mansi, Johannes Dominicus, *Sacrorum Conciliorum* (Paris and Leipzig, 1901).
Marsden, George M., *Fundamentalism and American Culture* (New York: Oxford University Press, 1980).
Marshall, Christopher, *Beyond Retribution* (Grand Rapids, MI: Eerdmans, 2001).
Marsilius of Padua, *The Defender of Peace (Defensor Pacis)*, trans. Alan Gewirth (New York: Columbia University Press, 1956).
Masur, Louis P., *Rites of Execution* (New York: Oxford University Press, 1989).
Mauer, Mark, *Race to Incarcerate* (New York: New Press, 1999).
McCoy, Bowen, "The Parable of the Sadhu," *Harvard Business Review* 103 (1983), pp. 103–08.
McGowen, Randall, "The Body and Punishment in Eighteenth Century England," *The Journal of Modern History* 59 (1987), pp. 651–79.
________ "The Well-Ordered Prison," in Norval Morris and David Rothman (eds), *The Oxford History of the Prison* (New York: Oxford University Press, 1995), pp. 79–109.
McGrade, A.S., *The Political Thought of William of Ockham* (Cambridge: Cambridge University Press, 1974).

McNeill, John T. and Helena M. Gamer, *Medieval Handbooks of Penance* (New York: Columbia University Press, 1938).
Meeks, Wayne A., *The Origins of Christian Morality* (New Haven, Yale University Press, 1993).
Megivern, James J., *The Death Penalty: An Historical and Theological Survey* (New York: Paulist, 1987).
Melanchthon, Philip, "Loci Communes," in O'Donovan, Oliver and Joan Lockwood O'Donovan (eds), *From Irenaeus to Grotius: A Sourcebook in Christian Political Thought* (Grand Rapids, MI: Wm B. Eerdmans, 1999).
Melossi, Dario and Massimo Pavarini, *Prison and the Factory*, trans. Glynis Cousin (New York: Macmillan, 1981).
Merton, Thomas, *Seeds of Contemplation* (New York: Dell, 1953).
________ "Rain and the Rhinoceros," in *Raids on the Unspeakable* (New York: New Directions, 1964), pp. 9–23.
Milbank, John, *Being Reconciled* (London: Routledge, 2003).
Mill, John Stuart, *Utilitarianism* (Indianapolis: Bobbs-Merrill, 1957).
Montesquieu, Baron de, *The Spirit of the Laws*, trans. Thomas Nugent (New York: Colonial Press, 1899).
Moore, R.I., *The Formation of a Persecuting Society* (London: Basil Blackwell, 1987).
Moyise, Steve, *Evoking Scripture* (London and New York: T&T Clark, 2008).
Muffs, Yochanan, *The Personhood of God* (Woodstock, VT: Jewish Lights, 2005).
Murphy, Jeffrie, "Christian Love and Criminal Punishment," in John Witte, Jr. and Frank S. Alexander (eds), *Christianity and the Law: An Introduction* (Cambridge: Cambridge University Press, 2008), pp. 219–35.
Murphy, Roland E., O. Carm., *The Book of Job* (New York: Paulist, 1999).
Myers, Ched, *Binding the Strong Man: A Political Reading of Mark's Story of Jesus* (Maryknoll, NY: Orbis, 1988).
Neusner, Jacob, *Torah* (Philadelphia: Fortress, 1985).
Newman, Graeme, *Just and Painful* (New York: Harrow and Heston, 1995).
Nicholas of Kues, "The Catholic Concordance," in O'Donovan, Oliver and Joan Lockwood O'Donovan (eds), *From Irenaeus to Grotius: A Sourcebook in Christian Political Thought* (Grand Rapids, MI: Wm B. Eerdmans, 1999).
Niebuhr, H. Richard, *Christ and Culture* (New York: Harper & Row, 1951).
________ *The Kingdom of God in America* (New York: Harper, 1959).
Niebuhr, Reinhold, *Moral Man and Immoral Society* (New York: Charles Scribner's Sons, 1932).
________ *The Nature and Destiny of Man* (2 vols, New York: Charles Scribner's Sons, 1949).
________ *An Interpretation of Christian Ethics* (San Francisco: Harper & Row, 1963).
Noll, Stephen F., "Doctrine of Angels," in *Dictionary for Theological Interpretation*, ed. Kevin Van Hoozer (London: Society for Promoting Christian Knowledge, 2005), pp. 45–8.

Novak, David, "Law and Religion in Judaism," in John Witte, Jr. and Frank S. Alexander (eds), *Christianity and the Law: An Introduction* (Cambridge: Cambridge University Press, 2008), pp. 33–52.

Oakeshott, Michael, "Introduction," in Hobbes, Thomas, *Leviathan* (Oxford: Basil Blackwell, 1960), pp. vii–xlvi.

Oakley, Francis, *The Western Church in the Later Middle Ages* (Ithaca: Cornell University Press, 1979).

O'Donovan, Oliver, *The Ways of Judgment* (Grand Rapids, MI: William B. Eerdmans, 2005).

Origen, *Contra Celsum*, trans. Henry Chadwick (Cambridge: Cambridge University Press, 1953).

Osuna, Francisco de, *The Third Spiritual Alphabet*, trans. by a Benedictine of Stanbrook, NY (New York: Benziger, 1931).

Pachomius, Saint, *Pachomian Koinonia*, trans. Armand Veilleux (2 vols, Kalamazoo: Cistercian Publications, 1981).

Percival, Henry R., "The Seven Ecumenical Councils of the Early Church," in Philip Schaff and Henry Wace (eds), *A Select Library of Nicene and Post-Nicene Fathers of the Christian Church* (Grand Rapids, MI: William B. Eerdmans, 1956).

Perrin, Norman, *Rediscovering the Teaching of Jesus* (New York: Harper & Row, 1967).

Peters, Edward, *Torture* (Philadelphia: University of Pennsylvania Press, 1985).

________ *Inquisition* (New York: The Free Press, 1988).

________ "Prison Before The Prison," in Norval Morris and David J. Rothman (eds), *The Oxford History of the Prison* (New York: Oxford University Press, 1995), pp. 3–47.

________ "Destruction of the Flesh—Salvation of the Spirit: The Paradoxes of Torture in Medieval Christian Society," in Alberto Ferreiro (ed.), *The Devil, Heresy, and Witchcraft in the Middle Ages* (Leiden: Brill, 1998), pp. 131–48.

Petersilia, Joan, *When Prisoners Come Home* (New York: Oxford University Press, 2003).

Pew Center on the States, *One in 100: Behind Bars in America 2008* (Washington, DC: Pew Center on the States, 2008).

Pinches, Charles R., *A Gathering of Memories* (Grand Rapids, MI: Brazos, 2006).

Pivar, David, *Purity Crusade: Sexual Morality and Social Control* (Westport, CT: Greenwood Press, 1973).

Pollock, Frederick, *The History of English Law Before the Time of Edward I* (2 vols, Cambridge: Cambridge University Press, 1968).

Polycarp, "The Epistle of Polycarp to the Philippians," in *The Apostolic Fathers*, vol. 1, trans. Kirsopp Lake (Cambridge, MA: Harvard University Press, 1959).

Porter, Jean, *The Recovery of Virtue* (Louisville: Westminster/John Knox, 1990).

________ *Natural and Divine Law* (Grand Rapids: Eerdmans, 1999).

Poschmann, Bernhard, *Penance and the Anointing of the Sick*, trans. Francis Courtney, S.J. (New York: Herder & Herder, 1964).

Pound, Roscoe, *Interpretations of Legal History* (Cambridge, MA: Harvard University Press, 1923).

________ *An Introduction to the Philosophy of Law* (New Haven: Yale University Press, 1954).

Poupko, Chana Kasachkoff, "The Religious Basis of the Retributive Approach to Punishment," *The Thomist* 39 (1975), pp. 528–41.

Pseudo-Dionysius, *The Complete Works*, trans. Colm Luibheid (New York and Mahwah: Paulist, 1987).

Pugh, Ralph B., *Imprisonment in Medieval England* (Cambridge: Cambridge University Press, 1970).

Rahner, Karl, "The Prison Pastorate," in *Justice Reflections* 6 (2004), pp. 1–14.

________ "Penance in the Early Church," *Theological Investigations*, vol. XV, trans. Lionel Swain (New York: Crossroad, 1982).

Ramsey, Paul, *Basic Christian Ethics* (New York: Scribner's, 1954).

________ *The Just War* (New York: Scribner, 1968).

Ranulf, Svend, *Moral Indignation and Middle Class Psychology* (New York: Schocken, 1964).

Reno, R.R., "Doctrine of Sin," in *Dictionary for Theological Interpretation of the Bible*, ed. Kevin J. Vanhoozer (Grand Rapids, MI: Baker Academic, 2005), pp. 748–51.

Ricoeur, Paul, "Religion, Atheism, and Faith," in *The Conflict of Interpretations*, trans. Charles Freilich (Chicago: Northwestern University Press, 1974), pp. 440–67.

Ristroph, Alice, "Desert, Democracy, and Sentencing Reform," *Journal of Criminal Law and Criminology* 96 (2006), pp. 1293–352.

Robinson, John A.T., *Wrestling with Romans* (Philadelphia: Westminster Press, 1979).

Rohr, Richard, *Adams's Return* (New York: Crossroad, 2004).

________ *The Naked Now* (New York: Crossroad, 2009).

Rousseau, Jean Jacques, *The Social Contract*, trans. Willmoore Kendall (Chicago: Henry Regnery, 1954).

Rufinus the Canonist, "Summa Decretum," in O'Donovan, Oliver and Joan Lockwood O'Donovan (eds), *From Irenaeus to Grotius: A Sourcebook in Christian Political Thought* (Grand Rapids, MI: Wm B. Eerdmans, 1999).

Rusche, Georg and Otto Kirchheimer, *Punishment and Social Structure* (New York: Russell & Russell, 1968).

Ryan, Columba P., O.P., "The Traditional Concept of Natural Law: An Interpretation," in Ronald Hamel and Kenneth Himes (eds), *Introduction to Christian Ethics* (Ramsey, NJ: Paulist Press, 1989), pp. 413–27.

Ryan, Mary P., *Cradle of the Middle Class* (New York: Cambridge University Press, 1981).

"S. Quintino Martyre," in *Acta Sanctorum*, 31 Octobris (Paris, 1883).

"Sanctus Leonardus," in *Acta Sanctorum*, 6 Novembris (Brussels, 1910).

Sanders, E.P., *Paul, the Law, and the Jewish People* (Philadelphia, Fortress, 1983).

Schleiermacher, Friedrich, *On Religion: Speeches to its Cultured Despisers*, trans. Richard Crouter (Cambridge: Cambridge University Press, 1988).
Schreiner, Thomas, *New Testament Theology* (Grand Rapids, MI: Baker Academic, 2008).
Schutz, Alfred, *On Phenomenology and Social Relations* (Chicago: University of Chicago Press, 1970).
Sellin, Thorsten, "Dom Jean Mabillon: A Prison Reformer of the Seventeenth Century," *Journal of the Institute of Criminal Law and Criminology* 17 (1927), pp. 581–602.
________ *Pioneering in Penology* (Philadelphia: University of Pennsylvania Press, 1944).
________ *Slavery and the Penal System* (New York: Elsevier, 1976).
Senior, Donald, *Jesus: A Gospel Portrait* (New York: Paulist, 1992).
Shaffern, Robert W., *Law and Justice from Antiquity to the Enlightenment* (Lanham, MD: Roman & Littlefield, 2009).
Shoham, Shlomo, *The Mark of Cain* (Jerusalem: Israel Universities Press, 1970).
Simmonds, N.E., *Law as a Moral Idea* (Oxford: Oxford University Press, 2007).
Simon, Jonathan, *Governing Through Crime: How the War on Crime Transformed American Democracy and Created a Culture of Fear* (New York: Oxford University Press, 2007).
Simons, Menno, "Admonition on Church Discipline," in *The Complete Writings of Menno Simons*, trans. Leonard Verduin (Scottdale, PA: Herald Press, 1956), pp. 409–18.
Skotnicki, Andrew, "Foundations Once Destroyed: The Catholic Church and Criminal Justice," *Theological Studies* 65 (2004), pp. 792–816.
________ "God's Prisoners: Penal Confinement and the Creation of Purgatory," *Modern Theology* 22 (2006), pp. 85–110.
________ *Criminal Justice and the Catholic Church* (Lanham, MD: Rowman & Littlefield, 2008).
Smith, Adam, "The Theory of Moral Sentiments," in D.D. Raphael (ed.), *British Moralists 1650–1800*, vol. II (Oxford: Clarendon, 1969).
________ *The Wealth of Nations* (London: Penguin, 1970).
Smith, L.M., *Cluny in the Eleventh and Twelfth Centuries* (London: Philip Allen, 1930).
Snyder, T. Richard, *The Protestant Ethic and the Spirit of Punishment* (Grand Rapids: Eerdmans, 2001).
Sobrino, Jon, *Christology at the Crossroads* (Maryknoll, NY: Orbis, 1976).
Soering, Jens, *The Convict Christ* (Maryknoll, NY: Orbis, 2006).
________ *The Church of the Second Chance* (New York: Lantern Books, 2008).
Somerville, J.P., "From Suarez to Filmer: A Reappraisal," *Historical Journal* 25 (1982), pp. 525–40.
Southern, R.W., *Saint Anselm and His Biographer* (Cambridge, UK: Cambridge University Press, 1963).

Spinoza, Benedict de, *The Political Works*, ed. and trans. A.G. Wernham (Oxford: Clarendon, 1958).

Spierenburg, Pieter, *The Spectacle of Suffering* (Cambridge: Cambridge University Press, 1984).

________ *The Prison Experience* (New Brunswick, NJ: Rutgers University Press, 1991).

Spohn, William, *Go and Do Likewise* (New York: Continuum, 1999).

Stackhouse, John G., *Making the Best of It* (New York: Oxford University Press, 2008).

Stark, Rodney and William Sims Bainbridge, *The Future of Religion* (Berkeley: University of California Press, 1985).

Stout, Jeffrey, *Ethics After Babel* (Boston: Beacon Press, 1988).

Strayer, Joseph, *On the Medieval Origins of the Modern State* (Princeton, NJ: Princeton University Press, 1970).

Stuntz, William J., "The Pathological Politics of Criminal Law," *Michigan Law Review* 100 (2001), pp. 505–600.

Suarez, Francisco, S.J., "On Laws and God the Lawgiver," in *Selections from Three Works of Francisco Suarez, S.J.*, trans. Gwladys L. Williams, Ammi Brown, and John Waldron (Oxford: Clarendon, 1944).

Sumption, Jonathan, *Pilgrimage: An Image of Medieval Religion* (London: Faber & Faber, 1975).

Taylor, Charles, *A Secular Age* (Cambridge, MA: Belknap Press, 2007).

Taylor, Mark Lewis, *The Executed God* (Minneapolis: Fortress, 2001).

Tertullian, *On Penitence*, trans. Maurice Bevenot, S.J. (Westminster, MD: Newman Press, 1957).

________ *Apology*, trans. T.R. Glover (Cambridge, MA: Harvard University Press, 1960).

The Book of Sainte Foy, trans. Pamela Sheingorn (Philadelphia: University of Pennsylvania Press, 1995).

The Cloud of Unknowing, ed. William Johnston (New York: Image Books, 1973).

The Miracles of Our Lady of Rocamadour, trans. Marcus Bell (Woodbridge, UK: Boydell Press, 1999).

The Schleitheim Confession, ed. and trans. John Howard Yoder (Scottdale PA: Herald Press, 1977).

"The Shepherd of Hermas," in *The Apostolic Fathers*, vol. II, trans. Kirsopp Lake (London: William Heinemann, 1959).

Theissen, Gerd, *Fortress Introduction to the New Testament* (Minneapolis: Fortress, 2003).

Tierney, Brian, *The Idea of Natural Rights* (Atlanta: Scholars Press, 1997).

________ "Natural Law and Natural Rights," John Witte, Jr. and Frank S. Alexander (eds), *Christianity and Law: An Introduction* (Cambridge: Cambridge University Press, 2008), pp. 89–103.

Tocqueville, Alexis de, *Democracy in America* (2 vols, New York: Alfred A. Knopf, 1945).

Tonry, Michael, "Purposes and Functions of Sentencing," in Michael Tonry (ed.), *Crime and Justice: A Review of Research* 34 (Chicago: University of Chicago Press, 2006), pp. 1–53.

Toral, Jorge Crespo, *Towards Freedom* (Washington, DC: Prison Fellowship International, 2000).

Troeltsch, Ernst, *The Social Teaching of the Christian Churches*, trans. Olive Wyon (2 vols, Chicago: University of Chicago Press, 1960).

Turner, Victor, *The Ritual Process* (Ithaca: Cornell University Press, 1969).

Ullmann, Walter, *The Growth of Papal Government in the Middle Ages* (London: Methuen & Co., 1955).

________ *Law and Politics in the Middle Ages* (Ithaca: Cornell University Press, 1975).

Van De Wiel, Constant, *History of Canon Law* (Louvain: Peeters, 1991).

VanderKam, James C., *An Introduction to Early Judaism* (Grand Rapids, MI: William B. Eerdmans, 2001).

Vogel, Cyril, "Sin and Penance," in Philippe Delhaye et al., *Pastoral Treatment of Sin* (New York: Desclee, 1968), pp. 177–282.

Volf, Miroslav, *The End of Memory: Remembering Rightly in a Violent World* (Grand Rapids: Eerdmans, 2006).

Von Rad, Gerhard, "Some Aspects of the Old Testament World-View," in *The Problem of the Hexateuch*, trans. E.W. Trueman Dicken (New York: McGraw Hill, 1966), pp. 144–65.

Walzer, Michael, *The Revolution of the Saints* (Cambridge, MA: Harvard University Press, 1965).

________ *Exodus and Revolution* (New York: Basic, 1994).

Watson, Alan, *The Evolution of Law* (Baltimore: Johns Hopkins University Press, 1987).

Watson, F., *Paul and the Hermeneutics of Faith* (London and New York: T&T Clark, 2004).

Weber, Max, "The Protestant Sects and the Spirit of Capitalism," in H.H. Gerth and C. Wright Mills, *From Max Weber* (New York: Oxford, 1946), pp. 302–22.

________ "The Social Psychology of the World's Religions," in H.H. Gerth and C. Wright Mills, *From Max Weber* (New York: Oxford, 1946), pp. 267–301.

________ *The Protestant Ethic and the Spirit of Capitalism*, trans. Talcott Parsons (New York: Charles Scribner's Sons, 1958).

________ *Economy and Society*, trans. Guenther Roth and Hans Wittich (2 vols, Berkeley: University of California Press, 1978).

Whitman, James, *Harsh Justice* (New York: Oxford University Press, 2003).

________ *The Origins of Reasonable Doubt* (New Haven: Yale University Press, 2008).

William of Ockham, *Quodlibetical Questions*, trans. Alfred J. Freddos and Francis E. Kelley (New Haven: Yale University Press, 1991).

________ *On the Power of Emperors and Popes*, trans. Annabel S. Brett (Bristol, UK: Thoemms, 1998).

________ "Eight Questions on Papal Power," in O'Donovan, Oliver and Joan Lockwood O'Donovan (eds), *From Irenaeus to Grotius: A Sourcebook in Christian Political Thought* (Grand Rapids, MI: Wm B. Eerdmans, 1999).

Wittberg, Patricia, *The Rise and Decline of Catholic Religious Orders* (Albany: State University of New York Press, 1994).

Witte, John, Jr., *God's Joust, God's Justice: Law and Religion in the Western Tradition* (Grand Rapids: Eerdmans, 2006).

________ "Introduction," in John Witte, Jr. and Frank S. Alexander (eds), *Christianity and the Law: An Introduction* (Cambridge: Cambridge University Press, 2008), pp. 1–32.

Wolf, Eric R., *Europe and the People Without History* (Berkeley: University of California Press, 1982).

Wuthnow, Robert, *Producing the Sacred: An Essay on Public Religion* (Champagne: University of Illinois Press, 1994).

Wycliffe, John, "Civil Lordship," in O'Donovan, Oliver and Joan Lockwood O'Donovan (eds), *From Irenaeus to Grotius: A Sourcebook in Christian Political Thought* (Grand Rapids, MI: Wm B. Eerdmans, 1999).

Yoder, John Howard, "A People in the World: Theological Interpretation," in *The Concept of the Believer's Church*, ed. Leo Garret, Jr. (Scottdale, PA: Herald Press, 1969), pp. 252–83.

Zahl, Paul M., *Grace in Practice* (Grand Rapids: Eerdmans, 2007).

Zehr, Howard, *The Little Book of Restorative Justice* (Intercourse, PA: Good Books, 2002).

Zimring, Franklin E., *Crime is not the Problem* (New York: Oxford University Press, 1997).

________ *American Juvenile Justice* (New York: Oxford University Press, 2005).

Index

For Product Safety Concerns and Information please contact our EU representative GPSR@taylorandfrancis.com
Taylor & Francis Verlag GmbH, Kaufingerstraße 24, 80331 München, Germany

www.ingramcontent.com/pod-product-compliance
Ingram Content Group UK Ltd.
Pitfield, Milton Keynes, MK11 3LW, UK
UKHW022128190926
475702UK00013B/1693
9781138110700

Lie Detection and the Law

This book develops a sociological account of lie detection practices and uses this to think about lying more generally. Bringing together insights from sociology, social history, socio-legal studies and science and technology studies (STS), it explores how torture and technology have been used to try to discern the truth. It examines a variety of socio-legal practices, including trial by ordeal in Europe, the American criminal jury trial, police interrogations using the polygraph machine, and the post-conviction management of sex offenders in the USA and the UK. Moving across these different contexts, it articulates how uncertainties in the use of lie detection technologies are managed, and the complex roles they play in legal spaces. Alongside this story, the book surveys some of the different ways in which lying is understood in philosophy, law and social order. *Lie Detection and the Law* will be of interest to STS researchers, socio-legal scholars, criminologists and sociologists, as well as others working at the intersections of law and science.

Andrew Balmer is Senior Lecturer in Sociology at the University of Manchester. He is a member of the Morgan Centre for Research into Everyday Lives.

Part of the Law, Science and Society series
Series editors: John Paterson, *University of Aberdeen, UK*
Julian Webb, *University of Melbourne, Australia*

A GlassHouse book

For information about the series and details of previous and forthcoming titles, see www.routledge.com/law/series/CAV16